# USING APPS FOR LEARNING ACROSS THE CURRICULUM

## A Literacy-Based Framework and Guide

*Richard Beach and David O'Brien*

Routledge
Taylor & Francis Group

NEW YORK AND LONDON

First published 2015
by Routledge
711 Third Avenue, New York, NY 10017

and by Routledge
2 Park Square, Milton Park, Abingdon, Oxon OX14 4RN

*Routledge is an imprint of the Taylor & Francis Group, an informa business*

*Library of Congress Cataloging in Publication Data*
Beach, Richard.
Using apps for learning across the curriculum: a literacy-based framework and guide/Richard
Beach, David O'Brien.
pages cm
Includes bibliographical references and index.
1. Application software. 2. Internet in education. 3. Educational technology.
4. Tablet computers. I. O'Brien, David G. II. Title.
QA76.76.A65B38 2014
371.33—dc23
2014015384

ISBN: 978-1-138-78262-4 (hbk)
ISBN: 978-1-138-78263-1 (pbk)
ISBN: 978-1-315-76912-7 (ebk)

Typeset in Bembo
by Swales & Willis Ltd, Exeter, Devon, UK

# CONTENTS

# PREFACE

Students are increasingly using mobile devices in the classroom for academic purposes. These devices are ubiquitous; portable; have intuitive touch features; and allow for image, audio, and video productions. Given this increased use of mobile devices, teachers are also employing apps supported by these devices.

However, overwhelmed with the availability of hundreds of thousands of apps—as of 2014, about 500,000 iOS apps and about 600,000 Android apps—teachers face the challenge of knowing how and why to use apps to foster learning in their classrooms. The purpose of this book is to provide a framework for thinking about how to employ these apps in ways that will foster learning with literacy across the curriculum. In thinking about the uses of apps, we focus on how apps foster use of literacy practices involved in accessing/assessing information, reading, writing, engaging in discussion, creating and reading images, using audio/video, and using games/simulation. For example, we describe how uses of annotation apps for responding to texts can be used to engage students in collaborative discussions about those texts.

Also, we describe how use of these literacy practices supports students in acquiring certain disciplinary literacies unique to English language arts, social studies, science, math, art, and music. For example, use of the affordances of mapping apps is supportive of learning geography in social studies classes while use of the affordances of drawing apps is supportive of learning in art classes.

We believe that our book is unique in that it goes beyond simply describing apps as found in app recommendation sites or books about apps to provide a framework for thinking about the uses of apps within the larger context of literacy learning across the curriculum. Teachers from different subject matter areas can use this framework to collaboratively devise activities supporting cross-disciplinary literacy learning so that students are using the same or similar apps in different courses. For example, teachers can plan activities involving use of annotation apps for students to share and build on each other's synthesis responses to their reading.

Teachers can also use this framework for devising criteria to assess students' learning in terms of their ability to employ certain literacy practices, for example, assessing students on their ability to employ annotation apps to synthesize their understanding of texts.

This book also provides readers with a number of features related to suggestions for using apps in the classroom through:

- descriptions of uses of app affordances supporting particular literacy practices related to accessing information, reading, writing, discussing, image/audio/video production, gaming, and reflection associated with learning in different subject matter areas for further resources and reading on uses of apps;
- connections between use of certain literacy practices and addressing the Common Core Standards;
- examples of classroom uses of apps demonstrating how students learn to employ disciplinary literacies through their uses of apps;
- links to apps designed for use in fostering specific literacy practices for iOS apps, to the iTunes Store; Android apps, to the Google Play Store; and Chrome OS apps, to the Chrome Store;
- links to resources and further reading on uses of apps on the book's website http://usingipads.pbworks.com and a blog http://www.appsforlearningliteracies.com for further discussion of topics in the book.

# OVERVIEW OF THE BOOK

*Part I: A Literacy-Based Framework for Using Apps* provides a framework for the book (Chapters 1 to 3).

Chapter 1 presents the idea that the affordances of apps—how apps support literacy learning— reside not in the apps themselves but in how you design activities that exploit the uses of certain apps. This means that rather than let an app itself drive your activity, it is your activity that drives how and why you are using a certain app.

Chapter 2 describes how uses of app affordances can foster uses of literacy practices to help students acquire disciplinary literacies as they study English language arts, social sciences, natural sciences, math, world/second language, art, music, physical education, etc.

Chapter 3 provides strategies for planning instruction and creating activities that exploit these app affordances based on determination of students' prior experiences, knowledge, needs, abilities, and interests. It also describes how devising activities using app affordances fosters learning different disciplinary literacies in ways that support implementation of the Common Core Standards.

In *Part II: Guidelines and Classroom Examples for Using Apps*, Chapters 4 to 11 look at uses of apps to foster use of certain specific literacy practices in the classroom.

Chapter 4 describes the use of apps to foster accessing and assessing information through the use of online database searches, including the ability to identify relevant key terms and assess the validity of information acquired.

Chapter 5 discusses the uses of apps to help students learn to read digitally through defining purposes for processing links in texts; synthesizing ideas through uses of note-taking, annotation, mind-mapping, tagging, and social networking apps; and acquiring the ability to select online texts relevant to one's needs and interests.

Chapter 6 is about the uses of apps for creating digital texts: blog posts, reports, wiki contributions, tweets, collaborative writing, digital stories, etc., within and across different disciplines.

Chapter 7 explains uses of apps to foster online synchronous and asynchronous discussion apps, as well as apps to assist English language learners.

Chapter 8 presents different literacy practices that revolve around the use and production of images to support multimodal learning through use of photo, drawing, poster, presentation, and comic-creation apps.

Chapter 9 describes the uses of audio and video communication apps to access audio and video productions and to create podcasts and videos; it also discusses the use of text-to-speech apps to assist learning disabled students.

Chapter 10 focuses on uses of simulations/game apps to engage students in role-play and problem-solving learning.

Chapter 11 looks at how to employ different apps to foster reflection and assessment through use of annotations, podcasts, screencasting software, chat sites, or videoconferencing apps to provide feedback on students' work, as well as e-portfolio apps to foster reflection on long-term learning.

*Part III: Professional Development* (Chapter 12) provides suggested resources for teaching professionals on using apps in the classroom: online training sites, educators' blogs, wikis, videos, podcasts, Twitter posts, forums, and curriculum resource sites, as well as the creation of a personal learning network (PLN) for collaboratively acquiring and sharing teaching ideas.

# ACKNOWLEDGMENTS

We wish to acknowledge our acquisitions editor Naomi Silverman and her assistant, Christina Chronister, of Routledge for their support of this project. And, we would like to thank our reviewers, William Ian O'Byrne and one anonymous reviewer, for their helpful feedback and suggestions for revisions; for project-managing the book, Caroline Watson; and for copy-editing the book, Ian Howe.

# PART I

# A Literacy-Based Framework for Using Apps

# 1

# INTRODUCTION

## Defining Purposes for Learning With Literacies Through Use of Apps

In their English language arts classrooms at West Junior High School, in Hopkins, Minnesota, Sara Speicher and Julie Walthour (2013) use the Subtext *http://tinyurl.com/9ykogpm* app to organize and support their students' responses to their reading. They use this app to have their students:

- access books from their local public library using OverDrive or Baker & Taylor or upload PDFs or ePub documents;
- share books or texts with peers and access the class's "group shelf";
- edit book covers by adding their own photos to those covers;
- share their responses to books or texts through highlighting, tagging, and annotating passages from texts;
- export their written responses to Google Docs;
- access discussion question, quizzes, polls, links, or videos added by teachers.

They can also acquire articles, curriculum materials, assessment tools for tracking student work, and text-to-speech tools in the Premium Subtext version.

The use of the Subtext app represents an example of one of thousands of apps available to support literacy learning in different subjects, the focus of this book.

In this chapter, we describe a number of frameworks for thinking about how use of apps can support learning with different literacy practices related to accessing information, reading, writing, speaking/listening, creating images/audio/videos, and reflecting on learning, practices relevant to learning in all subjects.

## Determining How and Why to Use Apps in the Classroom

A critical factor in teachers' use of apps is often discussed as tech integration—how well one selects an app that *affords* the best use of a particular tool to meet an instructional goal while engaging students. One recent study of the use of tablets with fifth-graders showed that some teachers use tablets in limited ways like calendar-keeping, grade-checking, and educational games, while other teachers employ tablets for note-taking, class polls, and videos, differences that reflected teachers' different attitudes about the value of use of technology in instruction (Schwartz, 2013).

In using a particular app with a teacher's guidance, students learn how and why they are using an app so when they are outside the classroom, they know which app is best for a particular project. For example, when a student employs the iOS *http://tinyurl.com/a6z4tsu* or Android *http://tinyurl.com/mrltgkl* Explain Everything screencasting app to visually enact how they solved a math problem, when they are outside the classroom, and need to create a visual display of their learning, they might turn to use of this screencasting app to achieve that purpose. So teachers need a clear purpose for using each app in order to convey those purposes to students.

## Defining Purposes in Terms of App Affordances

In this book, we propose that, as teachers or preservice teachers, you should plan and select apps based on what we're defining as *app affordances*. Unfortunately, apps are often selected for a particular use based on how they are labeled rather than on the possibilities they hold in well-designed instruction. All of those lists such as "50 Popular iPad Apps For Struggling Readers and Writers" describe these apps but fail to consider the degree to which they actually support certain kinds of literacy learning. When we peruse these lists, we find apps with some helpful tools, some apps that afford some engagement with lots of teacher guidance, and some apps based on totally faulty assumptions of reading instruction. Few of them have the affordances for fostering engaging, learning, and instruction based on what the app designer put into them.

## App Affordances as Action Possibilities for Your Activity

The primary problem is that the affordances of apps are not simply "in" the app based on the assumption that use of X app will result in Y learning. The affordances of apps depend on how you design an activity in ways that exploit uses of an app for purposes unique to your activity.

In coining the use of the concept of affordance, James Gibson (1986) argued that how an object presents itself in a certain context and point in time influences what it affords. Affordances are action possibilities available in the environment, independent of one's ability to perceive them. If you are tired from a long walk on the beach, a piece of driftwood affords rest—a place to sit; once rested, as the sun goes down and you start to feel chilled, a piece of wood might afford warmth when used as fuel for a fire. The driftwood affords a lot more than rest or warmth, depending on how it presents itself, in relation to what you need, and the extent to which you relate to it in a way that actualizes the affordance.

Instructional designers of apps, and, to a certain extent, teachers thinking like instructional designers, assume that the design of instruction, if carefully planned, can help them predict student learning and engagement outcomes. Of course, to an extent that is true, especially if the designers are armed with both ample instructional experience and in-depth knowledge of the domain the apps are supposed to tap into. Design, from the perspective of app designers, focuses more on the features incorporated into the app—the app-as-object, with a goal that a carefully designed app will predict some consistent outcomes when used for its intended purpose. Sometimes this happens, sometimes not.

We therefore discuss app affordances in this book in terms of both *design* and *use*—the features designed into the app and the design-in-use. For example, a well-designed app that affords annotating and note-taking related to a text supports the use of writing as a literacy practice. However, the specific instructional lessons and tasks you set up afford writing as a way to support learning because you are *inviting* students to use specific practices, afforded by the app in classroom activities.

The design-in-use affordances, which are not implicit in the app design, might not become apparent until you use the app for a specific purpose, as part of an instructional activity. App designers, although they might anticipate affordances of an app, cannot know for sure about what will actually happen with an app in use; and some apps are used in ways that designers never intended or imagined.

Just as the traditional classroom chalkboard affords teachers and students the opportunity to share their writing on the chalkboard for their class, so apps and mobile devices afford a range of opportunities for possible practices by the way the app, and the various tools it contains, *presents itself* to the student or the way the student *enacts* a particular use as needed. A popular note-taking app like Evernote iOS *http://tinyurl.com/cxo6req* and Android *http://tinyurl.com/dyspv8p* allows students to not only clip texts from websites, but also to record their notes related to these clips and to then share the notes with peers. However, students might not enact the most useful, purposeful affordances unless they are engaged in a collaborative activity that involves the use of note-taking to share with their peers.

## Selecting and Using Apps Based on Your Learning Objectives

Thus instructional activity is essential for defining app affordances. As illustrated below, rather than selecting an app because you want students to use that app for an activity (Option A), we suggest that you begin with the activity designed to achieve your particular learning objectives and find those apps that afford the best engagement and learning within the activity (Option B).

**Option A: App affordances → Activity**

**Option B: Activity → App affordances**

Focusing on instructional activities and what students will learn from participating in activities as the basis for selecting apps means not using apps as technology tools for their own sake, but rather using apps to enhance learning (Dickens & Churches, 2011).

The same apps may be used for multiple purposes, depending on purposes driving an activity. For example, while note-taking apps such as Evernote might be used to record and share notes, how your students use note-taking apps will vary according to the goals for classroom activities. Teachers should specify the anticipated affordances of uses of apps related to a particular instructional need. With the design-in-use aspect, you need to carefully observe and record affordances that you did not anticipate but that might emerge once students use the apps.

In planning instruction, you have a major role in selecting apps and determining the kinds of affordances associated with the use of apps. For example, a math instructor wants students to share their problem-solving process through creating a written record and an audio, think-aloud narrative for solving a math problem. These will be shared with peers and the instructor (Fusch, 2011). Based on this instructor's need, someone assisting this instructor suggests the use of the iOS app, Underscore Notify *http://tinyurl.com/olzn4t5* that students can use to create handwritten notes with a stylus and record their think-aloud narrative for solving the problem for sharing with peers and the instructor. This Underscore Notify app therefore provided the affordance of synthesizing/sharing information through writing to learn in math courses.

All of this suggests the need to define affordances in terms of *how* apps are being used to foster literacy learning in the classroom. Apps can certainly be used to foster traditional "drill and practice" forms of learning.

At the same time, apps have the potential to foster more engaging kinds of learning. In describing the uses of apps, Mark Prensky (2012) posits that apps have the following affordances in fostering learning:

> Apps can be designed for very specific purposes. My son learned his alphabets in two languages by tracing letters.
> Apps will soon exist across the entire school curriculum, that can be downloaded piece by piece as needed, and discarded when they have served their purpose.
> Apps increasingly come with intuitive, touch and voice controlled interfaces.
> Apps recruit all the other features of the devices they are on, such as the camera, the videocam, voice recording, phone, Wi-Fi connection, Twitter and Skype, for example.

Apps can incorporate capabilities from the cloud: text to voice, voice to text, voice recognition, storage, computing capacity, etc.

Apps can do everything computers or books can, incorporating all of those tools' capabilities, and far more. (p. 2)

Prensky's descriptions of these different uses of apps have a lot to do with the technical features of the devices themselves, such as the touch interface, use of recording/camera features, cloud-storage, and portability. At the same time, as he notes, apps are "designed for very specific purposes," so that they can be used to mediate specific kinds of literacy learning, the focus of this book.

## Defining App Affordances in Terms of Literacy Practices

In this book, we define app affordances associated with design of classroom activities in terms of certain *literacy practices*. We use the word *practices* rather than *skills* or *strategies*. Skills often represent a fixed corpus of what you know how to do, regardless of a particular context or situation, and strategies are often presented as the generic complements to skills, that is, particular plans for becoming more skilled. *Practices* puts more of a focus on literacy *enactments* that are played as part of participation and repetition in social contexts or events. As Barton and Hamilton (2000) noted:

> literacy practices are what people do with literacy. However, practices are not observable units of behaviour since they also involve values, attitudes, feelings, and social relationships . . . this include people's awareness of literacy, constructions of literacy and discourses of literacy, how people talk about and make sense of literacy. (p. 7)

For example, a group of students created a video public service announcement about the use of sexist language to show in their school. To do so, they decided to script and shoot some role-play incidents in which they portrayed the use of sexist language in hallway interactions. In creating these videos using the iMovie app, they employed a range of different literacy practices involved in working collaboratively as a team: defining their rhetorical purposes in creating their videos, reading and writing scripts, creating visual storyboards, engaging in role-plays, and shooting and editing videos.

Literacy practices involve the situated processes fostering learning, in monitoring understanding, in making transformations from understanding to articulations of that understanding through language, both spoken and written. Hence, these practices are both cognitive and social, and what one understands is mediated by social action and interaction, in a given activity, within a certain cultural context. For example, when students are working collaboratively with others in creating videos, they need to be able to determine who is responsible for which tasks and know how to support each other in a positive manner for the benefit of the group.

This focus on practices goes beyond a traditional focus on skills, knowledge of forms, or cognitive strategies to emphasize the socially situated nature of learning—how one learns in a community given shared beliefs, values, and goals within a cultural group. For example, students learn the literacy practices of engaging in online discussions with others through active participation in these discussions. Because literacy practices are socially mediated, when you plan instruction, you determine how the affordances of certain apps will foster literacy practices of students' engagement in social contexts that actively involve students in learning. And for the purposes of this book, a discipline also embodies cultural characteristics which we explain in more detail later as part of disciplinary literacy.

## Device Affordances

App affordances build on or exploit the affordances of iOS and Android devices themselves, affordances such as intuitive touch, portability, audio/video production, etc., not possible on other technological devices. Given the fact that most adolescents own their own device and the increased use of BYOD (bring your own device), students are accustomed to using devices outside of school for social networking, texting, or creating photos/videos (Nielsen & Webb, 2011). Kalantzis and Cope (2012) describe these students as members of a "Generation P," based on their active uses of mobile devices in a "participatory culture" (Jenkins, 2006):

> They have at hand ubiquitous mobile devices, connected to the new social media and allowing them to communicate with people at a distance from them at any time of day and anywhere . . . Generation P do as much by writing as reading in their spare time—and reading and writing are fused as integrated practices in social networking sites, blogs, and text messages. (pp. 9, 10)

This active participation mediated by uses of mobile devices provides them with a sense of agency outside of school that contrasts with self-perceptions based on schooled literacy, as measured on standardized tests.

Rather than adopt a simplistic binary in which schools are perceived as limiting students' uses of mobile devices, we believe that schools can and are valuing literacy practices employed outside of school in the home, community, or workplace in ways that can engage students through *exploiting uses of mobile devices they are currently using.* This use of mobile devices for both social and academic purposes gives students agency in meeting personally relevant goals, and can even improve their sanctioned literacy practices. This engagement and agency can be supported through multimodal, digital literacy practices, like social networking, video production, and texting. For example, while some research findings position texting on smartphones as inconsistent with or even a negative influence on school writing, a more positive "new literacies" practice views texting as simply different from school writing (Wood, Kemp, & Plester, 2013).

Prensky's affordances for apps have much to do with the affordances of different mobile devices—tablets, smartphones, and iPod Touches, as well as Chromebooks for use with Android apps and apps associated with Google Apps for Education. The vast majority of secondary students have access to smartphones. The 2013 Speak Up Survey found that 89% of high schools students have personal access to Internet-connected smart phones; 60%, access to laptops; and 50%, access to tablets (Riedel, 2014). Sixty percent of students use mobile devices for research; 43%, for educational games; and 40%, for collaboration with their peers; about one third access videos on their own for assistance in completing homework; 23% access teacher-created video.

## Ubiquity

Mobile devices such as tablets and smartphones are so flexible and used in so many ways that students are more and more likely to own them, a reflection of their ubiquity. A study by the Pew Research Center's Internet and American Life Project (Rainie, 2012) found that by January, 2012, 29% of households owned some type of tablet or e-reader. Students are upgrading to smartphones because smartphones are now more affordable and youth want access not only to texting but Facebook and YouTube. Because smartphones are actually powerful little computers, jumping from a lower class of technology to smartphones to engage in popular social activities means that now students have tools to foster learning both within and outside the classroom. Since the devices are both powerful and small, students can access them at anytime and anyplace (Brooks-Young, 2010; Dickens & Churches, 2011; Nielsen & Webb, 2011).

Ubiquitous access anytime or anyplace serves to alter how and where learning occurs. As Waters (2011) noted:

> It alters the places where learning takes place and expectations about where learning can take place. When something is perceived to be available all the time, anywhere, on any device, it changes the way that anybody, but particularly students, thinks about how they can access the information and media they want on the schedule they want. (p. 1)

## Engagement

A central goal for instruction and for our book is the need to engage students in their learning. We believe that uses of iOS, Android, or Chrome OS apps can enhance student engagement if these apps are employed to foster students' active participation in responding to and producing texts. Much of this engagement derives from active use and construction of multimodal texts, a key affordance of many apps. One study of eighth-grade students in an English class in Millis, Massachusetts who were using iPad apps, including the iOS Popplet Lite *http:// tinyurl.com/9wc9ztq* app to create storyboards, found that while some students were unmotivated and off-task in class prior to using the iPads, they were more motivated and on-task when using the iPads in class because students were more actively involved with learning with the iPads (Magley, 2011). Students were more likely to engage in discussions of current events because they had immediate access to current news and events on their iPads during class: 64% of students reported that they were more interested in doing their school work with the iPad than without the iPad; 60% reported that they spent more time on their school work when using their iPad than when working without their iPad.

## Portability

Because of advances in processor technology and battery technology, mobile devices are small and light, yet powerful enough to be comparable to computers. Students can use them in school and at home, as well as on field trips, museum visits, etc. A Pew Internet and American Life survey (Madden, 2013) found that 37% of teenagers have smartphones that provide them with online connections; 78% of teens have cell phones that allow them to send text messages, but not surf the Web. The portability and mobility of these phones alters how students can acquire information and learn in that they are no longer limited to certain physical spaces. Because college students at Notre Dame University had immediate access to their iPads in and outside of classrooms, they could readily access information and share thoughts with peers to a greater degree than when they were using traditional textbooks (Angst & Malinowski, 2010). Students also reported that the use of iPads made their classes more interesting, fostered exploration of additional topics, and helped them better manage their time.

This means that students can use devices to record thoughts, take notes, interact with/text others, take photos/videos, etc., without being limited by space and time. One study of adolescent students' uses of smartphones conducted by the StudyBlue online student assistance site found that students with access to smartphones studied 40 minutes more per week than did students without access to smartphones (StudyBlue, 2011). One reason for this increase in study time is that students can use their smartphones when they are commuting, exercising, or engaged in other activities. In the StudyBlue study, 50% of students used their smartphones to study when they were going to bed or waking up; 19% used smartphones in the bathroom; and 17% used them when they were exercising.

Students can also use smartphones or tablets when they are engaged in school-sponsored activities. For example, when conducting science or geography field trips, students can employ GPS devices on their smartphones to locate certain places to study or take photos, and then record data on their iPads. They will also have access to the same digital content across all subjects throughout the school day, so that they can draw on the same content for use in any subject.

## Reachability

The fact that students and/or parents generally have access to mobile devices means that they are reachable to readily receive messages or texts. A study showed that 74% of university students in five countries indicated that reachability was what they "like most," and 60% indicated that communication was what they "like most" about their mobile phones (Baron, 2011). Teachers can use mobile devices to share information with students or parents through texting, voice-mail, e-mail, Twitter, podcasting/phonecasting tools, blogs, or course websites about assignments, deadlines, or homework to students, particularly when and if they need to receive last-minute information or changes in a scheduled task. Students can also use cell phones or texting to work collaboratively with others. Analysis of 20 students' cell-phone audio logs of how they employed digital tools for collaboration indicated that they most often used cell phones for working on texts, followed by Skype, instant-messaging, e-mail, and blogs (Conole, de Laat, Dillon, & Darby, 2006).

Also, teachers and/or students can contact and interact with other students, parents, or experts from all over the world. In contrast to phone calls, e-mails, face-to-face visits, or letters, tools such as texting can be convenient for students or parents because students and parents receive them on their phones so that they can readily access or respond to text messages (Nielsen & Webb, 2011). Schools also employ messaging systems such as SchoolMessenger for use in sending text or voice messages. In the OneVille Project in Somerville, Massachusetts all students in the district receive text messages from their schools and teachers about their work (Pollock, 2011). Students perceive these messages positively because they see them as an indication that the school and their teachers care about their work. At the same time, students may also perceive the need to be continually available for communication with others as a burden, as well as not a substitute for face-to-face interaction (Baron, 2011). When 375 students were given iPads at the Gibbon-Fairfax-Winthrop High School in Minnesota, students became so accustomed to e-mailing their teachers using their iPads and having their teachers respond that, because teachers were overwhelmed with e-mails, the school had to set up some guidelines related to students' uses of e-mail.

Clearly, mobile devices enhance instant communication between students, teachers, parents, and administrators. As indicated by their use outside of school, students are already motivated to use them; and both teachers and students are already familiar with uses of cell phone technologies. Learning to use cell phones for educational purposes in concert with norms for appropriate use of phones in schools can enhance students' learning and uses of social practices. Cell phone communications eliminate the cost of paper and provide ways for teachers and students to readily communicate with each other (Nielsen & Webb, 2011).

Students and parents can also use the Pearson PowerSchool Parent iOS *http://tinyurl.com/kgkjp77* and Android *http://tinyurl.com/kkyawcj* and PowerSchool Student iOS *http://tinyurl.com/k2cueka* and Android *http://tinyurl.com/loonk6s* apps to keep track of and share information about student attendance, school announcements, assignments, assignment scores, teacher comments, grades, etc.

## Information Access

Students can also use their mobile apps for readily accessing information from a range of different sources (search engines, databases, newspapers, magazines, etc.) now available through ubiquitous broadband access. With the iOS Siri app, students can verbally ask questions and receive answers. And, some of these tools not only provide information but also organize and identify patterns in that information. Once they access this information students can readily share that information with their peers, for example, a group of students all working on the same project.

In a teacher-research study of the benefits of using iPads on his students' reading and writing, James Harmon (2011) compared his high school students who used iPads for their reading and writing with students who did not use iPads. While he did not conduct statistical comparisons, Harmon found that the students who used iPads had higher scores on standardized tests for both reading and writing, had higher levels of motivation for reading and writing, and generated longer essays than the students who were not using iPads.

## Multimodality: Photos/Videos/Artwork/Music

Students can use mobile devices to view or take photos/video or create artwork/music for uses in a wide range of subjects, multimodality that serves to enhance student engagement. They can readily access images associated with topics they are studying. For example, the iOS The Elements: A Visual Exploration *http://tinyurl.com/n8kdrwh* app that portrays the periodic table for use in chemistry classes provides students with 3D images of different elements. And, given the portability of their mobile devices, students can take photos or record videos wherever and whenever they wish; the majority of all photos are now taken on smartphones. Students can also use apps to edit and share their images or videos, including annotations about those images or videos.

Rather than rely on print books or other texts, students can now access e-books/e-textbooks without having to haul around their print textbooks. All of their textbooks can now be loaded on one device. Moreover, e-book textbooks are becoming increasingly interactive in ways that combine print with links to websites or videos. Apple's free iBooks Author tool or the Inkling publishing platform is being used to transform textbooks via multimodal images and videos. Students can highlight and take notes in response to their readings, which they can save and share with other students using the same book. In addition to authors creating books, teachers can create their own interactive books for their students and students can write their own books.

## Redefining the Curriculum Through Technology Use

Valuing the use of apps in schools therefore entails redefining the curriculum in ways that value adopting literacies associated with understanding and producing digital texts. This does not mean abandoning a print-based approach but rather meshing the two in inventive ways.

One framework for thinking about this redesigned curriculum is the SAMR model, based on four phases or steps involved in uses of digital literacies in the curriculum formulated by Ruben Puentedura: "Substitution, Augmentation, Modification, Redefinition" (Puentedura, 2011).

1. *Substitution*: the computer stands in for another technological tool without a significant change in the tool's function.
2. *Augmentation*: the computer replaces another technological tool, with significant functionality increase.
3. *Modification*: the computer enables the redesign of significant portions of a task.
4. *Redefinition*: the computer allows for the creation of new tasks that would otherwise be inconceivable without the technology.

Puentedura (2011) argues that none of these phases is necessarily superior—the use of a Substitution tool may be appropriate given certain learning objectives. What is critical is how you determine the relationship between the use of the tool and your learning objectives—the fact that a Substitution tool will not serve to foster creating new tasks that can only be done using technology. For example, in adopting a class set of iPads for her elementary math classrooms in a Chicago school, Jennie Magiera (2011), drawing from the SAMR model, noted that she initially taught her status quo math curriculum with the iPads without changing that curriculum, an example of Substitution. She just used math apps to substitute her worksheets for learning math. When she realized that the use of these apps did not really take advantage of the affordances of using the iPad beyond Substitution and Augmentation to move to Modification and Redefinition of her existing curriculum, she decided that she needed to change her approach to using the iPads:

> Data collection from these apps is limited and the level of student cognition is often low. Consider then, a creation app like ShowMe. This app can be used to address a wide range of standards from math to science to literacy— and will engage students at the highest level of Bloom's Taxonomy— creation. Relating this back to SAMR—the content apps are all substituting or augmenting pencil and paper learning. A creation app such as ShowMe

is redefining teaching and learning. Thus one redefined lesson outweighing dozens of substitution or augmentation lessons. (p. 2)

Rather than think simply about integration of the iPads and math apps to reify her existing curriculum, Jennie was moving towards Modification and Redefinition of how students learned through social sharing of audio commentary and visual drawings of math problems using the ShowMe app in ways that exploited the affordances of the iPad features.

Another example of Modification and Redefinition augmented by two English language arts teachers occurred when they had their students create MySpace profiles, blog posts, and multimodal posters associated with the characters from literary texts they were reading (Lewis, 2011/2012). In doing so, they had redesigned their traditional essay literary analysis assignments into more multimodal assignments involving the use of digital literacies. One of the two teachers, Barb, noted:

> My goal is to have them think *of* the character and *like* the character and to make that happen in an interesting way that challenges them to go "outside the box" . . . there's no difference between that stick figure and a MySpace page except that MySpace asks him to go a little beyond, like, "Knowing what you know about this character, what books might he read? . . . what friends would he have, and what online chat rooms would he be in?" It's phenomenal. . . . You can think of it as, let's say you're Atticus Finch on your MySpace page, and I'm Tom Robinson [characters in *To Kill a Mockingbird*], we can be online friends and communicate that way. (p. 290)

Barb noted that the students were much more engaged with creating and sharing these profiles than they had been in the past when completing their essay analyses. At the same time, the students experienced tensions between employing a formal writing style associated with writing in school versus adopting a more informal style associated with language use in MySpace social networking or texting. When the other teacher, Caitlin, gave them an opportunity to choose to employ the style they were most comfortable using, many of the students chose to adopt a more formal style because they assumed that, in a school context, their teacher preferred them to use the more formal style and that, as someone of a different generation, the teacher may not have understood their use of a more informal style. The teachers also found that, in some cases, assuming that their students were attuned to current digital literacies was not always the case. In some cases, their students had not employed MySpace.

All of this suggests that redesigning print-based assignments into assignments involving uses of digital literacies involves complexities related to students' ability to navigate between different social contexts, as well as the degree to which use of digital tools builds on their interests and needs.

## iOS, Android OS, and Chrome OS Apps

In this book, given the increasing use of iPads, Android tablets, or Chromebooks over Mac or PC desktops or laptops in schools, we will be focusing primarily on use of iOS and Android OS apps, with some references to Chrome OS apps. Because many students now have their own smartphones or tablets, as well as their own tablets, and if your school has a BYOD (bring-your-own-device) policy, then many students will be able to use their iOS and Android smartphones or tablets, particularly for use with Android apps or iOS apps.

The iOS apps we discuss in this book are used on iPads, iPhones, and iPod Touches (most apps for iPhone will work on iPads and vice versa). These apps are accessed by links to the iTunes Store *http://tinyurl.com/bssljs6* for iOS apps (see also apps for instruction listed on iTunes Apps for Teachers *http://tinyurl.com/kkxz3sr*).

The Android OS apps are used with medium- to low-price devices using the Android OS—the Nexus 7 and 10, KUNO, Sony Xperia Tablet Z, Asus MeMO Pad HD 7, Asus Transformer Pad 300, Asus Transformer Prime, LG G Pad 3.8, Galaxy Tab 3, Galaxy Tab 10, Galaxy Note 8.0, and Evga Tegra Note 7 tablets or the Kindle Fire HD (note: Android apps for the Kindle Fire are available only at the Amazon Store *http://tinyurl.com/l3qy5n5*) as well as any number of different Android smartphones. These apps are available on the Google Play Store *http://tinyurl.com/cn9oc2t*. The Android Amplify Tablets, with a $199.00 version for use in the 2014–2015 school year, is linked to the Amplify curriculum system *http://www.amplify.com/curriculum* that includes activities for different subject matter areas.

The Chrome OS apps available on the Chrome WebStore *http://tinyurl.com/mylg6xz* (this requires installation of the Google Chrome browser for Mac OS *http://tinyurl.com/bqgtntg* or for Windows 8/7/Vista/XP *http://tinyurl.com/n53n4su*) operate based on the Chrome OS. While there are far fewer Chrome OS apps than iOS or Android apps, we include mention of a few of these Chrome OS apps given the rapid increase in the number of Chromebook models produced by Acer, HP, Samsung, Lenovo, and Google itself in schools (for a comparison of different Chromebooks see *http://tinyurl.com/af5kgef*), recognizing that Android apps as of Spring 2014 still cannot be used on Chromebooks. It should also be noted that most of the Chrome OS apps are free. And, as announced in Winter, 2014 (*http://tinyurl.com/qa7ukql*), Chrome OS apps will now be available for use on Android and Mac OS devices, so developers will be creating more Chrome OS apps.

The Chrome OS differs from the Chrome browser app in that, like Firefox or Internet Explorer, the Chrome browser app can be used across different platforms. It is used to run Chromebooks or Chromeboxes (desktop versions of Chromebooks), which are network computer devices that use solid state storage similar to what is found on a USB flash drive (Miller, 2013), so that the apps, which seem to be housed on the devices themselves, are actually just links to the Google Server.

This means that Chromebooks are primarily a linking device to the cloud, which means that most of them do not contain a hard disk drive, reducing their weight and the cost of the devices. It also means that there are fewer security issues with a Chromebook in that it is less difficult to infect a Chromebook because its apps are housed in the cloud as opposed to on the device, so that if there is a problem with an app, it is fixed by Google on their cloud, as opposed to having a problem with an app on an infected tablet (Root, 2013). And, if a tablet is lost or stolen, the information on those tablets can be accessed, while with the Chromebook, that information is stored in the cloud.

At the same time, there are still some advantages to iPad and Android tablets compared to Chromebooks (Low, 2013; Miller, 2013). Tablets have the advantages of being lighter and therefore more portable than Chromebooks; having a higher screen resolution and touch than Chromebooks (the Acer Chromebook C720P does have touch); far more apps than are available on the Chrome OS; the ability to work offline, versus Chromebooks, which require to be online and can be slow with slow connections; superior video editing features; and a longer battery life (10 hours for the iPad Air) than Chromebooks (4 to 6 hours). And, because students can still use their cloud-based Google Drive apps (Docs, Presentations, Forms, Numbers, etc.) on their tablets as well as on Chromebooks, the cloud-based feature of Chromebooks isn't necessarily a critical attribute.

Yet, the Chromebook, as previously noted, is less expensive than many tablets, has a touchpad for use with a cursor for pointing to features on a screen which is lacking in tablets, a larger screen than most tablets, includes an integrated keyboard for typing, and has USB ports lacking on tablets for students to bring their work on flash drives to load into the device. For students who are doing a lot of writing, particularly at the upper grades, the inclusion of a keyboard and mouse is an asset. Moreover, Chromebooks support use of Chrome OS apps and Google Apps for Education that can be easily loaded into carts of Chromebooks at the press of one button. And, because these apps are cloud-based, there is no need to update them, as is the case with tablets, since they are updated on the cloud.

Because this book is about the use of apps and not devices per se, we leave decisions about selection of devices up to you, recognizing that your choice and use of apps will vary according to the device you are using.

## Summary

In this chapter, we stress the idea that, in planning activities for use of apps in the classroom, it is your own activities that should determine how you exploit the affordances of particular apps to achieve your particular learning objectives, as opposed to just using an app for the sake of using that app. It is also the case that you can design activities that can exploit the affordances of mobile devices—ubiquity, engagement, portability, reachability, information access, and multimodality—to enhance students' learning; for example, the fact that they can capture images on a field trip with their smartphones or tablets for use in reflecting on what they learned on that field trip. We also posited how you can define your learning objectives in terms of different literacies constituting learning across the curriculum, something we explore in more detail in the next chapter.

## References

Angst, C., & Malinowski, E. (2010, August 23–October 8). Findings from eReader Project, Phase 1: Use of iPads in MGT40700, Project Management. University of Notre Dame Working Paper Series (pp. 1–17). Mendoza College of Business, University of Notre Dame. Retrieved from http://www.nd.edu/~cangst/NotreDame_iPad_Report_01-06-11.pdf

Baron, N. S. (2011). Concerns about mobile phones: A cross-national study. *First Monday*, *16*(8). Retrieved from http://firstmonday.org/htbin/cgiwrap/bin/ojs/index.php/fm/article/viewArticle/3335/3032

Barton, D., & Hamilton, M. (2000). *Situated literacies: Reading and writing in context*. New York: Psychology Press.

Brooks-Young, S. (2010). *Teaching with the tools kids really use: Learning with Web and mobile technologies*. Los Angeles: Corwin.

Conole, G., de Laat, M., Dillon, T., & Darby, J. (2006). Student experiences of technologies. Bristol, UK: Jisc. Retrieved from http://tinyurl.com/kchw74m

Dickens, H., & Churches, A. (2011). *Apps for learning: 40 best iPad, iPod Touch, iPhone apps*. Los Angeles: Corwin.

Fusch, D. (2011). Piloting the iPad. *Academic Impressions*, June. Retrieved from http://www.academicimpressions.com/hei_resources/0611-diagnostic.pdf

Gibson, J. J. (1986). *The ecological approach to visual perception*. New York: Taylor & Francis Group.

Harmon, J. (2011). Unlocking literacy with iPads. Euclid, OH: Euclid Public Schools. Retrieved from http://tinyurl.com/mklov33

Jenkins, H. (2006). *Convergence culture: Where old and new media collide*. New York: New York University Press.

Kalantzis, M., & Cope, B. (2012). *Literacies*. New York: Cambridge University Press.

Lewis, E. C. (2011/2012). Friending Atticus Finch: English teachers' perspectives on MySpace as a contemporary framework for literary analysis. *Journal of Adolescent & Adult Literacy*, *55*(4), 285–295.

Low, C. (2013, December 12). Chromebook vs. tablet: Which should you buy? [Web log post]. Retrieved from http://tinyurl.com/kwj5jun

Madden, M., Lenhart, A., Duggan, M., Cortesi, S., & Gasser, U. (2013) *Teens and technology 2013*. Washington, DC: Pew Research Center Internet and American Life Project. Retrieved from http://tinyurl.com/pkdsqv3

Magiera, J. (2011, October 30). Breaking down to rebuild: Redefining the innovative classroom [Web log post]. Retrieved from http://teachinglikeits2999.blogspot.com/2011/10/breaking-down-to-rebuild-redefining.html

Magley, G. (2011, October 3). Grade 8 mobile one-to-one with iPads: Component of the Millis schools personalized learning initiative. Millis, MA: Millisp Public Schools. Retrieved from http://tinyurl.com/k7jfato

Miller, M. (2013). *My Google Chromebook*, 2nd ed. Indianapolis, IN: Que Publishing.

Nielsen, L., & Webb, W. (2011). *Teaching generation text: Using cell phones to enhance learning.* New York: John Wiley.

Pollock, M. (2011). Research day: Exploring the potential of texting for student–teacher communication. The OneVille Project. Retrieved from http://wiki.oneville.org/main/The_OneVille_Project

Prensky, M. (2012). Eliminating the app gap. *Educational Technology*, January–February. Retrieved from http://tonyv.me/marcpapps

Puentedura, R. R. (2011). A matrix model for designing and assessing network-enhanced courses. Retrieved from http://www.hazlet.org/Page/6049

Rainie, L. (2012, January 23). Tablet and e-book reader ownership nearly double over the holiday gift-giving period. Washington, DC: Pew Research Center's Internet and American Life Project. Retrieved from http://tinyurl.com/cpt3yg4

Riedel, C. (2014, February 3). 10 major technology trends in education. *THE Journal*. Retrieved from http://tinyurl.com/m7aolss

Root, G (2013). *Cloud computing with Google Chrome.* Amazon Digital Services, Inc. Retrieved from http://tinyurl.com/n5pf7av

Schwartz, K. (2013, December 30). Tablets for fifth graders? Teachers try different tactics [Web log post]. Retrieved from http://tinyurl.com/obwrelj

Speicher, S., & Walthour, J. (2013, May 11). Subtext iPad app: Collaborative reading made easy. Edina, MN: Minnesota Google Summit. Retrieved from https://docs.google.com/document/d/1ebYMFGWcJh3YrwjucirQe00DrsK62Gwq9J7aAgEAW-w/pub

StudyBlue. (2011). StudyBlue study report. Retrieved December 7, 2011 from http://tinyurl.com/7l9vp8b

Waters, J. K. (2011). Broadband, social networks, and mobility have spawned a new kind of learner. *THE Journal*. Retrieved from http://tinyurl.com/8xfjcga

Wood, C., Kemp, N., & Plester, B. (2013). *Text messaging and literacy: The evidence.* New York: Routledge.

# 2

# ACQUIRING DISCIPLINARY LITERACIES THROUGH USE OF APPS

In Chapter 1, we described how students acquire use of literacy practices through activities mediated by app affordances. In this chapter, we describe how use of these literacy practices differs across different disciplines. As a teacher, it is helpful to know how to build on those literacy practices that will support students' learning in your particular discipline.

Literacy practices differ across disciplines because members of different disciplines employ different ways of knowing, thinking, and believing (Draper, Broomhead, Jensen, Nokes, & Siebert, 2010; Moje, 2011; Shanahan, Shanahan, & Misischia, 2011). Scientists adopt an empirical approach to defining and testing hypotheses while historians analyze the cultural, political, and economic forces shaping a historical event. Accessing and assessing information in science based on empirical criteria is very different from accessing and assessing information in studying historical events or literary texts.

Mathematicians know how to read graphs given their knowledge of the meaning of shifting lines in a graph, while literary critics apply knowledge of poetic devices in analyzing poems. Reading graphs in math involves quite different practices from synthesizing the meaning of a poem. And, mathematicians have little interest in sourcing—that is, checking the credibility and accuracy of the source of a math report—while historians or scientists have a strong interest in sourcing given the critical need to determine the perspective or approach adopted by a historian or scientist in their research across multiple sources of information.

Chemists draw on knowledge of chemical elements and reactions to write their analysis of chemical reactions while psychologists use experimental methods to test out hypotheses about human actions. Writing a chemistry lab report entails different genre conventions from writing a psychology research report.

## App Affordances Fostering Uses of Literacy Practices for Acquiring Disciplinary Literacies

Given these differences in uses of literacy practices unique to your particular subject matter, in this chapter we discuss how the use of apps can foster learning literacy practices in different disciplines; learning described in terms of disciplinary literacies. By *disciplinary literacies*, we therefore mean those particular literacy practices unique to certain disciplines as subcultures, domains, or communities that value certain ways of knowing and thinking (O'Brien, Stewart, & Moje, 1995).

Elizabeth Moje (2012) has identified a number of different literacy practices associated with uses of disciplinary literacies for learning in different subjects:

- *Problem framing.* Framing problems requires identifying the specific nature and reasons for a problem—for example, in the field of environmental sciences the problem might be increased carbon dioxide that causes climate change. Framing problems also involves the knowledge of where and how to access knowledge relevant to addressing a problem, and the ability to visually represent a problem, topic, or issue.
- *Knowledge elicitation.* Learning in any discipline entails drawing on prior knowledge of a discipline—for example, what one knows about a historical period to explain a certain event in that period. Students draw on this prior knowledge in using search engines or databases to find information about a certain topic or issue.
- *Visualizing.* Learning in disciplines also involves the ability to understand and produce visual representations of information or data—graphs, charts, figures, illustrations, photos, videos, etc., to infer knowledge, ideas, or story themes represented by these visual representations.
- *Synthesizing across texts.* Students also need to know how to synthesize ideas that they have learned across different texts, such as how different texts provide competing perspectives on the same topic or issue, or how author A refutes author B.
- *Summarizing and producing/communicating knowledge.* Finally, students need to know how to summarize what they learn from different texts to generate their own knowledge, as well as how to clearly communicate that knowledge to their audiences.

Students acquire these disciplinary literacies as soon as they encounter texts and literacy practices specific to individual disciplines, certainly starting in grade three and becoming more finely tuned in grades four and five as they begin more directed study in specific subjects. As they study specific subjects, they adopt roles and stances as new members of disciplinary communities associated with sociologists, psychologists, historians, literary critics, anthropologists, biologists, chemists, mathematicians, artists, musicians, and athletes.

Students learn these disciplinary literacies not as sets of abstract principles or static practices tied to conceptual knowledge, but rather through participation in activities or events valued within disciplinary communities. As members of these communities, students participate in situated cognition (Lave & Wenger, 2013) in which knowledge is constructed by doing, mediated through the use of "real world" sets of tools and ways of knowing and thinking specific to a discipline (Gee & Hayes, 2011).

## Learning Through Tool Mediation

This concept of situated cognition or situated learning is consistent with creating authentic learning activities mediated by uses of app affordances, just as students have learned to use other kinds of tools mediating their learning. By mediating, we mean the ways in which tools themselves are designed to foster certain disciplinary literacies.

Students are continually acquiring uses of a range of different tools mediating their learning. For example, in a literature class, students learn how to analyze portrayals of gender differences in a novel by adopting the tool of a feminist critical perspective; in a biology class, they might learn how to use a microscope as a tool to identify cells, simple organisms, or bacteria on slides; or, in engaging in a debate, students might employ note cards as tools to cite valid, credible evidence to support their positions, adopt an authoritative stance, or to refute counter-arguments to gain their audience's identification. In these situations students learn to equate the use of tools mediating their disciplinary literacy practices with engaging in particular tasks. The next time students encounter a similar situation, they know to employ those disciplinary literacy practices relevant to that situation.

### Activity → App affordances → Literacy practices → Disciplinary literacies

How then can you help students use apps to employ those literacy practices specific to acquiring these disciplinary literacies? In planning activities, you can design activities that exploit certain app affordances for learning literacy practices unique to your specific discipline.

For example, if you teach chemistry, when students in a chemistry class are using writing apps for note-taking, mind-mapping, blog posts, or collaborative/extended writing, they are using these apps in very different ways from writing in a history class given the differences in scientific and historical arguments. Writing a chemistry report involves the use of concise descriptions and the report of visual observations through charts or graphs, often including images. In contrast, writing in a history class often requires references to and analysis of competing interpretations of events, including references to, and analysis of, different sources for these interpretations. Thus, your effective use of writing apps depends on your ability to employ them in ways that are consistent with those disciplinary literacies constituting your subject.

## The Common Core State Standards and Disciplinary Literacies

One component of the 6–12 English Language Arts Common Core State Standards (Council of Chief State School Officers and National Governors' Association, 2010a) is a section for grades 6 to 12, entitled *Literacy in History/ Social Studies, Science, and Technical Subjects*. These standards related to disciplinary texts and reading the text are posed as English language arts standards, not as social studies standards or science standards; they are named and defined as residing *within* the English language arts. Second, because they are included as part of English language arts standards, the specific standards include descriptive definitions found in 30 years of reading and writing methods texts. For example, the standards for grades 6 to 8 in social studies include the following: "Determine the meaning of words and phrases as they are used in a text, including vocabulary specific to domains related to history/social studies" and "Describe how a text presents information (e.g., sequentially, comparatively, causally)."

These are reasonable, but teachers and other educators should realize that the strategies that are selected and the way they are defined are from descriptive definitions from literacy rather than from within the disciplines that they apply to. The language used to name the standards and the descriptions of the competences come from the field of literacy rather than the disciplines (for resources related to implementation of the English language arts standards see *http://englishccss. pbworks.com*).

It is also the case that the use of apps in math class serves to address the Common Core Standards for Mathematics (Council of Chief State School Officers and National Governors' Association, 2010b). One component of those standards focuses on uses of technology tools to engage in mathematical analysis:

> Mathematically proficient high school students analyze graphs of functions and solutions generated using a graphing calculator. They detect possible errors by strategically using estimation and other mathematical knowledge. When making mathematical models, they know that technology can enable them to visualize the results of varying assumptions, explore consequences, and compare predictions with data. (p. 7)

As we discuss in this book, students can employ apps such as the iOS Graphing Calculator HD *http://tinyurl.com/mb6z7l7* or Android Graphing Calculator by Mathlab *http://tinyurl.com/bc839zu* to conduct their calculations on the devices as opposed to having to employ a separate calculator.

In this book, while we begin Chapters 4 to 10 by listing those English Language Arts Common Core State Standards relevant to the focus of each of these chapters, we caution that implementing these standards in a social studies or science class requires recognizing the disciplinary literacies unique to social studies or science instruction. Because this book is focused on literacy practices, we reference the English language arts standards, recognizing that some of our discussion of use of math apps does address the math standards.

## App Affordances as Mediating Tools

Students' use of app affordances *mediates* their use of disciplinary literacies. Take, for example, the use of apps for highlighting, annotating, and creating notes about texts such as iAnnotate PDF, GoodReader, Readdle, Notetaker HD, UPAD, or smartNote Free. One affordance of these apps is that they make it easy for students to readily add annotations to specific, highlighted sections of a text. They therefore mediate students' adoption of more active roles as readers who are formulating their responses to texts. Moreover, they contain features that allow students to readily store all of their annotations/notes in an archive, mediating the organization of their thinking so that they can then return to their annotations/notes to look for certain patterns or key ideas in their thinking. And, the apps contain features that allow students to easily share their annotations/notes with peers, mediating collaborative construction of knowledge.

At the same time, *how* students use affordances of these annotation apps will vary according to different disciplinary literacies. Students annotating a short story use annotation/note-taking apps to focus on consistent uses of literary techniques or character actions that create a repository of annotations that can then be used to interpret a writer's consistent literary style or thematic focus. By contrast, in annotating a news report of a study of voting differences in presidential elections based on race, class, gender, and age, students in a social studies class focus on how the results of their study are connected to their own understanding of how race, class, gender, and age differences influence other types of behavior; this focus draws on students' knowledge of groups in society.

## Mediating Peer Interactions

Students also acquire disciplinary literacies using apps with the affordances that mediate their peer interactions as members of communities of practice (Lave & Wenger, 2013; Wenger, 1999), as we just noted, and of "passionate affinity spaces" (Gee & Hayes, 2011). Gee and Hayes (2011) describe these spaces as occurring when:

> People organize themselves in the real world and/or via the Internet (or a virtual world) to learn something connected to a shared endeavor, interest, or passion. The people have an affinity (attraction) to the shared endeavor, interest, or passion first and foremost and then to others because of their shared affinity. (p. 69)

Gee and Hayes posit that, in these "affinity spaces," people can participate because of their shared interests with the other members, as opposed to whether they have certain official credentials or because of perceiving a space as closed according to restrictions. Members in passionate affinity spaces share a common passion or interest in achieving certain shared goals, for example, addressing an issue facing their school or community.

As is the case with the use of annotation/note-taking apps that mediate sharing of annotations/notes with peers, one of the prime affordances of many screen-casting apps such as VoiceThread, ShowMe, or Explain Everything is that they allow students to add audio or written comments to a text, image, or video for sharing with their peers. Or, they can use online discussion or collaborative writing apps to interact with each other to socially share and create texts. And, in playing app games, they often play collaboratively as team members.

## Mediating Construction of Shared, Situated Knowledge

Apps also have the affordances for mediating students' construction of shared, situated knowledge. For example, in using Twitter Apps such as Twitter, Tweet-Caster, Tweetbot, Tweetdeck, Twitteriffic, or HootSuite, students are sharing information leading to the collaborative construction of knowledge. This knowledge is "distributed" in that different members share their own knowledge or expertise, so that no one member is expected to know everything.

This knowledge is also "situated" in that it is valued within a community or affinity space consistent with that community's or space's way of knowing and thinking. For example, scientists have a strong commitment to a "shared domain of interest" (Wenger, 1999) associated with the need to provide empirical evidence for their claims.

## Mediating Acquiring Academic Language

Learning these specific ways of knowing involves the acquisition of academic language as a "premium literacy" that goes beyond "fundamental literacy" acquired at an early age (Gee, 2011). The ability to effectively employ this academic language as a "premium literacy" is critical to students' future success in school or the workplace. As James Gee (2011) argues:

Traditional literacy (reading and writing) has and still does come in two grades. One grade leads to working class jobs, once a good thing when there were unions and benefits, but now not such a good thing when it means low pay and no benefits, usually in service work. The other grade leads to more meaningful work and more financial success. What distinguishes these grades of literacy? The premium grade involves mastery of so-called "academic language," the forms of language used in research, empirical reasoning and logical argumentation. Now, I am well aware that nearly everyone hates "academic language" (things like "Hornworms exhibit a significant amount of variation," rather than "Hornworms sure vary a lot in how well they grow"), but when they are in good jobs, they are there because they got through their high school chemistry book and argued and debated their way out of a good college. (p. 1)

In addition to acquiring specific ways of knowing and using language unique to particular disciplines, students also acquire roles, norms, beliefs, and goals constituting participation in communities or spaces associated with disciplinary practices. For example, when students use game apps involving playing with other players, they are learning how to operate within a community of practice of players who follow or adopt certain roles, norms, and goals associated with winning the game. And, students who are novices learn to observe veteran players of the game to acquire practices through imitation. As they experience set-backs or failures, they learn to reflect on their uses of practices to change or grow.

## Uses of Apps Within Disciplinary Literacies

Given our focus on uses of apps to foster learning literacy practices, we now turn to describing how to foster uses of literacy practices through app affordances according to disciplinary literacies. (For resources on fostering literacy learning across the curriculum see *http://tinyurl.com/7crlxzy* as well as, from the National Center for Literacy Education *http://tinyurl.com/kbyd4cv*).

### Sciences

Take, for example, apps for fostering uses of writing practices supporting learning in science. Students might use note-taking apps such as the iOS bundled app, Notes, for a biology project related to observing water pollution in a local river. Students may then use their notes as well as photos linked to those notes to capture precise, concrete descriptions and even images of instances of pollution in the river. Or, students learn to read science research reports based on the knowledge of how scientists conduct empirical research through formulating guiding questions and hypotheses and gathering data to test hypotheses.

Students can also employ their smartphone or tablet devices in conjunction with certain apps for performing certain science observations and experiments. One advantage of the use of apps in science is their support of the affordances of portability so that students can conduct observations and analyses in different sites, along with using the affordances of multimodality of use of images, audio, or video to collect data and then collaboratively share that data. For example, students can use the the the iOS *http://tinyurl.com/nmo8b5v* or Android *http://tinyurl.com/kqhdu7r* Distant Suns or the iOS *http://tinyurl.com/cqjryr7* or Android *http://tinyurl.com/nxe5gr7* Star Walk apps for observing the stars or planets in astronomy. Or, for observing the mitosis process of cells, students can employ the iOS *http://tinyurl.com/msxpqrs* or Android *http://tinyurl.com/n7jgywq* Mitosis apps.

For studying the influence of climate change, students can use the iOS Adventure Learning *http://tinyurl.com/q9gunaa* app that includes descriptions of trips to the Arctic to study the influence of climate change on that region; see Henrickson (2014) for a description of the develpment of that app. And, they can access information about climate change on iOS *http://tinyurl.com/p9qrzqp* or Android *http://tinyurl.com/aylzjrj* NASA Earth Now, the iOS World Bank Climate Change DataFinder *http://tinyurl.com/mm5ujl5*, the Android Climate Change Challenge *http://tinyurl.com/ohwaymz*, or the iOS Painting with Time: Climate Change *http://tinyurl.com/oqop8e3* that involves users viewing the impact of climate change by themselves changing images of glaciers, land areas, or weather events.

Sam Gliksman (2013) cites a number of examples of use of devices and apps for taking photos of their observations or experiments for uses in scientific analysis, or collecting data to store and share on their devices:

- Use measurement sensors from PASCO *http://tinyurl.com/kluqsey* to connect to the iOS *http://tinyurl.com/kqwldq2* or Android *http://tinyurl.com/mzproae* SPARKvue HD apps using the PASCO bluetooth interface to send measurement data to an iPad or Android device, for example, measurements of carbon dioxide levels, temperature, or force.
- Use the ProScope Mobile *http://tinyurl.com/lfbmbws* digital microscope to send images or video to the iOS AirMicroPad *http://tinyurl.com/llsw86o* app for analysis of those images or video on their iPads.
- Use the Vernier Video Physics *http://tinyurl.com/momgvbe* app to capture video of moving objects to collect data on movement and force.
- Use the Monster Physics *http://tinyurl.com/c5r5mf7* app with younger students to have them build machines based on knowledge of physics principles.
- For Science iOS apps: *http://tinyurl.com/mvjad3a*
- For iOS middle school science apps: *http://tinyurl.com/n6hdtos*
- For iOS high school science apps: *http://tinyurl.com/lh9zetx*
- For APPitic science iOS apps: *http://tinyurl.com/kntrawv*
- For Google Play Store science Android apps: *http://tinyurl.com/m9zcrjy*

## Math

In a math class, in reading a mathematical analysis of phenomena, students may be focusing more on the graphic representations of those phenomena to address the Common Core Math Standards. In using the Notes app in a math class, a math teacher may project notes about a math problem as "chalk talk" in modeling ways of solving a math problem. In contrast to the use of note-taking in a biology class to capture specific observations, the note-taking in your math class is used to openly display your thought processes to students regarding certain mathematical proofs to solve a problem.

For learning algebra, students can use the iOS Algebra Touch *http://tinyurl. com/mash5wu* or Android Algebra Tutor *http://tinyurl.com/lcwc7pf* apps that model and support algebraic thinking by breaking down the processes involved in solving equations.

For learning geometry, students can use the iOS *http://tinyurl.com/n3tfx4u* or Android *http://tinyurl.com/q4gmnej* Geometry Pad, iOS Geometry *http://tinyurl. com/n8zq4uf*, iOS Geometry Pro *http://tinyurl.com/qck53z8*, or Android Pocket Geometry *http://tinyurl.com/mfmb3yz* apps providing them with calculation and drawing tools to create geometric shapes. And they can play the iOS *http://tinyurl. com/kmal4pm* and Android *http://tinyurl.com/n33y6f5* Geometry Dash game that requires knowledge of geometry to move quickly through a series of challenges.

Or students may employ a graphics construction app to create their own representation of the same phenomena so that they understand how graphics serve to communicate information. Expert math readers apply their knowledge of math in focusing their attention on relevant information in the text to avoid misinterpretation; they attend to graphics to interpret information and assess the accuracy of the information; and they reread the text to assess the relevance of the information. (For a description of these literacy practices specific to mathematics, see the Minds of Modern Mathematics *http://tinyurl.com/kt26lug* app that provides a history of the development of mathematics and how math is employed in science, music, art, architecture, and culture.)

- For math iOS apps: *http://tinyurl.com/lrlxmwh*
- For iOS middle school math apps: *http://tinyurl.com/n6hdtos*
- For iOS high school math apps: *http://tinyurl.com/lh9zetx*
- For AppSearch math apps: *http://tinyurl.com/pmj5j5j*
- For Google Play Store math Android apps: *http://tinyurl.com/lrqhjuw*

## Social Studies

In social studies, three key disciplinary literacies include determining the source of information about an event, corroboration, and contextualization of information about events (Draper et al., 2010). In determining the source of information about events, students need to consider who acquired the information about an event, how they acquired that information, and how those factors influenced their rendering in text. Corroboration involves the ability to compare and contrast conflicting information about an event, cross-checking that information against other information or previous accounts of an event. Contextualization involves framing an event in terms of larger cultural, political, economic, geographical, and historical contexts or forces.

Social studies teachers foster the kinds of thinking employed by history experts, for example, analysis of the perspectives employed in explaining an event using the Storify browser *https://storify.com* site and Android Storify Viewer *http://tinyurl.com/luq7xg8* apps that capture different news interpretations of the same current event to have students contrast the perspectives employed in interpreting that event.

- For social studies iOS apps: *http://tinyurl.com/kzojkzl*
- For iOS middle school social studies apps: *http://tinyurl.com/n6hdtos*
- For iOS high school social studies apps: *http://tinyurl.com/lh9zetx*
- For APPitic social studies iOS apps: *http://tinyurl.com/mhxpw2*
- For Google Play Store social studies Android apps: *http://tinyurl.com/mg6zccm*

## Second Languages

Central to second language/English language learner (ELL) instruction are opportunities for students to practice use of language for a range of different communication purposes. Second language teachers can employ the speaking/listening apps described in Chapter 7 to foster discussions in different languages. And, they can employ speech-to-text apps for students to perceive their translations in written form as well as text-to-speech apps to listen to their written translations.

- For second language iOS apps: *http://tinyurl.com/m56zc49*
- For iOS middle school secondary language apps: *http://tinyurl.com/n6hdtos*
- For iOS high school second language apps: *http://tinyurl.com/lh9zetx*
- For APPitic Spanish iOS apps: *http://tinyurl.com/ka5alwa*
- For Google Play Store second languages Android apps: *http://tinyurl.com/ms4xls5*

## Art

Students can employ different art apps for accessing art museum collections such as the iOS *http://tinyurl.com/l448veq* Art Authority apps for access to one thousand different artists. And, they can employ apps such as the iOS Paper *http://tinyurl.com/ctqccqo* or Android Fresco Paint Pro *http://tinyurl.com/oshtla7* apps for drawing and painting using different colors and brush choices.

- For art iOS apps: *http://tinyurl.com/mfv3qte*
- For iOS middle school art apps: *http://tinyurl.com/n6hdtos*
- For iOS high school art apps: *http://tinyurl.com/lh9zetx*
- For APPitic art apps: *http://tinyurl.com/lw2xogd*
- For Google Play Store art Android apps: *http://tinyurl.com/lun84mx*

## Music

Students can use music apps to listen to different kinds of music as well as learn to read musical scores using sheet readers such as iOS forScore *http://tinyurl.com/n6yoemz* or Android MobileSheets *http://tinyurl.com/kxlnwko*. And, students can create their own music employing apps for a wide range of different instruments, including the iOS Ninja Jamm *http://tinyurl.com/n2tvlmc* and Android Music Player *http://tinyurl.com/kawu3rz* apps for remixing music.

- For music iOS apps: *http://tinyurl.com/m39neen*
- For iOS middle school music apps: *http://tinyurl.com/n6hdtos*
- For iOS high school music apps: *http://tinyurl.com/lh9zetx*
- For APPitic music apps: *http://tinyurl.com/lktpy39*
- For Google Play Store music Android apps: *http://tinyurl.com/l7aq642*

## Connections Between Disciplinary Literacies and App Affordances

To select those apps whose affordances are most relevant for devising activities specific to acquiring certain disciplinary literacies we refer readers to both general app recommendation sites and sites associated with specific disciplines on the book's website: *http://tinyurl.com/clxfsy9*; for the Apple Education Apps: *http://www.apple.com/education/apps*; for a summary handout on Google Docs that lists apps according to the chapter categories in this book: *http://tinyurl.com/6oxcn7z*.

In Table 2.1 below, we show how specific disciplinary literacy practices align with app affordances associated with the literacy practices described in each of Chapters 4 to 10, as well as some illustrative example for the humanities/arts, social sciences, and natural sciences.

## *Teachers Co-teaching With Literacy Teachers: Towards School-Wide Collaboration*

Content-area teachers may assume that teaching literacy practices is the job of the English language arts teacher. However, given a broader conception of literacy, students are actually actively employing literacy practices in all classrooms.

This suggests the need for literacy/English language arts and discipline-area teachers to engage in co-teaching or shared curriculum planning by working

**TABLE 2.1** Apps Supporting Learning of Different Discipinary Literacies

| Disciplinary Literacies Practices Supporting Learning | Apps and Affordances | Illustrative Uses |
| --- | --- | --- |
| **4. Accessing/analyzing information**<br><br>• Adopting an inquiry stance<br>• Defining a clear purpose and keyword categories for searches<br>• Subscribing to and sharing on information sites<br>• Recognizing differences in information across different disciplines<br>• Analyzing and using information sources | **Search apps**: Provide access to information from databases<br><br>**Social bookmarking apps**: Enable tagging, annotating, and sharing information with others<br><br>**QR code apps**: Provide access to and sharing of information using QR codes<br><br>**Curation apps**: Enable one to access, store, and organize information and news stories based on topics<br><br>**Apps for multimodal access**: Provide access to images, audio, and video (see also Chapter 8/9): for use in media projects | **Humanities/Arts; Social sciences; Natural sciences**: Acquiring online information for use in discussing or generating text-based or multimodal reports on topics, issues, or themes |
| **5. Synthesizing/ connecting texts**<br><br>• Accessing information through interactive or "enhanced" e-books/ audiobooks<br>• Synthesizing information using note-taking/annotation apps for constructing and sharing knowledge<br>• Making intertextual connections between texts to identify related topics, issues, or themes<br>• Responding to and appreciating comics/ graphic novels | **E-book/audiobook apps**: Provide interactive learning experiences<br><br>**Note-taking/annotation apps**: Provide tools to synthesize/summarize texts for oneself and others<br><br>**Comics/graphic novel apps**: Offer tools for writing and producing comic and/or graphic novel layouts for engaging to students | **Humanities/Arts**: Responding to literature/ nonfiction or media texts; creating intertextual connections based on ideas, conventions, author, or historical period<br><br>**Social sciences**: Responding to historical, psychological, sociological, or cultural/ political texts based on the validity/recency of, and approaches to content of the texts<br><br>**Natural sciences**: Analyzing and responding to scientific reports |
| **6. Producing and editing written texts**<br><br>• Generating and developing information and ideas in one's own words | **Note-taking/outlining apps**: Enable the recording of information/observations<br><br>**Dictating/translating apps**: Provide tools for recording | **Humanities/Arts**: Producing essays/ literary texts; formulating opinions/ideas; sharing information |

- Recording specific reactions and observations.

- Adopting a sense of voice to communicate meaning.

- Acquiring proficiency in a different language

- Employing visual representations

- Defining the logical relationships between concepts or ideas

- Collaboratively developing or expanding topics

- Using hyperlinks and images

- Providing and receiving feedback to foster self-assessing

- Editing and formatting drafts to enhance readability to engage audiences

7. **Discussing ideas through constructing roles and relating to/ collaborating with others to learn**

- Developing a sense of voice

- Employing dialogic exchange of ideas

- Collaboratively developing and extending topics

- Making intertextual connections

- Reflecting on the relevancy of discussion material for reports

thoughts and ideas; can provide both audio and speech-to-print output

**Annotation apps**: Enable summarizing responses

**Mind-mapping apps**: Offer tools for defining aspects of a topic or text, showing connections, and defining types of relationships between and among aspects of topics

**Blogging/Twitter apps**: Allow sharing of information/ formulating opinions/ideas

**Extended/collaborative writing apps**: Facilitate producing/editing texts

**Literary writing apps**: Provide tools for creating stories, poems, and plays

**Editing apps**: Allow authors multiple ways to enhance text readability and formatting

**Publishing/presentation apps**: Create engaging text

**Discussion apps**: Provide ways of sharing discussions in asynchronous and synchronous forums

**Audio/videoconference apps**: Enable online environments that mimic face-to-face interactions

**Texting/Twitter/micro-blogging apps**: Enable the sharing of short written messages

**Backchannel/whiteboard apps**: Allow a forum for sharing background information in relation to presentations

**Survey/clicker apps**: Provide tools for acquiring group opinion data on issues

**Social sciences**: Producing historical, psychological, sociological, or cultural/political texts; formulating opinions/ ideas; sharing information

**Natural sciences**: Producing science reports or other representations of data

**Humanities/Arts**: Engaging in discussions to respond to literature, media, or the arts, as well as critiquing texts and ideas

**Social sciences**: Sharing analyses of historical, social, and cultural events, topics, or issues

**Natural sciences**: Sharing and collaborating on analysis and production of scientific data

**TABLE 2.1** Continued

| Disciplinary Literacies Practices Supporting Learning | Apps and Affordances | Illustrative Uses |
| --- | --- | --- |
| **8. Producing and editing visual images**<br><br>• Finding relevant, engaging images<br>• Producing and editing engaging photos<br>• Critically responding to images<br>• Sharing responses to images<br>• Producing engaging drawings and paintings<br>• Generating engaging slideshows, albums, and presentations | **Image apps**: Facilitate the location identification, and sharing of images<br><br>**Response to image apps**: Offer ways of formulating and sharing annotation responses to images<br><br>**Infographic, charts, and graphs apps**: Presenting and organizing information and data in visually appealing ways<br><br>**Photo and photo editing apps**: Enhance the taking and editing of visually appealing photos<br><br>**Photo viewing and sharing apps**: Provide ways of organizing and presenting photos to audiences<br><br>**Drawing and painting apps**: Creating artistic productions to represent experiences and ideas.<br><br>**Presentation apps**: Provide ways to dynamically present information to engage and inform audiences | **Humanities/Arts**: Responding to and creating photos, drawings, or paintings for use in communicating ideas, stances, and aesthetics to others<br><br>**Social sciences**: Use of graphs or figures to represent empirical data; using photos or videos for historical or ethnographic research and display of events<br><br>**Natural sciences**: Uses of photo images or video to portray natural phenomena for sharing with others for analysis; using graphs or figures to represent empirical data from science experiments |
| **9. Producing and editing audio and video texts**<br><br>• Accessing relevant podcasts and audio book resources<br>• Using listening to understand information and ideas<br>• Exploring language learning and text-to-speech apps | **Streaming audio apps**: Provide access to music/presentations in real time<br><br>**Language learning apps**: Facilitate the learning and practice of different languages<br><br>**Text-to-speech apps**: Enable listening comprehension via audio versions of print text<br><br>**Dictation and audio note-taking apps**: Allow the generation of ideas through dictation and audio note-taking | **Humanities**: Responding to and creating audio and video productions associated with radio, music, and/or film history/appreciation; using literacy audio production (spoken-word poetry) or listening in literature classes<br><br>**Social sciences**: Using audio or video portrayals of past and current events to analyze these |

- Recording thoughts using dictation and audio note-taking apps
- Communicating to audiences by creating podcasts
- Developing a sense of voice through audio production
- Accessing and appreciating various music genres
- Producing music through use of music apps
- Using videos as a source for learning topics and ideas
- Creating and editing videos to communicate to others

**Podcast production apps**: Provide tools for creating podcasts and sharing information and ideas

**Music listening apps**: Enable online access to music

**Music production apps**: Offer tools for playing virtual instruments to create music

**Mixer apps**: Provide tools for mixing multiple music channels to create music remixes

**Accessing video apps**: Enable the location of and viewing of videos

**Video screencast apps**: Enable the creation of video screencasts for demonstrations and feedback

**Video production planning apps**: Facilitate the planning of productions and the use of scripts and storyboards

**Video editing apps**: Provide tools for editing videos

events; using audio or video productions to communicate information and ideas regarding social or civic issues

**Natural sciences**: Using audio or video to capture and portray natural phenomena for understanding these phenomena.

10. **Using games and simulations**

- Constructing identities
- Learning to collaborate
- Critiquing and redesigning systems

**Game/simulation apps**: Building/participating in towns, cities, worlds; language use; interactive fiction; movie/TV-based interactive fiction; role-play games; creating game apps

**Humanities**: Using games/simulations to engage in literary worlds involving inventive uses of language and adoption of different roles/perspectives

**Social sciences**: Using games/simulations to engage in problem-solving about civic or social issues, leading to entertaining alternative solutions to addressing civic and social problems

**Natural sciences**: Using games/simulations to apply knowledge of science to solving challenges or problems collaboratively to foster learning of disciplinary literacies. Literacy/English language arts teachers can provide teachers in other disciplines with ideas about uses of literacy practices relevant to the particular disciplinary literacies, and teachers in other disciplines can provide literacy/English language arts teachers with an understanding of these particular disciplinary literacies in ways that help literacy/English language arts teachers tailor their literacy practices to support those disciplinary literacies. Such collaboration is most likely to occur when teachers are collaboratively co-teaching or curriculum planning, something that is most likely to occur in middle school, in which teachers work as curriculum teams to plan interdisciplinary lessons.

One example of such co-teaching occurred when an English and a history teacher planned a co-taught lesson revolving around reading and writing historical fiction associated with the topic of slavery and the Civil War (Smith & Hauptman, 2009). Students in the English teacher's class read the historical novel, *From Slave Ship to Freedom Road* (Lester, 1998) as a text reflecting how the use of figurative language can engage readers. The history teacher had students write their own short historical fiction pieces based on their understanding of the characteristics of the historical novel they were reading in the English class. The English teacher helped her students understand the importance of applying critical perspectives, addressing issues such as accuracy, validity, and reliability in judging the response to the novel while the history teacher focused on the same criteria when the students were writing historical fiction.

This teacher collaboration is particularly important for sharing uses of apps across the curriculum; for example, by using photography apps in a science class to capture images of a chemistry experiment to include in a written report. Students can then also employ these apps to add images of a local historical site to their blog in a history class. This transfer of the disciplinary literacy of visual communication across different disciplines helps students recognize how visual images function to communicate meaning in different disciplines.

At the same time, students also learn how the use of visual communication may vary according to the literacy practices unique to different disciplines. For example, use of images to portray visually important aspects of a science experiment considers how the images serve to illustrate certain changes in chemical compounds when they are mixed together—therefore focusing on capturing change over time. This imaging is associated with the literacy practice of analyzing cause–effect relationships in science to support or disprove a hypothesis. In using images to portray a local historical site, for example, a local Civil War battlefield, the images are used more to capture the features of the terrain to provide some understanding of how that terrain influenced the events of the battle, an understanding associated with the literacy of interpreting factors shaping a historical event.

## Summary

In this chapter, we described the ways in which literacy practices vary according to differences in disciplinary practices—how reading science texts entails different ways of reading from reading social studies texts. Understanding the differences in students' use of these disciplinary literacy practices helps you determine how to use app affordances to support learning these different disciplinary literacies.

In the next chapter we'll describe ways of planning instruction based on uses of apps affordances to help students acquire disciplinary literacies. This planning involves identifying:

1.  your learning objectives or outcomes related to fostering authentic learning activities or tasks;
2.  disciplinary literacies related to using information, reading, writing, discussion, multimodality, and reflection to learn across the curriculum;
3.  affordances of relevant apps designed to foster uses of literacy practices associated with these disciplinary literacies;
4.  individual differences in students' knowledge, interests, needs, abilities, and potential engagement in using these apps;
5.  ways of modeling, scaffolding, and assessing uses of these affordances to foster uses of these disciplinary literacies.

## References

Council of Chief State School Officers and National Governors' Association. (2010a). *Common Core State Standards for English Language Arts & Literacy in History/Social Studies, Science, and Technical Subjects*. Washington, DC: Author. Retrieved from http://www.corestandards.org

Council of Chief State School Officers and National Governors' Association. (2010b). *Common Core Standards for Mathematics*. Washington, DC: Author. Retrieved from http://www.corestandards.org/Math

Draper, R. J., Broomhead, P., Jensen, A. P., Nokes, J. D., & Siebert, D. (Eds.). (2010). *(Re)Imagining content-area literacy instruction*. New York: Teachers College Press.

Gee, J. P. (2011, May 23). Digital natives, digital brains? *Huffington Post*. Retrieved from http://www.huffingtonpost.com/james-gee/digital-naties-digital-b_b_865263.html

Gee, J. P., & Hayes, E. R. (2011). *Language and learning in the digital age*. New York: Routledge.

Gliksman, S. (2013). *iPad in education for dummies*. Hoboken, NJ: John Wiley & Sons.

Henrickson, J. (2014). The conceptualization, design, and development of a K-12 adventure learning app. In C. Miller & A. Doering (Eds.), *The new landscape of mobile learning* (pp. 172–187). New York: Routledge.

Lave, J., & Wenger, E. (2013). *Situated learning: Legitimate peripheral participation*. New York: Cambridge University Press.

Lester, J. (1998). *From slave ship to freedom road*. New York: Dial Press.

Moje, E. B. (2011). Developing disciplinary discourses, literacies and identities: What's knowledge got to do with it? In M. G. L. Bonilla & K. Englander (Eds.), *Discourses and identities in contexts of educational change: Contributions from the United States and Mexico* (pp. 49–74). New York: Peter Lang.

Moje, E. B. (2012). The role of disciplinary literacy instruction: Delivering and expanding on the Common Core State Standards. Paper presented at the annual meeting of the International Reading Association, Chicago.

O'Brien, D. G., Stewart, R. A., & Moje, E. B. (1995). Why content literacy is difficult to infuse into the secondary school: Complexities of curriculum, pedagogy, and school culture. *Reading Research Quarterly, 30*, 442–463.

Shanahan, C., Shanahan, T., & Misischia, C. (2011). Analysis of expert readers in three disciplines: History, mathematics, and chemistry. *Journal of Literacy Research, 43*(4), 393–429.

Smith, A., & Hauptman, C. (2009). Complimentary co-creation: Collaborating to reach history and language arts goals. *The English Record, 59*(3), 18–33.

Wenger, E. (1999). *Communities of practice: Learning, meaning, and identity.* New York: Cambridge University Press.

# 3

# PLANNING INSTRUCTION USING APPS TO FOSTER LEARNING WITH LITERACY

In the last chapter, we argued that carefully considering app affordances on mobile devices can be used to help engage students in disciplinary literacies. We also argued that what is essential to fostering student learning is the quality of the activities you create that take advantage of these app affordances, not simply the use of apps for their own sake. How then can you plan instruction based on activities for engaging students through uses of app affordances?

## Questions for Engaging in the Planning Process

In this chapter, we describe how to plan instructional activities that build on the uses of app affordances for helping students learn uses of disciplinary literacies. To do so, we provide a set of questions that serve as a heuristic for thinking about planning instruction using apps, questions that need not be addressed in any particular order. These questions involve the following planning processes.

### Defining Learning Objectives

#### What Are My Learning Objectives?

What do you want your students to learn, to be able to know, to do, or believe, and how are these learning objectives related to your curriculum and state standards? In planning instruction, one initial step involves defining your learning objectives: What is it that you want your students to know, to be able to do, or to believe as a result of employing certain tasks or activities? Rather than simply planning these tasks or activities, you are thinking about what students *will learn* from engaging in these tasks or activities. For example, in a social studies class, in the study of the Civil War, students are reading two conflicting versions of Pickett's Charge in Gettysburg. One version blames Pickett for the outcome; one version vindicates him and blames General Lee, noting that Pickett's rendition of the battle was ordered destroyed by Lee. Your learning objective may be to help students recognize that there is no objective truth about historical events and that the construction of the meaning these events hold varies according to the interpretation of primary documents and a historian's own beliefs, expertise, credibility and agendas.

You would then use these learning objectives to develop assessment methods to determine whether your students have achieved the objectives. For example, to determine if they understand the concept of sourcing information about a historical event, you might assess if they understand that different versions or interpretations of the same events can vary according to different expertise or agendas of authors of primary texts and the historical syntheses of these texts. You may have students create their own opposing versions of an event, assessing their ability to do so. In defining learning objectives, you are also reflecting on how these objectives are related to your own and your school's larger curriculum goals or the ELA and Math Common Core State Standards (CCSS), in terms of how your objectives are consistent with the literacy practices associated with the reading, writing, speaking/listening, and language standards in the ELA standards (Beach, Haertling-Thein, & Webb, 2012). You can use a number of CCSS planning apps listed below.

---

## CCSS PLANNING APPS

**iOS**: Common Core State Standards *http://tinyurl.com/kg6xdbz*, Common Core Standards *http://tinyurl.com/kscl2dk*, Common Core Lesson Planner *http://tinyurl.com/mzhgpxz*, Apps for Common Core *http://tinyurl.com/nhtjt78*, Common Core ConceptBANK *http://tinyurl.com/ku6ajq5*

**Android**: Common Core *http://tinyurl.com/kfg5j3q*, Common Core Lesson Planner *http://tinyurl.com/kdmuyn7*, Common Core Resource Search *http://tinyurl.com/lq8m8zd*, Common Core Assessment *http://tinyurl.com/mtf6wyb*

**Chrome OS**: Next Lesson Common Core *http://tinyurl.com/mnyr7aq*

---

These apps can help you identify standards related to your learning objectives to then provide relevant resources and activities for addressing those standards.

You can also collaborate with colleagues in your school to build on what students are learning in other classes. For example, if students are engaging in perspective-taking activities in responding to literature in their English classes, you can ask them to reflect on how such a literary perspective-taking experience is related to a critical sourcing activity like analyzing competing versions of historical events in their social studies classes. Or, if students are learning report writing in their language arts class, the language arts teacher and science teacher can coordinate their instruction so aspects of report writing learned in the language arts can transfer to writing practices in a science class, like writing lab reports. Similarly, if you are teaching a math class and you know your students are using digital mapping and GPS tracking apps in their science classes, you can work with the science teacher on ways to use analysis of coordinates and numerical data of these digital mapping/GPS apps for a field trip.

## Identifying Disciplinary Literacies

### What Kinds of Authentic Learning Activities Can I Create to Achieve These Learning Objectives?

In creating activities that take advantage of app affordances, it is important to create authentic learning activities that involve students' active use of disciplinary literacies. By authentic learning activities we mean *activities that address complex, ill-defined problems consistent with the complications of everyday life.* You can provide students the opportunity to address complex problems through activities similar to those that engage all of us in lived-world situations. In actual experiences in the lived world, many of these problems require extensive, long-term work; for example, how to create a marketing plan for a new product, how to cope with an increase in rats or other rodents in a sewer system, approaches to addressing the lack of bike paths in a town or city, or ways to provide instruction for students who lack basic computer skills, etc. (Herrington, Oliver, & Reeves, 2010).

In designing activities for students, it is useful to distinguish between school-based tasks versus more practical, authentic tasks associated with lived-world situations (Herrington et al., 2010). School-based tasks often involve well-structured "textbook" conditions, whereas lived-world situations are more ill-defined and unstructured. School-based tasks often lack complexity and are decontextualized while real-world tasks tend to be grounded in specific contexts, so they are more complex. The result is that students often perceive school-based tasks as more artificial, even more irrelevant than real-world tasks. While it may always be a challenge to engage students in "real-world" tasks in a school context, Herrington et al. (2010) cite some examples of more authentic school tasks:

- Students in an introductory biology course studying new forms of microorganisms assume the role of a biologist who goes to a remote Siberian lake where microorganisms have been discovered that cannot be classified; students are provided with online images of those microorganisms and they must attempt to identify them. (p. 49)

- Students in a language course are seeking jobs, requiring them to employ their new language. (pp. 50–51)
- Students in a literature course assume the roles of editorial board members of an online journal focused on reviews and articles. They create guidelines and criteria for their peers submitting reviews and articles; the journal is then published at the end of the course. (p. 52)
- In a history course studying World War I, students study actual soldiers whose names are derived from a local memorial tower or plaque. Based on research about that soldier, students create a story about their service during and after the war. (p. 52)

The fact that the problems or issues addressed in these courses are complex and ill-defined means that students themselves must collaboratively engage in their own problem-solving and planning of tasks that enable them to addresses these problems. For example, in a social studies class, students may be concerned about the high number of foreclosed homes for sale in their own neighborhoods. To investigate the causes and consequences of having a high number of foreclosed homes for sale on the viability of their respective neighborhoods, they can gather data from their city's databases as well as real-estate databases on home values, home sales, crime, income levels, and so on. In studying older neighborhoods they can employ the iOS LookBackMaps *http://tinyurl.com/ovwqdn7* app to find historical images of the area to identify changes in the neighborhood and reasons for those changes. By sharing these data for all of their neighborhoods, students could then identify patterns associated with this issue, leading them to consider policies for addressing the problem.

To organize this approach for inquiry/problem-based instruction, you can have students share their information on a wiki. Or you can create a website using Google Sites and use the Knowledge Building Center template that provides students with categories related to sharing information about a given issue or problem. You can also provide students access to online resources associated with a certain problem or issue, for example, research on the effects of foreclosed homes on neighborhoods.

It is productive to have students produce a final product or outcome that provides some analysis, insights, and/or alternative solutions to problems or issues; the products or outcomes should be seen as valuable to actual audiences interested in these problems or issues. For example, students studying their neighborhoods could construct a website that not only provides data about the adverse effects of foreclosed homes on different neighborhoods, but also suggests some solutions for how homeowners could address the challenge of retaining ownership of their homes. The fact that students have some tangible product or outcome that could be of value for others serves to motivate students to work on their projects.

## Employing Disciplinary Literacies

### What Disciplinary Literacies Are Being Employed in Achieving These Learning Objectives?

In planning activities, you are also identifying those disciplinary literacies described in Chapter 2 that can be used to achieve your learning objectives. In doing so, you are determining how the uses of literacy practices of accessing/assessing information, reading, writing, discussing, multimodal production, simulation/games, and reflection are best employed to foster disciplinary literacies unique to a particular discipline. For example, in a science class, a teacher is having her students study the effects of pollution on the water quality in a local river. The students are taking water samples from different places along the river and then testing those samples in their school's lab for levels of pollution using the iOS Water Quality *http://tinyurl.com/m9ugm6j* or Android Water Quality Meter *http://tinyurl.com/nw38r7o* app.

Given the disciplinary literacy of science that entails use of accurate, concise written descriptions of observed phenomena, to help students in the collection of information, the teacher used the literacy practice of writing specific observations by having students take field notes on their devices. She also had them engage in the literacy practice of using images to communicate to others by having them take photos of the river using their devices. Students then used the screencasting iOS *http://tinyurl.com/a6z4tsu* or Android *http://tinyurl.com/mrltgkl* Explain Everything app to upload their photos and record their audio observations about these photos to share with her and their peers related to how the photos documented the types and levels of pollution in the river.

The teacher believed that using writing and visual communication to support learning would serve to engage students, encouraging them to capture, record, and reflect on the water sample data they were collecting. The teacher also believed that by using these disciplinary literacies the students would then transfer use of disciplinary literacies across their different subjects. That is, as tasks warranted, the students would remember how they used apps already and reapply them. For example, in their English class, students could use note-taking apps to record their responses to literature. Similarly, in a math class, students might use note-taking apps to record and share their thought processes and approaches in solving a problem. Or, in their social studies classes, students might use their visual communication apps to record images of a field trip to a local neighborhood to study issues facing that neighborhood.

This transfer is most likely to occur when teachers from different disciplines share with each other the disciplinary literacies and related apps they are using. To foster such interdisciplinary sharing and planning, it is useful to have your own and other teachers' curriculum available on a website so that all teachers have access to each other's curricula.

## Considering App Affordances

### What App Affordances Foster Uses of Specific Literacy Practices?

For all of this planning to work, you need to understand and build upon our framework relating app affordances to disciplinary literacy practices. As previously noted, each app or tool within an app that students use to support learning *affords* something; ideally, it provides a positive advantage, but it can also introduce, through a particular use or the way students approach it, a more negative affordance. These positive or negative affordances can be manifested in the design of a particular app, or tools that are part of that app.

But, we want to reemphasize, the affordance can be unanticipated and emerge from the *use* of the app given your particular activity. Thus, depending on your activity, the same app might positively afford something in one practice and negatively afford something in another practice. A note-taking app used to summarize the gist of an informational text in a health book chapter might afford students use of paraphrasing and synthesis, two processes that positively influence comprehension. The same app used in science to list technical terms in a chapter and write definitions of them likely will not afford learning of concepts that should be taught conceptually and reviewed as topically related sets.

You therefore need to carefully consider the disciplinary literacy practice in which the app is integral and tune in to whether the positive affordance emerges as anticipated, often through trial and error with careful observation. Hence, when using apps to engage students in literacy practices like accessing/assessing information, reading, writing, discussing, using and producing images, audio/video, participating in simulation/gaming, and reflecting, you are determining how these uses of app affordances foster specific literacy disciplinary literacy practices that support learning.

Identifying specific literacy practices helps you plan those activities that will support uses and learning of disciplinary literacies. For example, simply noting that you want to use reading to learn doesn't provide you with enough direction in planning activities. Specifying the literacy practices involved in reading to learn might include synthesizing and connecting key ideas in history texts using annotation apps. For example, annotation is a practice that can be an important part of reading to learn in history and that requires the ability to compare and contrast different interpretations of the same historical event—for example, the reasons the United States entered into the Vietnam War.

But the affordance of an annotation app such as the iOS *http://tinyurl.com/b7g38ma* or Android *http://tinyurl.com/an589j3* iAnnotate PDF app, although partly in the design of how it enables commentary on text, is contingent upon how the annotations are constructed, how often they appear, how they are related to the running text, and so on. If you want students in a social studies class to work collaboratively on identifying issues they perceived from reading about problems with the lack of mass transit in their city, to foster such collaboration of their written notes from their readings to create collective knowledge, you could select collaborative note-taking/annotation apps such as the iOS *http:// tinyurl.com/cxo6req* or Android *http://tinyurl.com/7mcj4ph* Evernote app or the iOS *http://tinyurl.com/mdesq6f* or Android *http://tinyurl.com/mggqmgu* Diigo app for sharing their responses to the readings. The fact that students are working collaboratively means that they can take advantage of the affordances of these note-taking apps to not only share their notes, but also to react to and combine their notes to create a composite set of notes, helping them identify areas of agreement about issues.

## Selecting Apps

### How Do I or My Students Select Those Apps Whose Affordances Best Support Students' Learning?

By now, you can see that a key part of planning involves determining those app affordances that will best foster the use of disciplinary literacies that are consistent with your learning objectives. For example, if students are studying astronomy in a science class, the teacher might want them to learn how to access and analyze data from their observations of the moons of Jupiter, synthesize the results of those observations, and then create their own images that support their syntheses of those observations. To help them observe and identify various stars and solar systems, the teacher might select apps such as the iOS *http://tinyurl.com/lzj36j6* or Android *http://tinyurl.com/95yxv47* SkyORB; iOS *http://tinyurl.com/cqjryr7* or Android *http://tinyurl.com/nxe5gr7* Star Walk; iOS SkyView Free *http://tinyurl. com/kz4thb5* or GoSkyWatch Planetarium *http://tinyurl.com/bch286r*; or the Android Sky Map *http://tinyurl.com/bnvqnfo* or Night Sky *http://tinyurl.com/ anc8yx5* apps.

In selecting apps based on their affordances supporting disciplinary literacies, it is also important to determine whether an app will engage students—will it increase their levels of involvement, participation, or creativity? Students' potential engagement may be related to an app's intuitive ease of use, degree of interactivity, visual appeal/design, facility for allowing students to readily share results with others, and its perceived purpose.

Let us look at purpose more closely: For example, if the perceived purpose is simply to impart information, followed by testing students on that information—as is the case with many "flash card" apps—students will likely be less engaged with those apps than with apps that don't so directly convey a particular pedagogical agenda. For example, younger students might be engaged in learning about states and countries due to the game-like features of the iOS *http://tinyurl.com/lr6z6zg* or Android *http://tinyurl.com/lgcn7qj* Stack the States or iOS *http://tinyurl.com/ kp3nz2y* or Android *http://tinyurl.com/n22cmxv* Stack the Countries apps.

In selecting apps, you are evaluating the apps based on criteria associated with their potential affordances consistent with your learning objectives, criteria such as those defined by Tony Vincent (2012):

- *Relevance*: The app's focus has a strong connection to the purpose for the app and is appropriate for the student.
- *Customization*: App offers complete flexibility to alter content and settings to meet student needs.
- *Feedback*: Student is provided specific feedback.
- *Thinking Skills*: App encourages the use of higher order thinking skills including creating, evaluating, and analyzing.
- *Usability*: Student can launch and operate the app independently.
- *Engagement*: Student is highly motivated to use the app.
- *Sharing*: Specific performance summary or student product is saved in the app and can be exported to the teacher or for an audience.

You can also engage students by giving them choices in planning activities themselves so that they have some say in defining learning objectives and selecting relevant apps to complete those objectives given the fact that they will ultimately need to make these decisions on their own outside of the classroom.

One useful tool to support their own planning is the iChoose *http://iChooseTech.Weebly.com* framework (Bisson & Vazquez, 2013; for a conference presentation on use of iChoose see *http://tinyurl.com/mp245g2*). Students can use this site to identify their goals related to employing certain practices: remember, understand, apply, analyze, evaluate, and create. Once they select a practice, they then respond to the following questions created with Google Forms: "What is your goal?," "Choose a digital tool" [to achieve that goal], "What materials will you need?" [digital devices or paper/pencil], "What skill or skills will you use?" "How will you show what you know?" and "I will be working individually/collaboratively."

Once students each complete a form in Google Forms, you have information about their selection of devices and tools so that you can group them based on their use of the same devices or tools. Based on the idea of the iChoose model, you can also create your own Google Forms questionnaire based on your particular students' abilities and needs; we would substitute practices described in this book for skills.

### Selecting and Evaluating Apps

### In Planning My Instruction, How Can I Find and Evaluate Apps Based on Criteria Related to Their Affordances?

Given the thousands of available apps, it is often difficult to select those apps that might serve your particular needs. We therefore suggest some app recommendation sites as well as criteria you can employ to assess the relevancy and quality of certain apps.

There are number of useful app recommendation sites listed below.

---

## APP RECOMMENDATION SITES

**iOS**: Apps in Education *http://appsineducation.blogspot.com*, APPitic *http://appitic.com*, Common Sense's Graphite *http://tinyurl.com/mpqoyyh*, AppGuides *http://appadvice.com/appguides*, iPads in Education *http://tinyurl.com/lhczvsl*, iPad Apps for Schools *http://ipadapps4school.com*, EdShelf *https://edshelf.com*, appoLearning *http://tinyurl.com/kkecned*, PlayBoard *http://tinyurl.com/lvery8e*, and Appadvice *http://tinyurl.com/m65hufl*

**Android**: Quixey *http://tinyurl.com/mvzuwhu*, PlayBoard *http://tinyurl.com/mcr9pj2*, APPvisor *http://tinyurl.com/mdr3hez*, AppAffinity *http://tinyurl.com/nxecsmh*

---

For general app recommendation sites on our website *http://tinyurl.com/cpk52su* and for recommendations of apps organized by subject matter *http://tinyurl.com/clxfsy9*. These links include some of our favorite sites for iOS and Android apps; we also recommend the Google Apps Documentation and Support *http://learn.googleapps.com* site for use of the Google apps.

One of the more useful app selection sites is AppCrawlr *http://appcrawlr.com*. You can search for apps based on selecting different menu options: device, price, in-app purchases, category, topic, "helps you," audience, and feature. Once you find certain apps consistent with your needs, you can also find other similar apps.

However, as we've argued, it is often best to determine the value of certain apps by going beyond these descriptions of apps to consider how these apps' affordances will serve to support your own learning objectives. For example, as part of their teacher education program, a group of science preservice teachers were asked to review and assess apps based on their own use of those apps (Baran & Khan, 2014). These included the iOS Project Noah *http://tinyurl.com/pb3bfrw* app for cataloging observed wildlife according to a range of different categories to determine matches with the Project Noah database and the iOS Element Matching *http://tinyurl.com/o4n8kjq* app for matching elements in the periodic table with certain symbols and atomic orbitals and charges, and eight other science apps according to criteria they developed: usability, integrating to curriculum, entertaining, engagement, usefulness for outdoors, clarity, relevance to real world, compatibility, content, and extras (p. 271). The apps that had the most positive assessments employed the affordances of portability/mobility and fostering interactivity and collaborative, collective data analysis.

## Learning to Use Apps

### How Do I Help Students Learn to Exploit Certain Apps Affordances Through Participation in Activities?

As we've argued, the affordances of apps are not simply *in* an app—what we just discussed as design features. Once you or your students have selected certain apps, you then create activities that help students learn to exploit certain app affordances for achieving your learning objectives.

In planning these activities, because students may not know how to employ a certain app, you can then model your own use of an app to exploit the affordances within a particular activity, scaffolding the activity based on students' particular ability level or zone of proximal development (ZPD) (Vygotsky, 1978). In doing so, you are making explicit your own thought processes on how you are using an app given certain affordances within an activity. For example, if students are using the iOS VoiceThread *http://tinyurl.com/nvun33b* app to collect photos of physical problems or deterioration within their school to then add and share audio or written annotations, you can model ways of responding to others' annotations through agreeing, extending, making connections, or challenging those annotations. You can also model how synthesizing ideas about the photos on Voice-Thread serves to define consistent patterns in their school, leading to formulating recommendations for addressing those problems to the school administration.

Consistent with the flipped classroom approach, you can also refer students to the many online video tutorials on YouTube or other video sites demonstrating use of certain apps. Or, you can use screencasting apps to create your own online video tutorials. To create screencast demonstrations of your use of iPad apps on a Mac, you can use Reflector or AirServer to mirror your iPad's screen to a Mac and then use a screencasting tool such as Screencast-O-Matic to record the screencast (Byrne, 2013).

## Accommodating Individual Differences

### How Do I Consider Students' Individual Differences in Selecting and Using Apps?

In planning classroom activities, it is also important to remember that your students differ in a range of factors including knowledge, abilities, interests, levels of engagement, goals, and learning preferences, just to mention a few. These variations in what students bring to the classroom challenges traditional instruction in which a teacher leads an entire class through a lesson, at least implicitly based on the assumption that all students are at the same starting point with the same degree of knowledge, abilities, interests, needs, and learning preferences, and that, at the end of the lesson, students will all arrive at the same completion point.

A relatively recent movement, called Universal Design for Learning (UDL), has changed the way many educators think about how to make the curriculum accessible to students with disabilities. Inspired by the Universal Design movement in architecture, the concept behind UDL is to make the curriculum accessible by designing it that way from the beginning using digital and/or multimedia technologies. For example, the traditional approach to making a book accessible to students with vision problems would be to provide a magnifying device.

Instead, the UDL approach would provide a digital version of the text that could be printed using a Braille printer, read on screen so that the font size and magnification could be adjusted, printed using a standard printer, include a foreign language translation, or even be read to the student using a screen reader. In this way, the text would be accessible to the blind, those with low vision, limited English ability, or even dyslexia. The UDL approach is focused on keeping the learning goal in mind when designing a curriculum. As Rose and Meyer (2000) put it,

> having electronic text where the computer can read all of the words aloud is a powerful way of making the text more accessible. But if the goal is to teach a dyslexic how to decode unfamiliar words, such accessibility may be counterproductive. (p. 68)

The ultimate goal of UDL is not to ensure access simply to the material, but to ensure access to the learning itself. It is important to note that universal does not mean one size fits all. Instead, UDL emphasizes incorporating multiple approaches to teaching a concept (Hall, Meyer, & Rose, 2012). More information on UDL is available at the Center for Applied Special Technology (CAST) *http://www.cast.org* website, including an online lesson plan development tool to assist teachers: *http://lessonbuilder.cast.org*.

While there is a need to personalize instruction in ways that accommodate these individual differences, personalized or "individualized" instruction has not been typical in standard textbook-driven curricula. The one-size-fits-all approach can be seriously disrupted with creative use of apps. Nevertheless, the idea of tailoring to each student's individual differences in a class of 35 students is overwhelming if not sometimes impossible.

One middle-ground alternative involves exploiting the uses of devices and apps so that students are working more on their own or in small groups to accomplish tasks in ways that are consistent with these individual differences. Each group is responsible for or is assigned to study a particular topic, issue, and/or text/film based on their use of disciplinary literacies facilitated by mobile devices. This shifts the focus of your instruction from direct instruction to all students doing the same thing over the same time period to organizing and facilitating group work based on your knowledge about students' individual differences.

Consistent with the use of the iChoose framework *http://iChooseTech.Weebly.com*, this places the onus on students to develop their own plans, learning objectives, use of tools/apps, schedules, and goals, subject to your approval and facilitation. Students can indicate their expertise in uses of certain devices and/or apps, and, given their knowledge or expertise, whether they can serve as peer tutors or instructors.

## Addressing the Needs of Struggling Readers and Writers

### How Can I Employ Apps to Help Struggling Readers and Writers?

You may also have students who struggle with reading and writing for a range of different reasons, including learning disabilities. Some of these students may be orally proficient but are apprehensive about reading and writing, or lack certain cognitive skills associated with comprehending or creating print texts. In working with these students, to build on their language proficiency to complete reading/writing tasks, you can use text-to-speech and speech-to-text apps to help these students in moving between oral and written discourse.

The text-to-speech (TTS) apps listed below transform print texts into audio for students who learn better from listening to rather than reading a text. For example, learning disability students are more likely to identify errors in their writing when they hear their writing as opposed to just reading their text (Graham, Harris, Fink, & MacArthur, 2003).

---

## TEXT-TO-SPEECH APPS

**iOS:** Speech Magnet *http://tinyurl.com/ltcg3jg*, iSpeech *http://tinyurl.com/lw76cy5*, Voice Dream Reader *http://tinyurl.com/crbdau8*, iReadWrite *http://tinyurl.com/ljya8m3*, Web Reader HD *http://tinyurl.com/m7xwkle*, Speak It *http://tinyurl.com/loabqh7*, Write & Say *http://tinyurl.com/77nzfry*, Voice Reader Text to Speech *http://tinyurl.com/79h9gea*, Voice Brief *http://tinyurl.com/mk7wcpm*, iSpeech *http://tinyurl.com/lw76cy5*, Talk to Me *http://tinyurl.com/2v8z26y*, NeoPaul *http://tinyurl.com/qg4w8mo*

**Android:** Google Text-to-Speech *http://tinyurl.com/mx38eba*, iSpeech *http://www.ispeech.org*, IVONA Text to Speech *http://tinyurl.com/mbcq84d*, Classic Text-to-Speech Engine *http://tinyurl.com/kr7faho*, Best Voices *http://tinyurl.com/m4hvkkq*

**Chrome OS:** SpeakIt *http://tinyurl.com/mpco47m*, Chrome Announcify *http://tinyurl.com/lo59lpb*, Readthewords *http://tinyurl.com/o29vc2k*, Natural Reader *http://tinyurl.com/kq3oubq*

---

The Speak it! apps reads aloud texts in four different voices (American Male, American Female, British Male, British Female). The app also highlights words as they are being read, and includes different playback rates and the ability to pause, something that is important for struggling readers. Students can use the vBookz PDF Voice Reader to listen to PDF files read aloud in 16 different languages; by saving their writing as PDFs, students can listen to their writing to note instances of missing or misspelled words.

The Voice Reader Text to Speech app provides readings in 21 languages using 32 different voices, as well as readings of PDF files. Students can use the Talk to Me or NeoPaul apps to hear words spoken to them as they are writing. These apps are particularly useful for working with students with learning needs related to processing or speaking language.

For students who are more proficient in their oral versus written text production and who have difficulty translating their speech into writing or with typing or spelling words, you can use the speech-to-text (STT) apps listed below for students to dictate their writing (Rosenberger, 2013).

---

## SPEECH-TO-TEXT APPS

**iOS**: Siri, Dragon Dictation *http://tinyurl.com/bwwbach*, iTalk Recorder *http://tinyurl.com/27u8qc8*, Best Dictation *http://tinyurl.com/6mjq3lh*, iProRecorder *http://tinyurl.com/7tq4led*, QuickVoice *http://tinyurl.com/2amq7x6*, Paper-Port Notes *http://tinyurl.com/94wvypf*, Voice Assistant *http://tinyurl.com/k4vjb8n*, Notability *http://tinyurl.com/7ewz5xo*

**Android**: ListNote Speech/Text *http://tinyurl.com/krtdw9z*, Dragon Mobile Assistant *http://tinyurl.com/92rxa5w*, Evernote for Android *http://tinyurl.com/7mcj4ph*, Vlingo for Android *http://tinyurl.com/2br3lwt*, ShoutOUT *http://tinyurl.com/c8kxtu7*, Speech to Text *http://tinyurl.com/kfy43ct*

**Chrome OS**: Dictation *http://tinyurl.com/kczsomo*, Voice Recognition *http://tinyurl.com/mbp8djz*, Dictatenote *http://tinyurl.com/mkvfn5x*, or Simple Dictation *http://tinyurl.com/mpjehb8*

---

## Special Learning Needs

### How Can I Use Operating Systems Accessibility Features and Apps to Accommodate Students' Special Learning Needs?

As you are planning your instruction, you can use a number of accessibility features and apps to provide for students' special learning needs. Descriptions of tools that are designed for use with special needs students are on our website: *http://tinyurl.com/le9jzdq*.

Apple has included some accessibility features in iOS. To access these features, go to Settings>General>Accessibility. Here, you will find features that make your iOS device more accessible to people with vision impairments, hearing impairments, and physical/motor impairments including features for Vision: VoiceOver, Zoom, Large Text, Invert Colors, Speak Selection, Speak-Autotext; Hearing: More Audio; Learning feature: Guided Access to disable the Home button as well as restrict touch input to certain areas of the screen; and Physical and Motor: Assistive Touch and Triple-click Home for returning to the home screen or to perform a different task.

For example, visually-impaired students can use the VoiceOver feature on the iPad to touch anything on their screen to have texts or the name of an app read aloud in 36 different languages, as well as to read aloud iBooks. And, for typing, VoiceOver will read aloud each character and word as they are typed. And, for hearing-impaired students, the Mono Audio feature provides students who have hearing loss in one ear to receive balanced stereo audio in the other ear. For students with physical disabilities, the Assistive Touch feature replaces the need to swipe or pinch the iPad screen with single touches and the Guided Access feature can be used to disable the Home button as well as restrict touch input to certain areas of the screen (Gliksman, 2013).

However, one limitation of these features is that their use may vary in using different apps. Analysis of the use of popular apps such as the iOS BrainPOP *http://tinyurl.com/lfbu9mw* video app and iOS Toontastic *http://tinyurl.com/m2zh4tx* animation production app found that while the VoiceOver feature did not work properly, the BrainPOP app did include captions and the Toontastic app provided specific step-by-step instructions for creating animations (Kumar & Owston, 2014).

The Android OS includes a built-in text-to-speech engine and a screen reader, along with other hardware accessibility features. Similarly, on the Chromebook, the Chrome OS Accessibility menu can enable "spoken feedback," "high contrast mode," and "screen magnifier." The spoken feedback works using ChromeVox, a built-in screen reader that describes what's happening on the screen and reads documents and webpages out loud (for a demonstration: *http://goo.gl/8BN20*). And, the Windows OS *http://www.microsoft.com/enable* and Office 2013 *http://tinyurl.com/jvtl5te* include similar accessibility features such as Windows Speech Recognition and Narrator for audio, Magnifier to enlarge portions of a screen, High Contrast to reduce eye strain, and Windows high DPI to enlarge text.

## Apps for Visually-Impaired Students

Visually-impaired students can employ the text-to-speech and speech-to-text apps listed above, recognizing that these apps may only work effectively for certain students (Hecker & Engstrom, 2005). You can also use the Digit-Eyes *http://tinyurl.com/n6t9slx* app for visually-impaired students to read aloud bar codes as well as for you to create bar codes to print out using the Digit-Eyes website *http://www.digit-eyes.com* to add bar codes providing audio identification of items in your classroom (Gliksman, 2013).

### Apps for Hearing-Impaired Students

Hearing-impaired students can employ speech-to-text apps or the iOS Sign Language Fun Learning *http://tinyurl.com/kbry8mr* or Android ASL American Sign Language *http://tinyurl.com/nu7cqn3* app that includes instruction for using American Sign Language for letters, numbers, animals, family members, transportation modes, nature scenes, and salutations (Windman, 2011)

### Apps for Students With Speech Impairments

There are also a number of apps designed to provide augmentative and alternative communication (AAC) students with language disorders who have difficulty with oral communication with visual and sonic aids, including the iOS *http://tinyurl.com/qhj82b9* and Android *http://tinyurl.com/cpfld7p* VizZle Player for use in devising lessons for providing visual and sonic support for students; iOS AutisMate *http://tinyurl.com/qj2c9bd*, iOS *http://tinyurl.com/o4rm825* and Android *http://tinyurl.com/qdsfsgu* Avaz for assisting autistic students with oral language communication; and the Abilipad *http://tinyurl.com/plzjcbz* app for writing using customized keyboards that include audio recordings of letter, word, sentence, or picture assigned to different keys (Boser & Wayland, 2014). And, the Proloquo2Go iOS *http://tinyurl.com/kx2yhyb* app contains a library of over 14,000 symbols, to enable students to communicate by selecting symbols rather than speech, and has natural voices to enhance communication.

### Lesson-Planning Apps

#### What Are Some Lesson-Planning Apps for Planning and Organizing My Lessons?

For planning and organizing instruction, you can also employ a number of different lesson-planning apps listed below that assist you in identifying objectives, connecting those objectives to standards, and devising activities, and then sharing these activities with students.

---

## APPS FOR LESSON PLANNING

**iOS**: Nearpod Teacher *http://tinyurl.com/mbkagra,* Socrative Lite *http:// tinyurl.com/c5ettwo,* GoClass *http://tinyurl.com/my2yvj8,* iLesson Plans *http:// tinyurl.com/l5twwo5,* Lesson Plans *http://tinyurl.com/kvyyk38,* Teacher-Plan *http://tinyurl.com/mpglojl,* My LessonPlan *http://tinyurl.com/n5pca63,* Lesson Planning *http://tinyurl.com/mswdwc9*

**Android**: Nearpod Teacher *http://tinyurl.com/lk8qrth,* Socrative *http://tinyurl. com/c5ettwo,* Daily Lesson Planner *http://tinyurl.com/mswdwc9,* Teacher Planner Lite *http://tinyurl.com/n62lglr,* Assignment Planner Pro *http://tinyurl. com/lq5rxx5,* Homework Planner *http://tinyurl.com/mlwp448,* SchoolTraq *http://tinyurl.com/lpdowcl,* SchoolBinder *http://tinyurl.com/lm9wxkc,* Semester Planner *http://tinyurl.com/k8caeqq,* PlanbookEdu Lesson Planner *http:// tinyurl.com/lp8oyx5*

---

For example, you can use the iOS and Android Nearpod Teacher to create lessons that are then connected to the students' devices. You can then see the students' responses in real time on your device as well as also obtain activity reports about the students' work. Or, you can use the iOS GoClass app as well as the desktop GoClass *http://tinyurl.com/lootby6* app, which includes use of The Lesson Plan feature, to import different online resources and pose questions, and then share these resources and questions to students' devices.

To create lessons involving contrasting and comparing topics, artifacts, ideas, or categories, you can use the Compare a Twist *http://tinyurl.com/knmszod* app to compare, for example, how vertebrates and invertebrates as categories differ from each other based on examples for each category.

There are also a number of curriculum repository sites that include lesson plans, teaching ideas, and links to different resources (for a list of curriculum resource sites see *http://tinyurl.com/ktpw4y5*). These include:

- ReadWriteThink *http://tinyurl.com/yb45dhu* site sponsored by the National Council of Teachers of English and the International Reading Association;
- Sophia *http://www.sophia.org,* which includes lesson plans that are submitted by teachers and are rated for quality by experts;
- Curriki *http://www.curriki.org,* Share My Lesson *http://www.sharemylesson. com,* and EdSitement *http://edsitement.neh.gov* also include an extensive number of lesson plans submitted by teachers for use in all subject matter areas;

- The Explore Learning *http://www.explorelearning.com* and Discovery Education *http://www.discoveryeducation.com* sites are particularly relevant for math and science;
- The PBS Learning Media *http://www.pbslearningmedia.org* site provides extensive video resources on topics in all subject areas, as well as well-designed lesson plans associated with these videos.

There are also academic social networking sites that provide you or your students with access to activities and resources based on different subjects. The iOS *http://tinyurl.com/kzy5na7* and Android *http://tinyurl.com/l6dn24f* Docsity apps support a site with 600,000 registered users and 300,000 documents for students to pose questions of other users or access documents, lectures notes, or videos across a wide range of different subjects. The iOS *http://tinyurl.com/nxhfv3r* and Android *http://tinyurl.com/cy7pp89* StudyBlue apps provide students with notes and flash-cards created by other students on different subjects. And, the iOS *http://tinyurl.com/k6rwbu6* and Android *http://tinyurl.com/m2j8rkz* Lynda.com apps provide older students with video-based instruction on a range of topics.

### Purchasing and Syncing Apps to Devices

#### How Do I Purchase Apps for Use in Schools and Then Add Them to Devices?

You obtain or purchase iOS apps at the iTunes Store (you still need to "purchase" an app even if it's free) using your Apple ID for your iTunes account (for iOS apps on the iTunes Store organized by grade level *http://tinyurl.com/lyl4h8c* and by subject *http://tinyurl.com/kznncwk*). You can also use the Apple Volume Purchase Program *http://tinyurl.com/ky8e7w2* that enables you to purchase 20 copies or more of a particular app at a bulk rate for use in schools without having to pay sales taxes (for tax-exempt schools/institutions). You can also enroll students in the school's Mobile Device Management *http://tinyurl.com/kd7mqaq* for sharing devices with students, installing e-mail accounts, configuring passcodes, and restoring their backup files/documents.

Once you purchase an app or book using your new Apple ID, you receive a code to distribute to your students as End Users. Your students then use the code at the iTunes Store to download the apps or books. With iOS 8, schools can purchase and assign apps wirelessly to users while keeping ownership of the license. And, students who choose to use their own Apple IDs can access apps (for descriptions of iOS 8 features *http://tinyurl.com/kvjfkct*).

For purchasing and obtaining licenses for apps, Apple provides three different models: the Personal Ownership model, Institutional Ownership model, and Layered Ownership model, models that differ according to who is considered to be purchasing or owning an app (for a presentation on the pros and cons of each of these models: Stephens, 2012 *http://tinyurl.com/n4ayh2r*). If you are just using your own devices and purchasing apps for your own personal use, then the Personal Ownership model is preferable. Under the Institutional Ownership model, a school assumes ownership of apps based on an institutional Apple ID and maintenance of apps (for a video of use of the Institutional Ownership model for synching apps to devices *http://tinyurl.com/klzww2n*). Because students need to be 13 and older when using this model, it is preferable for schools with students under age 13. However, the school must then do their own app purchasing or updating since they will not be using iCloud.

With the Layered Ownership model—a combination of the Personal Owner-ship and the Institutional Ownership models—both the school and you or your students can purchase and update apps, an option that encourages students to assume responsibility for maintaining their apps and devices, particularly if they are taking these devices home (for a video demonstration on use of the Layered Ownership model for synching apps *http://tinyurl.com/m83qku7*). With the use of iCloud backup with this model, syncing and updating is less time-consuming.

In Winter, 2014, Apple announced a series of changes for school IT admin-istrators or teachers in creating settings on iOS devices: *http://tinyurl.com/k4un6w9*. These included the "zero-touch" configuration for new iOS devices using the Device Enrollment Program *http://www.apple.com/education/it/vpp* replacing use of the Apple Configurator utility that means that administers or teachers can enroll iPads or iPhones simply by serial number or order number without having to remove devices from their boxes, as opposed to having to enroll each device itself by connecting to a computer running the Apple Con-figurator utility (for Apple's Device Enrollment Program Guide (PDF) *http://tinyurl.com/p7o55oo*).

Moreover, students can no longer uninstall their profiles, which is what occurred in the Los Angeles district when students "hacked" their iPads (Cun-ningham, 2014). And, students under age 13 can now be given their own Apple ID with parental approval, which means that they can receive apps or ebooks, use iTunes U, sync content to iCloud; at the same time, there are limitations not found with the standard Apple IDs.

To obtain or purchase Android apps, you go to the Google Play Store *http://tinyurl.com/cn9oc2t*. To use the Google Play Store, it is useful to review their terms of service and purchase options *http://tinyurl.com/c9pc45o*. For instructions on use of Google Apps in Education for Android devices *http://tinyurl.com/kuzhv4s*; administrators can use the Google Edu Device Setup *http://tinyurl.com/mdobrg3* app to add apps to devices.

And, you can obtain or purchase Chrome OS apps on the Chrome Web Store *http://tinyurl.com/ccmetrr*, recognizing that the Google Apps for Education *http://tinyurl.com/kaoufhw* are central apps for use of Chromebooks, as described on the Google Classroom site *http://tinyurl.com/l2j7mve*.

## Storing and Sharing Files on Devices

### How Can My Student Store and Share Their Work With Me on Their Devices?

One major challenge of using tablets or Chromebooks is that, in contrast to desktops or laptops, students cannot store their files on their tablets themselves. To address this issue, they therefore will be using cloud-based storage and sharing sites. For iOS devices, when students employ Pages, Keynote, Numbers, Mail, Notes, and Reminders, their work is automatically backed up on iCloud *http://tinyurl.com/m9knqeu* (up to 5 GB free storage); students can also work collaboratively using these apps. Students can also use cross-device apps on all devices, which is useful for students with different types of devices working collaboratively on the same files. These include:

- *Google Drive* for iOS *http://tinyurl.com/ckuvapt*, Android OS *http://tinyurl.com/crs5x2*, and Chrome OS *http://tinyurl.com/k2y92ku* (for use in sharing work using Google Docs, Presentations, Forms, Spreadsheets, Forms, Drawings, Lucid Graphs, Mindmeister Maps, Scripts, and WeVideo, as well as sharing video files; up to 5 GB free storage);
- *Dropbox* for iOS *http://tinyurl.com/a3bd3cp*, Android OS *http://tinyurl.com/7qlb8q3*, and Chrome OS *http://tinyurl.com/kect75t* (up to 2 GB free storage;
- *Box* for iOS *http://tinyurl.com/kzpwykx*, Android OS *http://tinyurl.com/83twm2a*, and Chrome OS *http://tinyurl.com/mofk88j* (up to 5 GB free storage;
- *Evernote* for iOS *http://tinyurl.com/cxo6req*, Android OS *http://tinyurl.com/dyspv8p*, and Chrome OS *http://tinyurl.com/kluts3h* (upload up to 60 MB of data each month, with unlimited free storage);
- *OneDrive* for iOS *http://tinyurl.com/kxfte6x*, Android OS *http://tinyurl.com/n2pzgu2*, and Chrome OS *http://tinyurl.com/ltd2cng* (up to 7 GB free storage);
- *Bitcasa* for iOS *http://tinyurl.com/mfjjsve*, Android OS *http://tinyurl.com/mtpb4af*, and Chrome OS *http://tinyurl.com/kzykwrz* (up to 5 GB free storage);
- *MEGA* for iOS *http://tinyurl.com/ny47swl*, Android OS *http://tinyurl.com/nh2tzym*, and Chrome OS *https://mega.co.nz/#chrome* (up to 50 GB free storage).

Many apps do include links to upload files to these sites, particularly to Dropbox, Box, and Evernote. To employ these cloud-based apps, students need to set up an account with these sites. While these cloud-based apps provide relatively generous free storage limits as noted above, if students are uploading video files, they need to recognize that longer video files can consume a lot of space.

One advantage of using some of the sites is that you can have students upload a file to a site and then provide them with feedback within a site, for example, using Comments or Google Voice within Google Docs, something we discuss in more detail in Chapter 11.

## Summary

In this chapter, we have described different steps for planning instruction for using apps for fostering the use of disciplinary literacies to support learning. While we have presented these steps in a sequential order, it is important to recognize that the steps are highly recursive. You may actually begin with later steps of selecting activities and then determine how those activities achieve certain learning objectives. Regardless of the steps you take in planning activities, a key focus is devising engaging activities that employ those app affordances that will best support those activities instead of simply using apps for their own sake.

Now that we've provided you with a general framework for thinking about affordances of apps that foster disciplinary literacies practices, in Chapters 4 to 11 we will home in on specific disciplinary literacies—accessing/assessing information, reading, writing, discussing, using images, using audio/video, games/simulation, and reflection—that support learning across the curriculum. For each of these chapters, we refer to some of the relevant Common Core State Standards addressed in the chapter, recognizing the limitations of those standards with regard to the disciplinary literacies unique to particular disciplines.

## References

Baran, E., & Khan, S. (2014). Going mobile in science teacher education. In C. Miller & A. Doering (Eds.), *The new landscape of mobile learning* (pp. 258–275). New York: Routledge.

Beach, R., Haertling-Thein, A., & Webb, A. (2012). *Teaching to exceed the English language arts Common Core State Standards.* New York: Routledge.

Bisson, R., & Vazquez, A. W. (2013, December 10). iChoose: Academic choice and iPads. Presentation at the annual TIES Conference, Minneapolis, MN.

Boser, K. I., & Wayland, S. (2014, March 20). 7 apps that teach literacy skills [Web log post]. Retrieved from http://tinyurl.com/o8l266p

Byrne, R. (2013). How to create screencast demos of iPad apps [Web log post]. Retrieved from http://tinyurl.com/kllldlv

Cunningham, A. (2014, February 27). Apple's new management features help locked-down iPads stay locked down [Web log post]. Retrieved from http://tinyurl.com/nzpy4pc

Gliksman, S. (2013). *iPad in education for dummies.* Hoboken, NJ: John Wiley & Sons.

Graham, S., Harris, K. R., Fink, B., & MacArthur, C. (2003). Primary grade teachers' instructional adaptations for struggling writers: A national survey. *Journal of Educational Psychology, 95*(2), 279–292.

Hall, T. E., Meyer, A., & Rose, D. H. (Eds.). (2012). *Universal design for learning in the classroom: Practical applications*. New York: Guilford Press.

Hecker, L. & Engstrom, E. U. (2005). Assistive technology and individuals with dyslexia. In J. R. Birsh (Ed.), *Multisensory teaching of basic language skills*, 2nd ed., Course Companion website from Paul H. Brookes Publishing Company. Retrieved from http://tinyurl.com/p3kuoby

Herrington, J., Reeves, T. C., & Oliver, R. (2010). *A guide to authentic e-learning*. New York: Routledge.

Kumar, K., & Owston, R. (2014). Accessibility evaluation of iOS apps for education. In C. Miller & A. Doering (Eds.), *The new landscape of mobile learning* (pp. 208–224). New York: Routledge.

Rose, D., & Meyer, A. (2000). Universal Design for Learning. *Journal of Special Education Technology, 15*(1), 67–70.

Rosenberger, R. (2013, October 7). Dictation technology will change writing instruction [Web log post]. Retrieved from http://tinyurl.com/lao4dfy

Stephens, C. (2012, June 7). Managing and supporting iPads in the classroom [Web log post]. Retrieved from http://tinyurl.com/n4ayh2r

Vincent, T. (2012, March 4). Ways to evaluate educational apps [Web log post]. Retrieved from http://learninginhand.com/blog/ways-to-evaluate-educational-apps.html

Vygotsky, L. (1978). *Mind in society: The development of higher psychological processes*. Cambridge, MA: Harvard University Press.

Windman, V. (2011, December 22). Apps and extras for iPad accessibility [Web log post]. Retrieved from http://tinyurl.com/8xb54yr

**PART II**

# Guidelines and Classroom Examples for Using Apps

# 4

# USING APPS FOR ACCESSING AND ASSESSING INFORMATION

In this chapter, we discuss the use of apps to foster disciplinary literacies practices involved in accessing and assessing online information, including data. When students write reports or essays, create presentations, or voice their opinions during discussions, they draw upon informational literacies that are essential for understanding and constructing knowledge in all disciplines. Most students need assistance with information literacies, particularly the affordances of apps that enable learning with these literacies. Students' abilities to effectively access and assess information often depend on the guidance you provide through your assignments or in modeling search strategies, methods for assessing the quality of information, and approaches to synthesizing and archiving relevant information for future access.

## English Language Arts Common Core State Standards Related to Accessing/Assessing Information

The 512 English language arts Common Core State Standards (Council of Chief State School Officers and National Governors' Association, 2010) for writing, reading, and speaking/listening include the following standards associated with accessing and assessing information:

- Perform short, focused research projects as well as more sustained research in response to a focused research question, demonstrating understanding of the material under investigation (writing standard). (p. 41)
- Gather relevant information from multiple print and digital sources, assess the credibility and accuracy of each source, and integrate and cite the information while avoiding plagiarism (writing standard). (p. 41)

- Draw evidence from literary or informational texts to support analysis, reflection, and research (writing standard). (p. 41)
- Integrate and evaluate content presented in diverse formats and media, including visually and quantitatively, as well as in words (reading standard). (p. 35)
- Integrate and evaluate information from multiple oral, visual, or multimodal sources in order to answer questions, solve problems, or build knowledge (speaking/listening standard). (p. 48)

To achieve these standards, students need to know how to engage in effective searches for relevant, valid information for use in generating knowledge. They also need to know how to assess and synthesize this information for creating reports or essays. They can do so by knowing how to employ a wide range of different apps for engaging in searches.

## The Changing Nature of Knowledge in Moving From a Print-Centric to a Digital World

Readily available information on the Web has changed how we acquire and assess information to create knowledge. Prior to the emergence of the Web, relatively few people like publishers, news organizations, the media, and library-media specialists had access to information and the concurrent control over dispensing it. As noted by David Weinberger (2012) those top-down, authoritative limits and controls have been replaced by a different, more egalitarian set of limits and controls. Weinberger agrees with Clay Shirky's (2008) assertion that the problem is not information *overload*, but *"filter failure."* Weinberger posits that there has always been information overload resulting in the ongoing need to filter information. However, the ways in which filters work in conducting searches has become more sophisticated, requiring that students understand how these filters work. For example, students need to know how to apply specific search terms to acquire relevant information.

## Engaging in Effective Searches

You may assume that students have the intuitive ability to engage in effective searches. Actually, many students lack strategies for engaging in searches, and they need some explicit instruction and modeling with demos or video tutorials on how to search. They need explicit instruction in how to search for and critically analyze search results in terms of accuracy, reliability, and bias of information in online reading environments (Leu, Kinzer, Coiro, Castek, & Henry, 2013).

While many search engines apps and sites generate the same information, they vary greatly in how much support or scaffolding they provide students for reading online or understanding information (Coiro & Fogleman, 2011). Some search engines provide information without providing students with scaffolding, while others provide scaffolding in the form of navigational tips, hypertexted definitions, titles and subtitles, commonly structured sections, summaries, relevant links, source information, and bibliographies, among others.

In using these search engines, students experience difficulties in finding relevant, valid results; they can also be overwhelmed with the sheer volume of thousands of hits. These problems occur because search engines simply crawl the Web for the most frequently accessed sites, which may not necessarily be the most valid sites for scholarly uses. And, since many of these sites are commercial, their primary purpose is to present information designed to sell products.

The problems inherent in search engines aside, students often lack the ability to effectively *use* search engines. They might browse a particular topic or issue without a sense of purpose or strategy. Not only do they need a purpose and strategy, but, as they are browsing, students need to critically reflect on the information they get to confirm that it meets their purposes as they search and make choices to select relevant links as they continue. Julie Coiro puts it this way: "It's not just point and click. It's point, read, think, click" (Coiro, 2003, p. 459).

One factor shaping students' use of effective search strategies is their socio-economic status. Students in lower-income homes with parents with less knowledge about the Internet, and with less access to a computer and to high-speed Internet access, lack the digital media skills associated with effective search demonstrated by students from higher income homes in which parents can model or support use of search strategies (Adler, 2014). A report from the Pew Research Internet Project (Zickuhr & Smith, 2012) found that adults earning less than $30,000 per year and those with less than a high school education are the least likely adults to have Internet access.

## Use of Google Search

Most students initially begin a search with Google: for the iOS *http://tinyurl.com/9rnjeqn*, Android *http://tinyurl.com/842ja43*, and Chrome OS Google Search *http://tinyurl.com/lue3htq* apps. Unfortunately, students (similar to the public at large) don't often take advantage of specific features of Google Search. And, they are less likely to employ Google Scholar *http://scholar.google.com* as opposed to Google to access scholarly material (Purdy, 2012)

To address the need to enhance use of search strategies, Google has also launched the Google Search Education *http://tinyurl.com/73wqndu* resource site that provides tutorials and professional development resources for employing Google Search. (For a *New York Times* Learning Network description *http://tinyurl.com/knc6bzz* on the use of Google and other search sites such as the *New York Times* itself for accessing information.)

Students need to know how to enter specific search terms to limit their search results. For example, they can enter a specific question, put quotes around a word or phrase, specify the range of dates, for example, "2009 . . . 2012," or exclude words using "not." They also can select categories related to searches for images, maps, videos, books, places, blogs, news, and discussions, as well as limiting their searches by availability of the information (past 24 hours, week, month, or year), as well as sorting by relevance or date.

When they use Google Advanced Search *http://www.google.com/advanced_search*, they can search for more specific information, searching for pages that have "all these words," "this exact word or phrase," "one or more of these words," or "but don't show pages that have . . . any of these unwanted words." They can choose to obtain certain file types (doc, ppt, pdf, etc.), search within a domain, or use the Timeline feature (selected after a search) to create a visual timeline based on information organized by years.

And, when they use the Google Instant feature *http://tinyurl.com/l7bvzjy* when they begin to type, certain optional words will appear related to the words they initially entered that they can select from for their search—so that the Google algorithms are predicting words associated with the topics of students' searches (Barseghian, 2011). Once students access a page that was the basis for their search, they can then locate the words on that page by using the Command or Control F function. And, they should also note alternative search categories in the left sidebar—images, videos, timeline, dictionary, related searches, etc. (Barseghian, 2011).

To search for scholarly material, students can employ Google Scholar, which will provide them with more scholarly items than is the case with Google Search. You can also set up a Google Custom Search *https://www.google.com/cse/all* site for your class for limiting and filtering searches to sites you believe are most relevant and valid for the topics or issues students are studying. Limiting the types or topics of sites helps students cope with the problem of being overwhelmed with too much information. (For advanced search strategies using Google: *http://tinyurl.com/mb6p4rd*).

## Using Browser Platforms/Apps

To engage in effective searches, students need to know about use of browser platforms/apps. The default browser platform for iPad and iPhone is Apple's Safari. To employ Safari, students need to know how to employ navigation and bookmarks toolbars, for example, how to save and share bookmarks to sites they want to later access. They also need to know how to add certain bookmarking apps such as Diigo or Evernote for highlighting and annotating websites. And, they need to know how to move between certain tabs that serve as a record of previously accessed sites.

The iOS *http://tinyurl.com/mv9x7gn* and Android *http://tinyurl.com/7qoewqh* Chrome Browser app, also the default browser platform for Chromebooks, includes voice search, easy movement between tabs, and sync search results between the iPad/iPhone and a desktop. There is a Firefox browser app for Android *http://tinyurl.com/bw3q9cd*, and extension for Chrome OS *http://tinyurl.com/k3nh7t9* (see the website for other browser platforms/apps).

---

## BROWSER PLATFORMS/APPS

iOS *http://tinyurl.com/m5g4hby* and Android *http://tinyurl.com/89yqcrv* Bing
iOS Rover *http://tinyurl.com/aatnxha*
iOS *http://tinyurl.com/mlfnfhf* and Android *http://tinyurl.com/ka6hgcr* Photon Flash Player Browser
iOS *http://tinyurl.com/cxqllbs* and Android *http://tinyurl.com/mfccaar* Skyfire
iOS *http://tinyurl.com/bp37ytn* and Android *http://tinyurl.com/cyx8umy* Wolfram Alpha
iOS *http://tinyurl.com/kmfrwwo* and Android *http://tinyurl.com/k8lyr8n* Yahoo Search and Chrome OS Yahoo Toolbar *http://tinyurl.com/k7cnoly*
iOS *http://tinyurl.com/lerwbel* and Android *http://tinyurl.com/m6yd7rx* Ask
iOS *http://tinyurl.com/lv696t6* and Android *http://tinyurl.com/okkwqzk* DuckDuckGo Search
iOS *http://tinyurl.com/b3eqhko* and Android *http://tinyurl.com/mw3gayo* Quora
iOS *http://tinyurl.com/ma78cxh* and Android *http://tinyurl.com/nx6xyug* Shelfster
iOS *http://tinyurl.com/6cee6xj* and Android *http://tinyurl.com/7xcs37p* Dolphin Browser
iOS Knowtilus Pro *http://tinyurl.com/6r3hy4z* (translates websites into 28 different languages) *http://tinyurl.com/6r3hy4z*
iOS *http://tinyurl.com/y6wpemb* and Android *http://tinyurl.com/cphghzs* Opera Mini

### For search engine apps that search across different search engines

iOS *http://tinyurl.com/l9lcgzb* and Android *http://tinyurl.com/kvah4us* Multisearch
iOS *http://tinyurl.com/kev8cbc* iSearch Engine
iOS iSearch *http://tinyurl.com/lc8yjzt*
iOS All Search Engines in One *http://tinyurl.com/mcv2kba*
iOS *http://tinyurl.com/n3p4xd8* and Android addon *http://tinyurl.com/k8vmsuy* Dogpile

---

## Using Academic Databases

One limitation of using these search engines is that they generate a lot of results based more on popularity of hits to a site rather than the academic or scholarly relevance of a site. (Students can use RefSeek *http://www.refseek.com* or iSeek Education *http://www.iseek.com* that provide only "academic" results, eliminating commercial or sponsored links; for 100 search sites for educational purposes: *http://tinyurl.com/ltnsbbh*).

Given the limitations of search engines, reference librarians suggest that students are better off using school library academic databases of specific articles, documents, or materials associated with a specific topic or subject. In most cases, students can access these databases through their libraries' sites.

---

### ACADEMIC DATABASES

InfoTrac Junior Edition *http://tinyurl.com/85pdras*, EBSCO Host *http://tinyurl.com/6xll2gt*, EBSCO Academic Search Premier *http://tinyurl.com/7olxb9c*, WorldCat *http://www.worldcat.org*, Gale/Cengage General Reference Center Gold *http://tinyurl.com/7lavs4f*, CQ Researcher *http://library.cqpress.com/cqresearcher*, and Jstor *http://www.jstor.org*

---

One advantage of these academic databases is that they search across different journals to generate composite results, providing students with access to journals that they could not access on search engines. However, if students do not have access to these journal subscriptions within these databases, they can also search "open access" journals listed in the Directory of Open Access Journals *http://www.doaj.org*—journals that provide free access to their articles.

To identify certain relevant databases for specific disciplines, students can employ searches on the Wikipedia list of academic databases *http://tinyurl.com/p8b8gb* or Infomine *http://infomine.ucr.edu* developed by the University of California to first identify a discipline and then conduct searches within that discipline, as well as use the Library of Congress's Ask a Librarian *http://tinyurl.com/14ev* site to obtain information based on academic databases. And, secondary students can go to the IPL2 for Teens *http://www.ipl.org/div/teen* site for topics relevant to adolescents. For different academic databases organized by disciplines see *http://tinyurl.com/km5znmu* (some of these databases are only available by library subscriptions).

## Using Audio Searches

Students can also employ audio searches using speech recognition tools, an option that is significant for students with learning disabilities. Students with access to an iPhone 4S or 5 or the 2012 iPad with at least iOS 6 can employ Siri to obtain information by posing questions (see the website for other audio search apps). In using voice searches, students need to clearly enunciate their requests as well as focus on use of specific nouns relevant to the search topics.

## AUDIO SEARCH APPS

**iOS**: Google Voice Search *http://tinyurl.com/a6v8gkz*, Dragon Go *http://tinyurl.com/lr484wc*, Voice Ask *http://tinyurl.com/lu24tj3*, Voice Search *http://tinyurl.com/m7wn6sm*, iSpirit *http://tinyurl.com/kz4ka4x*

**Android**: Google Voice Search *http://tinyurl.com/bm8jqpq*, Andy *http://tinyurl.com/kqoyo85*, Assistant *http://tinyurl.com/mv9zevf*, Jeannie *http://tinyurl.com/ofc3vk7*, Dragon Mobile Assistant *http://tinyurl.com/92rxa5w*, Voice Ask *http://tinyurl.com/cwffkw*, Sherpa *http://tinyurl.com/lwf6rfx*

**Chrome OS**: Voice Search *http://tinyurl.com/msfawan*

## Using QR/Barcodes Searches

Students can also employ QR or barcode searches when they encounter texts or sites with QR icons or barcodes. The QR codes are square box codes that are scanned or created by entering in a URL using QR search apps listed on the website. You can use QR codes to provide students with access to a wide range of documents: your assignments, blog posts, schedules, videos, maps, podcasts, directions, tutorials, websites, surveys, etc. (see Brendan Jones's (2011) collection *http://tinyurl.com/3u2ee5v* of different ideas for using QR codes in the classroom). You can embed images of QR codes in students' readings or textbooks to provide them with additional information, images, or videos that enhance their reading, creating a more interactive, multimodal version of a particular reading or textbook.

## QR CODE SEARCH APPS

**iOS**: QR Reader *http://tinyurl.com/cc8b8zg*, QuickScan *http://tinyurl.com/agog6bx*, QR Code Reader *http://tinyurl.com/kqb2sh4*, NeoReader *http://tinyurl.com/l53tvsn*, Scan *http://tinyurl.com/kp9yrvf*, QR Scanner *http://tinyurl.com/clj7f7u*, inigma *http://tinyurl.com/mqhejt9*, Qrafter *http://tinyurl.com/cslddr5*

**Android**: QR Droid *http://tinyurl.com/7hxspwd*, QR Code Reading for Android *http://tinyurl.com/7hxspwd*, RedLaser *http://tinyurl.com/7c8qlez*, QRBarcode Scanner *http://tinyurl.com/mx6d4bk*, QR Pal *http://tinyurl.com/785xnlz*

## Planning *How* to Search

To engage in effective searches, students must plan their searches to acquire desired results. Students often begin with broad, general topics or questions that will generate a lot of responses, requiring them to specify their topic by posing questions about particular aspects of their topic. In giving students writing assignments, it is helpful to provide them with relatively specific prompts. For example, rather than the prompt, *Describe life during the 1930s Great Depression in America*, the prompt, *Describe the unemployment rates, mean incomes, and employment possibilities in America from 1930 to 1940* gives students some more specific direction to guide their topical search in the research. Moreover, you could provide students with databases containing relevant information on employment, income, and job types to complete this assignment, as well as the suggestion that they consult with a reference librarian if necessary.

## Engaging in Inquiry-Based Searches

Central to students' work in school is their ability to access information for completing assignments. While students can certainly access information by reading print texts/books or by talking with others, given the availability of searchable databases, students are increasingly using online resources to access information. At the same time, they also need to be able to assess the validity and credibility of the information they obtain.

In accessing and assessing information, students are employing inquiry-based literacy practices (Beach & Myers, 2001). These practices include the ability to pose questions about a topic or issue driving their investigation. To frame their inquiry, students could list questions and then select those questions that most interest them. They can then use the iOS *http://tinyurl.com/mqn4mqh* or Android *http://tinyurl.com/o58g4bo* ChaCha, iOS *http://tinyurl.com/lerwbel* or Android *http://tinyurl.com/c995hev* ASK, iOS *http://tinyurl.com/b3eqhko* or Android *http://tinyurl.com/mw3ga* Quora apps to pose their questions. The iOS *http://tinyurl.com/arkqzvp* app and Android *http://tinyurl.com/l4te3x5* Thinkpal app provides students with assistance in posing questions. Students can use the iOS *http://tinyurl.com/lnlnkoo* or Android *http://tinyurl.com/nrstgzf* Near Me app to view questions posed by other students in their class who are working on related places or sites.

There are also online tools that assist students in formulating questions, for example, GO! OHIOInfo Ask! Act! Achieve! site *http://go.infohio.org*, Noodle-Tools NoodleQuest *http://www.noodletools.com/noodlequest*, or Information Fluency Wizards *http://21cif.com/tools*, and the Strategy Tutor sites *http://tinyurl.com/k7so5go* developed by the Center for Applied Special Technology (CAST) for assisting students who have special learning needs with online searches. And, students can engage in the Internet Search Challenge game *http://tinyurl.com/k9ua3y3* to learn search strategies.

If students are generating their own topics, while they may begin with broader questions, as they acquire more information, they could then pose more specific questions. For example, if they are seeking information about the development and evolution of jazz music, posing a question such as *How did jazz develop?* will generate a large number of answers. They then need to pose more specific questions, for example, *Who were some of the first jazz musicians?*

As they are identifying or refining their topics to shape their searches, they also need to clarify their purposes for their searches—what they want or hope to learn related to key topics or concepts, as well as criteria for what constitutes relevant versus less relevant results, given those purposes. For example, a student, Susan, is writing a paper on the positive and negative effects of offshore oil drilling off of the Florida coast. To frame her searches for information, she knows that she needs to find information that is based on scientific research, as opposed to information released by the oil industry. She also knows that she wants informed but alternative perspectives on the topic, even if the information might conflict with her own opposition to offshore oil drilling.

As is the case with the uses of keyword searches, in posing these questions to obtain information, students need to specify the wording of their questions so that they can obtain specific results. Students can also employ the Thinkpal or Near Me apps that help them pose questions about their topic or issue through providing directions and questions that enable students to adopt multiple perspectives on a topic or issue.

## Modeling Search Strategies

Rather than simply telling students about effective search strategies, you can show them how to engage in these strategies by modeling your own search processes. To do so, you may start with a general inquiry question such as *What are some reasons that immigration to the United States has slowed?* Because it's difficult if not impossible to engage in searches to answer this question, you may then describe the need to generate more specific questions that will focus your searches for specific information. For example, you can pose the question, *What were the numbers of immigrants coming from Mexico to the United States over the past two decades?*; a question that can focus your search on some specific data. Given that question, you may then unpack some of the explicit and implicit key concepts in that question: "immigration to the United States," or "Mexican immigration to the United States," that will provide some empirical data about changes in the numbers or rate of immigration over time. You can then model the use of entering in more specific questions to yield more specific results, for example, *How many immigrants came from Mexico to the United States from 1990 to 2014?*

You can then model the process of altering your search categories when you recognize that you're not obtaining desirable search results. For example, in using the above categories, if you're not obtaining official, government census data, you may include specific mention of the United States Census results, as in *Based on the United States Census results, how many immigrants came from Mexico to the United States from 1990 to 2014?*

One useful tool for modeling inquiry-based questions or activities is "pathfinders" or Webquests—specific inquiry-based assignments that contain links for collecting information for completing specific activities (Dodge, 2006) that provide students with directions on how and where to search for specific topics or to complete specific assignments (Valenza, 2005/2006). You can create pathfinders using TrackStar *http://tinyurl.com/mqfksaj* or LibGuides *http://springshare.com/libguides*, as well as Webquests using QuestGarden *http://questgarden.com*. You can also have students create their own pathfinders or Webquests for use by their peers.

## Judging Information Obtained

As students acquire information, they also need to engage in the disciplinary literacy practices of reading critically to judge the validity and credibility of that information. This requires that they critically analyze the value, sufficiency, relevancy, and validity of information they acquire (for an excellent overview of teaching critical analysis of online material, see Potter, 2012).

Engaging in critical analysis requires self-monitoring and metacognitive awareness, a challenge for students with memory, attention deficit, or spatial processing problems (McNabb, Thurber, Dibuz, McDermott, & Lee, 2006). These critical analysis practices include the ability to contrast primary and secondary sources—understanding the difference between an original report document versus a blog post opinion about that report. Students should also be able to assess critically the objectivity of a given analysis in a text, website, or video (Clark, 2013). They should understand how to critique the language employed in a given analysis, particularly the use of biased, deceptive language that distorts or oversimplifies factual information. To do so, students can contrast analyses by different authors writing about the same topic to determine different degrees of bias, distortion, or oversimplification.

To help students analyze arguments employed in a document, students can use Roland Paris's C-L-E-A-R model (*http://aix1.uottawa.ca/~rparis/critical.html*) for analyzing arguments: claims the author is making, logical structure of the argument, evidence provided, assumptions the author makes, and alternative arguments. For other resources on teaching critical analysis of online content see Howard Reingold: Critical Thinking *http://criticalthinking.iste.wikispaces.net*, Critical Thinking on the Web *http://austhink.com/critical*, University of British Columbia: Critical Thinking *http://learningcommons.ubc.ca/criticalthinking*, and Evaluating Websites *http://www.lib.berkeley.edu/TeachingLib/Guides/Internet/Evaluate.html*.

Students can also contrast the perspectives or biases in news stories about the same event by accessing reports from newspapers around the world available at the Newseum site: *http://www.newseum.org*. They can work in groups of three, with each student reading a different report—one from a local, one from a national, and one from outside the US about the same event (Chase & Laufenberg, 2011). Students can create notes as a synthesis from a source, focusing on factual information and stance, and then comparing notes, share the results of their analyses of differences in primary report documents to the class, along with reasons for those differences in terms of issues like a journalist's own research and use of sources.

One useful first step involves identifying the source or producer of a website. To do so, students need to find the "about us" or "who we are" links to determine who created a site (Leu et al., 2013). In many cases, a website might be produced by a commercial company selling certain products. The site may simply be providing users with information designed to promote the company's products. For example, a site may present medical self-help information about a certain medical problem, but doing so to sell its own product to "cure" that problem.

It's important to have students identify the source or creator of sites because these sites may provide false, misleading, inaccurate, or biased information (Kozdras & Welsh, 2008). For example, a Martin Luther King site *http://www. martinlutherking.org* is operated by white racists and contains racist misinformation about Dr. Martin Luther King. To help students become aware of the importance of identifying sources, you can show them examples of hoax sites as well as satiric sites by searching "hoax sites," for example, The Federal Vampire and Zombie Agency *http://www.fvza.org*, Feline Reactions to Bearded Men *http://tinyurl.com/9segr*, AFDB (Aluminum Foil Deflector Beanie) *http:// zapatopi.net/afdb*, and satirical sites such as The Onion *http://www.theonion.com* or the Church of the Flying Spaghetti Monster *http://www.venganza.org*. You can also have students, working in teams, each generate a list of hoax versus valid sites and then determine which team is best able to distinguish between the two (Potter, 2012).

To determine the source of information, students can search for an "About Us" link to identify the organization, group, or individual who produced the site. If the source of the site cannot be located, the fact that no information is given or is available may raise suspicions, or a camouflaged link with "XPi" in the top bar indicates that students could then search for information about the site on Google or Wikipedia or put out a query on Twitter or on discussion boards (Leu et al., 2013), or go to Web monitoring sites such as Snopes *http://www.snopes.com* that identify misinformation on sites.

Students also need to distinguish among the domain names .org, .edu, .com, and .gov in terms of the type of organization, group, or individual producing the site. In analyzing Wikipedia entries, students can look at the revision histories on entries to note deletions and additions as well as Talk Pages for discussions of misinformation.

To help students analyze search results, Esther Grassian (2006) of the UCLA Library has them pose questions such as:

- Who is the intended audience?
- What is the purpose of the site (e.g., news, information/factual, entertainment, social connection, opinion, education, experimentation, research, training, sales, marketing/advertising, recruitment, etc.)?
- What sorts of information or data does it contain?
- To what extent does the site fulfill its intended purpose?
- How valuable or useful is the site or item?
- Who created the site?
- Who owns the site?
- Who regulates the site?
- Are there rules or standards regarding the site and items or areas mounted, created, or utilized on the site?
- Is there a reporting mechanism in place regarding violation of rules and standards?
- Who is the author/creator/producer of individual items, collections of items or areas within the site?
- Can the identity of sponsors/authors/creators/producers be verified? If so, how?

## Engaging in Safe Searching

In modeling search strategies, you also need to demonstrate for students the practices of safe searching given the likelihood in any search of obtaining objectionable or pornographic sites, and emphasizing that when students encounter such sites in school, they need to exit them and note the search terms that led to them to avoid them in the future. Although school computers and networks have filters that block access to these sites, students can find ways around these filters. The other ongoing filtering and access issue is whether the filters also block access to non-objectionable information important for online projects and learning. Rather than assuming that the problem can be solved simply by filtering content or using censorship, it is important to take a proactive stance by addressing this issue as matter of student choice and attitudes—students need to take responsibility for their own actions by adopting safe searching techniques.

## Transferring and Summarizing Search Results to Notes

As students acquire online results, they need to synthesize, summarize, and transfer those results into notes for use in developing reports and other written products. When students are in a Web browser on a device, moving between the browser and a note-taking app can be a challenge. To address that challenge, students can employ the iOS Sling Note *http://tinyurl.com/l9gw5cd* app that visually positions the Web browser on the left side of the screen panel and a notepad on the right panel. Because the browser and notepad are side by side, students can more easily move back and forth between the two, for example, dragging clips or links from the Web to their notepad, and then exporting those notes as a PDF document; for a demonstration: *http://www.mobilebuster.com.*

Or, students can use the iOS *http://tinyurl.com/kw9ykqx* or Android *http:// tinyurl.com/k675s9y* Note Anytime app to take notes directly on a screen associated with a website. Similarly, if students are drafting a paper, they can employ the iOS PaperHelper *http://tinyurl.com/n3ac6h5* app that also provides a side-by-side format to move material from their Web browser searches to a draft.

In some cases, students will want to move text/image documents in print form into their digital notes or reports. To do so, they can use scanner apps such as the iOS Scanner Pro *http://tinyurl.com/lcy68r9* app. Students simply place the document on their iPad screen for scanning, which then produces a digital document for sharing or e-mailing to themselves.

## Using Wikipedia

In addition to academic databases, one major source for accessing information is Wikipedia: *http://www.wikipedia.org*: iOS *http://tinyurl.com/bo8bv68* and Android Wikipedia *http://tinyurl.com/m5agwxn* or Wikipedia Mobile *http://tinyurl.com/ kdwjnkd* apps. While Wikipedia should not be perceived to be the definitive or sole source for scholarly information, it is often an excellent starting point for understanding key concepts or issues and identifying key terms and other resources. Contrary to criticism, Wikipedia is highly vetted by editors who peruse entries for errors or misinformation, often adding corrections relatively quickly.

Younger students often have difficulty using Wikipedia because they can be overwhelmed by the sheer amount of information as well as entries written at a relatively high readability level. To address this challenge, students can employ numerous apps designed to assist students in accessing and using Wikipedia. For example, the iOS Qwiki *http://tinyurl.com/kc3oape* app includes videos, images, graphs, and entries for millions of topics written at a relatively accessible level, as well as enhancing comprehension through uses of images.

---

### WIKIPEDIA APPS

**iOS**: Articles for iPad *http://tinyurl.com/kd4gzod*, Wikibot *http://tinyurl. com/jwk6t6s*, Wikiview *http://tinyurl.com/lxbrq6h*, Wikipedia Mobile *http:// tinyurl.com/bo8bv68*, Wikipanion Plus *http://tinyurl.com/mnomr5h*, Wiki Offline *http://tinyurl.com/m7jvw4p*

**Android**: Gwiki *http://tinyurl.com/lpyxj6c*, Wikidroid *http://tinyurl.com/ avqww26*, Wikipedia for Tablet *http://tinyurl.com/q6e38pm*, and WikiMobile *http://tinyurl.com/lko5t9w*

---

You can also create study guides for use with Wikipedia searches using the iOS StudyGuideMe *http://tinyurl.com/l4hfcqd* app for providing students with study guides for topics in Wikipedia entries. To use the app, you enter search terms and the material from Wikipedia shown on one side of the screen is transferred into a study guide format on the right side of the screen. Students can respond to the study guide prompts in writing a paper.

Students can also study the revision history on Wikipedia to note the changes that are made to a certain entry, as well as comments that are made as to why certain changes were made. By studying the revision history, students begin to appreciate the ways in which Wikipedia entries are vetted by others who create a revision.

As we note in Chapter 6 on writing to learn, students can edit existing Wikipedia entries based on their research on certain topics. They can also create their own entries, for example, creating an entry about their school, town/city, or a local event.

## Using Social Bookmarking Browser Apps for Storing, Annotating, and Sharing Information

Another important set of apps for supporting searches involves the use of social bookmarking browser apps. Students can use social bookmarking apps for saving links to websites relevant to their needs based on certain topics or groups, resulting in building up collections of sites for use in their work. And, they can also use social bookmarking tools to add tags to these sites, highlight texts, and add annotations to websites or texts for sharing responses with others.

---

## SOCIAL BOOKMARKING APPS

iOS *http://tinyurl.com/mksh786* and Android *http://tinyurl.com/mggqmgu* Diigo (Diigo add-ons for use with browsers *https://www.diigo.com/tools*)
iOS *http://tinyurl.com/m9qdf3k* and Android *http://tinyurl.com/kj4mzk5* Delicious
iOS *http://tinyurl.com/q9pbydr* and Android *http://tinyurl.com/qfuatrv* Digg
iOS *http://tinyurl.com/cs2zoxf* and Android *http://tinyurl.com/7y967az* Stumbleupon
Yahoo! Bookmarks *http://tinyurl.com/8ywkslu*, jogtheweb *http://www.job theweb.com*

---

One of the most popular of these social bookmarking apps is the Diigo Browser app. Students can add Diigo to Safari on their iPads or Android devices, as well as on Firefox, Chrome, or Internet Explorer browsers. Students can bookmark websites to save them to their own accounts or to share with others using Twitter, Facebook, or Evernote. To begin with Diigo, you should set up a free educator account at *https://www.diigo.com/education*, which you can use to create student accounts that do not require an email address and are therefore private. Students can then highlight text and add sticky-note annotations to share with peers. As we briefly noted, these highlighting and annotation tools afford literacy practices like reading and writing that can enhance both learning and engagement.

## Using Tags With Social Bookmarking

In sharing bookmarks, students need to learn how to employ specific keyword tags identifying the primary topical focus of a link, tags that facilitate students' searches for relevant material. For example, for their civil rights history project, students may tag sites using terms such as civil rights, sit-ins, nonviolent, Martin Luther King, Southern Christian Leadership Conference (SCLC), and so on.

When students are tagging links, they are also presented with generic tags typically associated with the link they are tagging, tags that others have assigned to that link. Students can also add their own unique tags consistent with the focus of their own projects.

These tags can then be used to create tag clouds for a collection of links for inclusion on a website or blog that show those words in different-size fonts that represent different degrees to which a tag was referenced—frequently referenced words are then larger than less frequently referenced words. Students can also use add hashtags, words, or phrases following the symbol # to identify groups and topics to their tweets for searching each other's tweets in Twitter.

One issue in the use of tags is whether they should be generated from the bottom up by users—what are known as a folksonomy tags, defined as a set of terms or categories developed collaboratively by users of a group based on their own experience or expertise, that differ from official library taxonomies associated with library classification or keyword systems. The advantages of folksonomies is that they are available to the public and users can readily create them for their own use without having to adhere to existing taxonomies.

On the other hand, such individualized folksonomy tagging can generate idiosyncratic tags that are not searchable, are not valid or standardized, or are not logically related to each other (Berger & Trexler, 2010). The advantages of tags based on existing taxonomies is that they are created by experts who are familiar with a field, discipline, or topic; they are valid and standardized, and they reflect logical, hierarchical relationships between categories. However, conforming to such taxonomies excludes bottom-up involvement and requires taggers to learn these categories (Berger & Trexler, 2010).

## Using RSS Feeds to Subscribe to Information Sources

The use of these search engine and social bookmarking tools involves students in searching the Web for information. Rather than having to continually search for information, students can employ RSS feeds to subscribe to sites, blogs, wikis, or news outlets that "feed" information automatically to them using "feed reader" apps.

---

### RSS FEED READERS APPS

iOS *http://tinyurl.com/n8qqa5a* and Android *http://tinyurl.com/aws7s2x* Feedly
iOS *http://tinyurl.com/lw42629* and Android *http://tinyurl.com/ap9x8sd* gReader
iOS *http://tinyurl.com/m5rzaec* and Android *http://tinyurl.com/lm89s2z* RSS Reader
iOS Reeder 2 *http://tinyurl.com/lj5d26a*, Android Press *http://tinyurl.com/cl3dor3*

---

Students can select certain topics within these apps, which will then pull in material from a range of sources. Students can then use them to subscribe to specific sites, blogs, wikis, or news outlets by using "Add subscription" and then copying and pasting in the blog's feed URL. They can also collect their feeds by creating a folder on their bookmarks bar. When they find a news site—for example, the *New York Times*—they click on the RSS feed icon next to the refresh icon within the URL box. They then go to their bookmarks link to save that feed URL to their folder. They can also add other news outlets' RSS feeds to their folder. When they open that folder, they can search for certain items using the search options in the right column.

## Using Curation Apps

Students can also access information on certain topics or current news using the curation apps listed below, which themselves employ RSS feeds to access information and curate news items. Curation apps therefore adopt a "push" model to provide students with information based on topics of interest.

## CURATION APPS

---

iOS *http://tinyurl.com/6sf5z9r* and Android *http://tinyurl.com/kdp3wql*
Pearltrees
iOS *http://tinyurl.com/6ndawuq* and Android *http://tinyurl.com/bvcsgcg*
Flipboard
iOS *http://tinyurl.com/lwfq88u* and Android *http://tinyurl.com/lr3f9oh*
Learnist
iOS *http://tinyurl.com/yb7r6u5* and Android *http://tinyurl.com/mun9gfp*
Zinio
iOS *http://tinyurl.com/79qn9zg* and Android *http://tinyurl.com/7vacsas*
Zite
iOS *http://tinyurl.com/lu4khuz* and Android *http://tinyurl.com/6s4gz2*
Google Currents
iOS *http://tinyurl.com/7zpuhe5* and Android *http://tinyurl.com/mrsbagq*
LiveBinders
iOS *http://tinyurl.com/7ef7qjk* and Android *http://tinyurl.com/lvqxxxu*
Scoop.it!
iOS *http://tinyurl.com/9vrp9np* and Android *http://tinyurl.com/la4twa2*
Pinterest
iOS *http://tinyurl.com/mqg5rln* and Android *http://tinyurl.com/luq7xg8*
Storify
iOS Educlipper *http://tinyurl.com/l728m3d*

---

Certain curation apps have features that are particularly useful in the classroom. The iOS EduClipper app, along with the *https://www.educlipper.net* site for use on other devices, is designed to encourage students to add or "clip" online material to "boards" for sharing with peers. You can also create lessons for students organized around certain topics based on their clips. And, students can create portfolios based on their stored work for reflecting on their learning across time.

Similarly, students can use the iOS and Android Learnist apps to access material sites such as Wikipedia entries or TED Talks videos, to create their own or to add onto others' "learnings" or "learn boards." And, students can use the popular iOS and Android Pinterest apps to post or "pin" online images or images from cameras to visual pinboards about certain topics or events, or to share interests. Students can also collaboratively create pinboards, adding images to a single pinboard, for example, images associated with their projects.

Students can also use the iOS and Android Flipboard apps to select certain topics for accessing current stories or news items based on those topics (Davis, 2011). They can also add links to other content sources such as Facebook, Twitter, or blogs to create a central hub for organizing their information, as well as create a classroom magazine (Fryer, 2012), something they can also do using the iOS and Android Scoop.it! apps.

Students can also use the iOS and Android Storify apps to gather videos of current news stories organized by the news topic so that they can see a number of different stories on the same topic. With Storify they can contrast the coverage of certain stories by different media outlets as well as outlets from different parts of the world. Students can discuss differences in selection of images, interviewees, competing perspectives, and the language employed in covering a story.

The increased use of these curation apps is changing how media or app producers are generating and editing information. Tim Carmody (2011) argues that the use of these curation apps represents a shift in how users acquire information that in turn shapes the ways in which information is generated and edited. Given the mobility of devices, users can acquire this information across a range of different devices and locations, for example, between their iPad and iPhone so that they can access their iPhone while waiting in a coffeeshop line. While in the past people acquired the information provided for them by the media, now people can personalize the types of information they are receiving, with personalization depending on their needs, interests, and location. He quotes Flipboard founder Mike McCue's description of his use of Flipboard:

> It's a mix of what's going on in the world and what's going on in your world, fused together. And it might seem weird that I'm looking at a picture of my daughters, and then the next flip I'm reading a story about Iran. But to me as a reader, when I'm standing in line waiting to get my coffee, those things are what I care about.

The use of curation apps changes how media producers define the context for accessing and analyzing information (Carmody, 2011). Rather than simply perceiving context as providing background information for a story, media, or app, producers now perceive context in terms of five factors: medium, location, time, the social, and identity.

Central to students' successful use of these curation apps is the ability to define those topics relevant to students' projects. Given the large number of stories or news items available on these curation apps, students need to narrow down their focus to acquire those items that will be more useful for their work.

## Summary

In this chapter, we discussed ways for students to use apps to access, assess, collect, and store online information and material for use in the classroom. Students will need explicit instruction on use of effective search strategies to go beyond simply accessing Google, particularly in terms of using academic databases and critically analyzing their search results. Students also need to know how to employ social bookmarking tools to collect and tag sites relevant to their work, as well as exploiting the benefits of "push" tools such as curation apps for accessing information.

## References

Adler, B. (2014, March 6). News literacy declines with socioeconomic status. *Columbia Journalism Review*. Retrieved from http://tinyurl.com/mj5bvv5

Barseghian, T. (2011, December 27). 12 ways to be more search savvy [Web log post]. Retrieved from http://tinyurl.com/kztemc5

Beach, R., & Myers, J. (2001). *Inquiry based English instruction: Engaging students in life and literature*. New York: Teachers College Press.

Berger, P., & Trexler, S. (2010). *Choosing Web 2.0 tools for learning and teaching in a digital world*. Santa Barbara, CA: Libraries Unlimited.

Carmody, T. (2011, December 9). The future of context: Mobile reading from Google to Flipboard to FLUD. *Wired Magazine*. Retrieved from http://www.wired.com/2011/12/google-to-flipboard-to-flud

Chase, Z., & Laufenberg, D. (2011). Embracing the squishiness of digital literacy. *Journal of Adolescent & Adult Literacy*, *54*(7), 535–537.

Clark, H. (2013, October 16). Do your students know how to search? [Web log post]. Retrieved from http://www.edudemic.com/student-search-skills

Coiro, J. (2003). Reading comprehension on the Internet: Exploring our understanding of reading comprehension to encompass new literacies. *The Reading Teacher*, *56*(5), 458–464.

Coiro, J., & Fogleman, J. (2011). Using websites wisely. *Educational Leadership*, *68*(5), 34–38.

Council of Chief State School Officers and National Governors' Association. (2010). *Common Core State Standards for English Language Arts & Literacy in History/Social Studies, Science, and Technical Subjects*. Washington, DC: Author. Retrieved from http://www.corestandards.org

Davis, V. (2011, April 27). 15 fantastic ways to use Flipboard [Web log post]. Retrieved from http://tinyurl.com/l75ksfz

Dodge, B. (2006, November 26). The Webquest portal [Web log post]. Retrieved from http://webquest.org/index.php

Fryer, W. (2012, January 21). Create a custom digital newspaper on your iPad with Flipboard & Google Reader [Web log post]. Retrieved from http://tinyurl.com/7jxhlyj

Grassian, E. (2006, October 9). Thinking critically about Web 2.0 and beyond. UCLA Library. Retrieved from http://www2.library.ucla.edu/libraries/college/11605_12008.cfm

Jones, B. (2011, July 24). 40 interesting ways to use QR codes in the classroom [Web log post]. Retrieved from http://tinyurl.com/3u2ee5v

Kozdras, D., & Welsh, J. L. (2008). Hoax or no hoax? Strategies for online comprehension and evaluation. *ReadWriteThink*. Retrieved from http://tinyurl.com/29lbz7c

Leu, D. J., Jr., Kinzer, C. K., Coiro, J., Castek, J., & Henry, L. A. (2013). New literacies: A dual-level theory of the changing nature of literacy, instruction, and assessment. In R. B. Ruddell & D. Alvermann (Eds.), *Theoretical Models and Processes of Reading* (6th ed.). Newark, DE: International Reading Association.

McNabb, M. L., Thurber, B. B., Dibuz, B., McDermott, P., & Lee, C. A. (2006). *Literacy learning in networked classrooms: Using the Internet with middle level students.* Newark, DE: International Reading Association.

Potter, M. J. (2012). Developing critical thinking through Web research skills. Microsoft Education. Retrieved from http://www.microsoft.com/education/en-bn/teachers/guides/Pages/Critical-thinking.aspx

Purdy, J. P. (2012). Why first-year college students select online research resources as their favorite. *First Monday, 17*(9). Retrieved from http://www.firstmonday.org/ojs/index.php/fm/article/view/4088/3289

Shirky, C. (2008, September 18). "It's not information overload. It's filter failure." Web 2.0 Expo, New York. Retrieved from http://www.youtube.com/watch?v=LabqeJEOQyI

Valenza, J. K. (2005/2006). Pathfinders, streaming video: Welcome to the 21st century school library. *Educational Leadership, 63*(4), 54–59.

Weinberger, D. (2012). *Too big to know: Rethinking knowledge now that the facts aren't the facts, experts are everywhere, and the smartest person in the room is the room.* New York: Basic Books.

Zickuhr, K., & Smith, A. (2012, April 13). Digital differences. Washington, DC: Pew Research Internet Project. Retrieved from http://tinyurl.com/ka69q5g

# 5

# USING APPS FOR READING DIGITALLY

Central to reading is comprehension—the ability to interact with or transact with texts in ways that engage the reader and result in understanding. The term *text* has been synonymous with *print*. Historically, until recently, reading in general as well as within various disciplines referred to understanding printed artifacts; the term *texts* meant books or other printed materials consisting of words, sentences, and paragraphs, on pages, with pages stacked and bound. Print was arranged in a linear fashion to be approached from left to right on each page and from front to back in books and other documents. With digital reading and reading in virtual spaces, the history of what reading means, what research says about it, and the typical artifacts it has been applied to, must be re-examined and our stances and definitions of reading reconfigured.

The English language arts standards from the ELA Common Core State Standards (CCSS) (Council of Chief State School Officers and National Governors' Association, 2010) below point to the importance of students learning to construct meaning with texts. However, in the standards, *text* is synonymous with *print*, whereas in digital reading texts are multimodal representations of meaning. A key issue that is engendering a lot of discussion is the CCSS notion of close reading which directs the reader back to the print text at different levels of comprehension, citing the importance of evidence in the text. In digital reading, the print text might be one source of information supplemented with other kinds of information represented in different modalities, like reading images and video.

The notion of close reading as stated in the CCSS, although sometimes important to reading print text as part of a multimodal reading experience, is actually contradictory to a lot of the reading that occurs online across modalities, across Web pages, across reading spaces in apps, and across social network posts (Leu, Kinzer, Coiro, Castek, & Henry, 2013). Reading in these environments is often designed to produce a unique intertextual understanding or intermedial understanding that would not be possible with the close reading of a singular print text.

The notion of text complexity in the CCSS has also been discussed at length in multiple forums. The idea is that students should be challenged with complex texts to hone their reading skills and strategies. But, again, this notion of text complexity is tied to text features of print texts whereas reading digitally entails reading texts that are complex because they are multimodal, are linked to other texts via an online search, and might represent a range of accessibility and genre types that afford different kinds of challenges.

## English Language Arts Common Core State Standards for Reading

### Key Ideas and Details

1. Read closely to determine what the text says explicitly and to make logical inferences from it; cite specific textual evidence when writing or speaking to support conclusions drawn from the text.
2. Determine central ideas or themes of a text and analyze their development; summarize the key supporting details and ideas.
3. Analyze in detail where, when, why, and how events, ideas, and characters develop and interact over the course of a text.

### Craft and Structure

4. Interpret words and phrases as they are used in a text, including determining technical, connotative, and figurative meanings, and explain how specific word choices shape meaning or tone.
5. Analyze the structure of texts, including how specific sentences, paragraphs, and larger portions of the text (e.g., a section or chapter) relate to each other and the whole.
6. Assess how point of view or purpose shapes the content and style of a text.

### Integration of Knowledge and Ideas

7. Synthesize and apply information presented in diverse ways (e.g., through words, images, graphs, and video) in print and digital sources in order to answer questions, solve problems, or compare modes of presentation.
8. Delineate and evaluate the reasoning and rhetoric within a text, including assessing whether the evidence provided is relevant and sufficient to support the text's claims.
9. Analyze how two or more texts address similar themes or topics in order to build knowledge or to compare the approaches the authors take.

## Range and Level of Text Complexity

10. Read complex texts independently, proficiently, and fluently, sustaining concentration, monitoring comprehension, and, when useful, rereading.

*(Council of Chief State School Officers and*
*National Governors' Association, 2010, p. 31)*

These standards embody the importance of students knowing how to make inferences or define common themes across different texts, to make intertextual connections, and draw inferences from those connections. And the standards emphasize the importance of students being able to recognize uses of various text structures and use textual or literary techniques that they can employ in their own writing. The standards also emphasize the importance of close reading—reading to pay attention to what the text offers, its word choice and structure, and the ability to synthesize important information; understand the differences between important theses, themes, or points and details; and understand features and devices unique to narrative texts.

## Challenging and Engaging Digital Reading Contexts

As we move from reading print texts to the reading of hypertexts, multimodal texts, or media intertexts, the rules and processes for what constitutes reading change drastically. Hence what skilled readers do in print environments and what they do in online and digital environments, although sharing some components, are quite different. Soon *most* of students' reading of both informational and narrative texts will occur in digital environments either in apps or online. Digital texts differ from those of print texts in that they require different kinds of literacy practices. For example, digital texts can be both multimodal and intermedial. What students read can be print or some other modality like visual or various combinations of print and other modalities; but digital texts can also be intermedial because the text you comprehend is a *constructed* text that represents a reader's *synthesis* of multimodal information say, across Web pages or various parts of apps.

In digital environments, texts are more likely to take the form of portable textoids rather than longer print text with traditionally defined features—like text structure, organization signaling, headings, subheadings, and the like. These portable textoids are easily read, reread, changed, and passed on. They are also easily transformed into other modalities (Kress, 2003).

## Apps for Generating Annotations

As noted above, one important digital reading practice is the ability to synthesize the meaning of texts. Students can use annotation apps to engage in what Fisher and Cook (2007) describe as *annotexting*, synthesizing responses to and interpretations of texts, as well as sharing these annotations with others. Some apps also allow for multimodal annotation. A reader can read a print text, and annotate it with an audio annotation. Then someone might listen to the audio annotation after reading the original text and respond to the audio annotation with a text annotation. Annotexting in this sense can provide multimodal affordances, allowing a range of students with modality preferences to respond to a text and create a synthesis from it. But the most compelling affordance is that each text read can be reshaped, repurposed, and re-presented based on various readers' stances and their senses of what different audiences might want to read.

### Text Annotation Apps

The text annotation apps listed below allow students to type, handwrite, or in some apps, insert an audio annotation in texts, particularly PDFs. Once affixed, the annotations can be shared with readers.

---

## ANNOTATION APPS

**iOS**: iAnnotate *http://tinyurl.com/mmdw2mr*, Adobe Reader *http://tinyurl.com/lhoyya2*, GoodReader *http://tinyurl.com/c8h9lqg*, Readdle *http://tinyurl.com/n7rwv5f*, DocAS Lite *http://tinyurl.com/n88lwgx*, PDF Review *http://tinyurl.com/kgwd4ad*, PDF Max *http://tinyurl.com/llcww9d*, AnnoDoc Lite *http://tinyurl.com/kg8qef9*, UPAD Lite *http://tinyurl.com/nxv9bao*, and PDF Notes *http://tinyurl.com/l32lnx6*

**Android**: iAnnotate *http://tinyurl.com/kgwd4ad*, Adobe Reader *http://tinyurl.com/7g373kq*, PDF Reader *http://tinyurl.com/bslzgmp*, qPDF Notes *http://tinyurl.com/bmmbq8l*, ezPDF Reader *http://tinyurl.com/czra7c3*, RepliGo PDF Reader *http://tinyurl.com/773z9es*, FoxIt Mobile *http://tinyurl.com/cv2op98*

---

The iOS and Android iAnnotate apps involve multimodal annotation in print, handwrittten text, and audio annotations in PDFs, as well as highlighting of texts, underlining, and bookmarking. Another, somewhat simpler, free PDF annotation app is DocAS for highlighting, underlining, typing/handwriting annotations, and exporting students' files to Dropbox or Google Docs. Students can also use GoodReader and Readdle apps that provide for both typed and handwritten annotations, as well as adding different drawings, lines, or boxes, and syncing to iCloud, Dropbox, or Google Docs.

## Social Bookmarking Apps

As described in Chapter 4, students can use social bookmarking apps such as Diigo iOS *http://tinyurl.com/mksh786* and Android *http://tinyurl.com/mggqmgu* or Delicious iOS *http://tinyurl.com/m9qdf3k* and Android http://tinyurl.com/kj4mzk5 apps, or Digg iOS *http://tinyurl.com/q9pbydr* and Android *http://tinyurl.com/qfuatrv* apps, or Educlipper *https://www.educlipper.net* to highlight sections of a text and then add annotations often in the form of "sticky notes" as with Diigo, to those highlighted sections.

Annotating, if planned carefully, should encourage students to construct their own meanings based on their purposes for reading—for example, formulating ideas for writing a paper or collaboratively planning a group presentation. Because the purpose for reading shapes the nature or focus of annotations, it is useful to provide students some direction for why they are annotating texts related to your assignments or activities.

One powerful and flexible approach to annotating can be adapted from a time-tested reading annotation strategy called REAP (Eanet & Manzo, 1976): **R**ead, **E**ncode, **A**nnotate, **P**onder. When the strategy was originally introduced, Eanet and Manzo (1976) introduced the following types of annotations: *Summary* annotations that attempt to capture the main gist in a concise way; *Question* annotations that focus on an important thesis but require a question that, if answered, gets to the thesis, and so on; *Thesis* annotations that call for an incisive statement that cuts to the core of a piece; *Heuristic* annotations that capture the author's intention in her or his own words (for further information about REAP from Cengage see *http://tinyurl.com/pdscff6*).

## Summary Annotation

States the basic message in brief form.

**App adaptation**: Have students read up to the point in a text in which they are prepared to summarize an important point or gist. Then, using an annotation app, they can write the summary and post it for peers. Variation: Pre-read the text before the students read it and pre-mark points at which to write summary annotations. When they read the text up to each point, they write summary annotations.

## Question Annotation

A main point that is answered in the reading passage when the author responds to the annotator's question.

**App adaptation**: As students read, they can pose key questions that the text, up to the point of the annotation, answers; other students can actually respond to the questions in annotations posed by peers by answering the questions as responses to existing annotations.

## Thesis Annotation

Concise statement of the author's main point—the most important point the author is trying to put across to the reader. For narrative text this could be the theme.

**App adaptation**: Students must read a complete section of a text that holds together and conveys a thesis. At the end of that text they can write a thesis annotation. Unlike the summary annotation, this cannot be an ongoing series of annotations that summarize as they read but must occur at the end of the relevant section of text like a subsection or division of a chapter, for example.

## Critical Annotation

The annotator's response to the author's thesis; these can be organized around whether the annotator agrees, disagrees, or agrees in part with a sentence or two that supports the thesis position of the annotator.

**App adaptation**: Like in the question annotation adaptation, this annotation could involve one set of students writing thesis annotations and another set reading the text and then writing critical annotations as comments on existing thesis annotations.

By sharing these annotations, students are exposed to different interpretations reflecting different perspectives and purposes for reading. This sharing can then lead to challenging one's interpretations, leading to further revisions and development of interpretations. For example, in sharing their annotations about a poem, students may discover quite different meanings formulated by their peers, resulting in altering and further developing their own interpretations.

In his first-year college composition class, Paul Morris (2012) uses annotations to foster students' dialogic responses to their reading. To encourage his students to go beyond using annotations to simply restate ideas in a text, he provided his students with a template for predicting, questioning, clarifying, summarizing, and making connections to their prior knowledge or other texts.

Morris found that students have difficulty generating annotations as questions. To help his students learn to pose questions, he employs a fishbowl discussion activity. Students first put their questions from their annotations onto anonymous index cards. He then has the students create an inner circle and an outer circle for the fishbowl discussion. Students in the inner circle disseminate their index card questions and then respond to these questions. Students in the outer circle observe their discussion and identify the kinds of questions students in the inner circle are employing, i.e., whether those questions are open-ended versus closed questions, clarification versus interpretation questions, etc., and how these different kinds of questions generate certain kinds of responses. Engaging in these observations fosters further meta-awareness of different types of annotations to employ.

He also has his students engage in paired "think-alouds" in which students pair up and one student creates oral annotations while the other student transcribes their annotations (students could also use audio recording apps to record their own "think-alouds").

From engaging in these activities, his students learn to recognize the range of different reading literacy practices they can employ in creating their annotations: predicting, questioning, clarifying, summarizing, and making connections to their prior knowledge or other texts that serve to foster dialogic thinking in his class. He quotes one student who noted that "it's like reading two novels—the original novel and the one I'm writing in the margin" (p. 386).

## Student Uses of Annotation Apps: Diigo and DocAS Lite

Seventh-grade students in Melanie Swandby's science class at an urban California school, made up of 67% Latino students, 17% African American students, 8% Asian students, and 3% white students, engaged in a project in which they were studying the pros and cons for use of wind energy (Castek & Beach, 2013a). Students read a series of essays written specifically for this project—a pro essay arguing that wind power has a number of positive benefits and a con essay arguing that wind power is not cost effective and has negative effects. In terms of disciplinary literacies, as described in Chapter 2, the ability to read these essays as science reports requires that students know how to generate questions or hypotheses as well as address those questions based on empirical data. And, reading these science texts requires the ability to interpret visual images or graphs portraying data (Shanahan, Shanahan, & Misischia, 2011).

The goal for this lesson was to help students learn how to use annotations to formulate interpretations from these pro–con essays to generate their own positions on the issue of the positive versus negative effects of wind power. The students knew that they were using their annotations to develop materials for writing arguments that were for or against the issue of the use of wind to generate power.

Students were provided with an overview of the benefits of annotating the essays, as well as different ways in which they could annotate the articles by modeling annotations on a projector, including the uses of posing questions to obtain responses from their peers. Students then read the pro article describing the benefits of wind power—that it provides free, renewable, green energy that reduces dependence on fossil fuels, and added annotations.

### Use of Diigo Sticky Notes to Engage in Collaborative Discussion

To complete their annotations, students used the Diigo social bookmarking/annotation app with their iPads to annotate essays by posing questions. As previously noted, the Diigo app allows students to add and share sticky note annotations within their own classroom groups. Students could therefore respond to each other's questions with their own annotations.

The fact that students were collaboratively responding to these essays reflects the importance of collaborative responses to online texts. By reading each other's annotations, students were exposed to alternative response practices that might differ from their own, resulting in their acquiring new ways of interpreting texts (Coiro, Castek, & Guzniczak, 2011).

When students added their annotations to the article, their annotations showed up as sticky notes. For example, as shown in Figure 5.1, Vanni Tran added her annotation, "if we get our energy from burning coal and oil, how are we supposed to go green."

Other students then used sticky notes to pose questions or make comments:

| | |
|---|---|
| *Francisco Lopez-Luna:* | "What is promising alternative?" |
| *Daisy Cardenas:* | "What are some things that use energy or power?" |
| *Juan Carlos Ortiz:* | "What are some things that use energy or power?" "I use my lights when I wake up because it's all dark and I can't see." "I agree that everybody should use wind power." |
| *Bryant Maldonado:* | "I use electricity before coming to school." "Don't wind turbines kill birds?" |
| *Matthew Chhom:* | "How does wind power generate energy?" |
| *Moises Espinoza:* | "If we burn gas it creates carbon dioxide and goes to the sky but it doesn't leave it's stay there and creates heat and that might be a reason why there is no snow in Lake Tahoe." |

Students also responded to each other's annotations. For example, in response to the article about the negative reactions to the appearance of wind turbines (Figure 5.2), Steven Martinez asked, "Why are they complaining about the

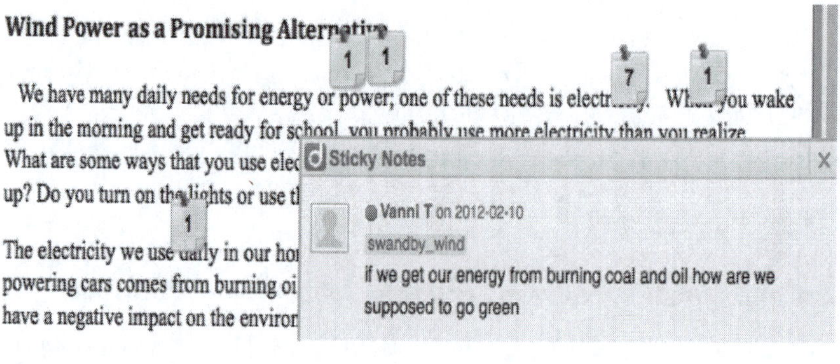

FIGURE 5.1   Student's Sticky-Note Annotations in Response to Wind-Power Essay

*Source:* Reprinted with permission from Vanni Tran.

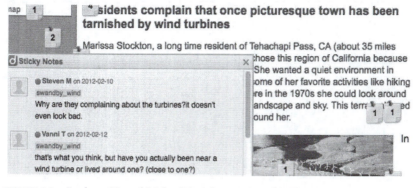

**FIGURE 5.2** Students Use of Sticky-Note Annotations for Discussion
*Source:* Reprinted with permission from Vanni Tran and Steven Martinez.

turbines? It doesn't even look bad." Vanni Tran then responded, "that's what you think, but have you actually been near a wind turbine or lived around one? (close to one?)."

Students then used the notebook feature in Diigo and the iOS DocAS *http:// tinyurl.com/pxd92jg* app to synthesize thinking and formulate arguments for or against use of wind power drawing on evidence from both the pro and the con articles. Students were told to skim back through the articles to identify key points to help them support their pro or con positions on whether wind power is a good alternative energy source.

Students then drew on these annotations to write summary reports using the DocAS Notebook. One student noted that:

> Everything has something bad about it, wind energy is renewable but sometimes it is a waste of energy. In my opinion, it's a bad thing because if one of the wind turbines is broken, there's no law for that company to fix them. Yes, some people might say it's renewable and causes no pollution. Wind energy has some things that are good about it but overall it's a waste of space and money to build. (Castek & Beach, 2013a, p. 560)

In this student's writing he drew on his own and others' annotations as prewriting as prewriting to address the pros and cons of wind turbines by citing reasons for his claims. Analysis of the students' Diigo annotations indicated that 34% of their annotations consisted of questioning; 22% integrating/connecting; 13% evaluating; 10% determining important ideas; 9% inferring; 8% reacting to others' comments; and 4% monitoring (Castek & Beach, 2013b). The fact that the most prevalent use of their annotations involved posing questions suggested they were engaged in the inquiry process of formulating questions that led to the collection of evidence or data to address these questions. Students also used their annotations for "integrating/connecting" and "inferring" to apply their own personal experience and prior knowledge to the issue.

Analysis of the DocAS annotations indicated that the types of online reading strategies employed in their annotations led to their adoption of similar strategies or stances in their summary written arguments. For example, one student's annotations were all categorized as "questioning," which reflected a critical stance related to the cost of wind turbines, disturbance of people and animals, and the fact that broken wind turbines are not removed. This student adopted the same critical stance in her summary to argue that wind power is not an effective energy source. All of another student's annotations were categorized as "evaluating," reflecting her own personal judgments about the negative effects of turbines and resulting in her adopting a negative stance on turbines as "not a good energy source."

## Students' Use of E-books

There has also been an increased use of e-books by the reading public. While young adults are more likely to read e-books, including accessing e-books on mobile devices, readers are still reading print books (Zickuhr & Rainie, 2014). Most e-book readers read their e-books on an e-reader or tablet as opposed to a computer, particularly given the increased ownership and use of tablet readers, with 32% of adults owning a Kindle or Nook (Zickuhr & Rainie, 2014).

### E-books as Apps

There is also an increased use of apps themselves as e-books that include videos and graphs, for example, on the effects of climate change on the earth. The multimodal essay, "Fish: a Tap Essay" for the iPhone (*http://www.robinsloan.com/fish*) by Robin Sloan contrasts living versus loving something on the Web.

One recent development in the uses of apps to foster and enhance reading e-books is evident with the Citia *http://citia.com/about.html* "e-reading system." Citia can be used to provide summaries of nonfiction/technical books, as evident in their app of the book *What Technology Wants http://tinyurl.com/pobwad9* by Kevin Kelly (2012). Readers are presented with a stack of "idea cards" summarizing key ideas in a book as well as providing links, videos, and visual maps representing intertextual links between key ideas in the book that can be shared with others using Twitter or Facebook.

While it could be argued that Citia shortchanges reading an entire book as opposed to summaries from the book, reading a Citia summary does not preclude readers from reading the entire book. As is the case with shared annotations of books, Citia also represents an experiment in new ways of reading and sharing ideas from books.

## Accessing E-books

In addition to the use of textbooks, in lieu of having students buy books, for example, novels for a literature class, you can now have your students readily access free e-books as books in the public domain or as no longer copyrighted from a range of different sources for reading on their phone or tablet, as well as excerpts of copyrighted books. They can search for books on the sites and apps listed below.

---

### SITE FOR ACCESSING E-BOOKS

**Web-based sites:** Amazon Kindle *http://tinyurl.com/kxm6wfd*, the iTunes bookstore *http://tinyurl.com/mm9gk3g*, Google Books *http://books. google.com*, Google Books on the Google Play Store *http://tinyurl.com/ 7xmjyan*, Project Gutenberg *http://www.gutenberg.org*, Manybooks *http:// manybooks.net*, Free e-books *http://www.free-ebooks.net*, Goodreads *http://www.goodreads.com*, Obooko *http://www.obooko.com*, WHSmith *http://tinyurl.com/kys8rm2*, Barnes and Noble Nook books *http://tinyurl. com/7mrgptq*

**iOS:** Kindle *http://tinyurl.com/ar4lo8f*, Nook *http://tinyurl.com/kt4x2x5*, Goodreads *http://tinyurl.com/d83vgpf*, Kobo *http://tinyurl.com/nelnrrl*, Google Play Books *http://tinyurl.com/99ae4fo*, Wattpad *http://tinyurl.com/ mqw3mle*, iBooks *http://tinyurl.com/cb9olpf*, Free Books *http://tinyurl.com/ bvtqlpe*, Free Books Search *http://tinyurl.com/o3zdbsn*, e-book Reader and Free Epub Books *http://tinyurl.com/kegwn4v*, Oyster *http://tinyurl.com/ k65mbft*, International Children's Digital Library Free Books *http://tinyurl. com/k5hjkrx*

**Android:** Kindle *http://tinyurl.com/cjooext*, Nook *http://tinyurl.com/6m7a9hj*, Goodreads *http://tinyurl.com/lsux7wm*, Kobo *http://tinyurl.com/qal5fd2*, Android Free Books to Read *http://tinyurl.com/7l44lre*, Google Play Books *http://tinyurl.com/chxwpsk*, Wattpad *http://tinyurl.com/l2pz72y*, Aldiko *http://tinyurl.com/mv4rq77*, FBReader *http://tinyurl.com/oxgj75l*

---

You and your students can also use the free Subtext *http://tinyurl.com/9ykogpm* app described in Chapter 1 to access books on the Google eBookstore; assess bestsellers with author/expert notes; share their own responses with their peers, teachers, authors, and experts; and access links to related material, as well as preview their friends' books. You can also use Subtext to create your own closed group for your class to have students engage in discussions of books linked to specific pages of a book; share notes that only you and your students will see; or add assignments, polls, or discussion prompts; as well as have students add their own links to websites related to a book. And, for working with younger students, you can use the BiblioNasium *https://www.biblionasium.com* site for accessing books according to reading levels as well as having students share their book recommendations.

There are also a number of apps listed below that are designed to assist students in reading these digital texts, particularly as PDF files.

---

## PDF READERS

**iOS**: Adobe Reader *http://tinyurl.com/bkwehxf*, FastPdf+ *http://tinyurl.com/m5ff44b*, SmileyDocs *http://tinyurl.com/kp4y5vm*, iPDFs *http://tinyurl.com/m4sbakd*, Flip Reader *http://tinyurl.com/n77xuct*, SimplyPDF *http://tinyurl.com/lnn747n*

**Android**: Adobe Reader *http://tinyurl.com/7g373kq*, PDF Reader *http://tinyurl.com/bslzgmp*, Radaee Reader *http://tinyurl.com/m5ff44b*, BeamReader *http://tinyurl.com/btwjtkl*, or Universal Book Reader *http://tinyurl.com/k7qdg7j*, PDF Viewer *http://tinyurl.com/kjoo3oa*, Radaee Reader *http://tinyurl.com/lbzg3bc*, RepliGo PDF Reader *http://tinyurl.com/lbzg3bc*

---

### Accessing Library E-books

One important aspect of accessing or promoting books is having students access their school or local public library to access library catalogues and obtain books. You or your students can also download free e-books from their local public or school library using the OverDrive Media Console *http://omc.overdrive.com* app as well as the iOS iMLS HD *http://tinyurl.com/l5zyn26* app to access a school library that uses Junior Librarian.net or Eclipse.net services. This app provides the ability to search the library catalogue, reserve/renew books, obtain recommendations for new books based on a previous loan record as well as lists of popular books, share book reviews and related resources, and view videos by book authors.

The iOS *http://tinyurl.com/o3dnmvk* and Android *http://tinyurl.com/kh9hz9z* AccessMyLibrary: School Edition app provides access to those school libraries that employ the Gale online information system to obtain access to e-books and online database resources. School libraries can sign up for the Brain Hive *http://tinyurl.com/kah83ec* on-demand e-book service that provides access to 100,000 e-books.

## Use of E-books in the Classroom

It is also the case that more e-books are being used in the classroom, as well as the use of apps by teachers for creating e-books for specific use in their classroom. While these e-books afford highlighting, annotation, and note-taking tools, the jury is still out on whether these features, presented as "just-in-time" tools, offer both positive and negative affordances in terms of comprehending the text.

School districts and states are recognizing that they may save money by moving to online textbooks for use on mobile devices. Spurred by Apple's development of the iBooks Author app, the textbook industry is publishing more online textbooks to meet this demand. Houghton Mifflin, Pearson, and McGraw-Hill, who control 85% of the $3.2 billion K-12 textbook market, are all publishing textbooks for the iPad (Denison, 2012).

Other online publishers include the following:

- Inkling *http://tinyurl.com/made8ve* publishes e-book textbooks that include a lot of interactive features similar to those on iBooks.
- FlexBooks *http://www.ck12.org/teacher*, produced by the non-profit CK-12 Foundation creating open-content books, particularly aligned with the STEM movement.
- Scholastic iOS *http://tinyurl.com/kpsr3un* and Android *http://tinyurl.com/mn4cpu8* Storia app provides access to Scholastic's e-books for elementary and middle school students.
- Kno Textbooks iOS *http://tinyurl.com/mqsznrg* and Android *http://tinyurl.com/adem7wp* textbook/PDF reader app designed for use in reading textbooks that include note-taking, annotations, search, and quizzes.
- VitalSource Bookshelf iOS *http://tinyurl.com/q8oel3s* and Android *http://tinyurl.com/8f6lnxs* app can be used to download and access VitalSource e-books.

## Affordances of Online Textbooks

A current marketing strategy is to position traditional print textbooks as boring, outdated, static, lacking in interactive features, and impractical due to their physical weight (see our blog post, "Apple iBook Textbooks: What is a Textbook": *http://tinyurl.com/bllr2he*). We caution that we must carefully assess both the positive and negative affordances of the rapidly emerging e-textbooks and apps that contain e-text features, particularly those touted as supporting learning. Below, we briefly touch on some negative and positive affordances of specific apps or features of apps. These e-textbooks share a number of different affordances not available with print textbooks:

### Interactive Media

### 3-D Images/Graphics, Videos, Keynote Presentations, and Virtual Demonstrations/Tours

These multimedia features are intended to actively engage students in, for example, manipulating a 3-D image of a molecule in a biology textbook, or viewing videos about the topics they are studying. For example, the iOS *X is for X-Ray http://tinyurl.com/kykh2e2* app book published by Touch Press, includes X-ray versions of images. The iOS *Bobo Explores Light http://tinyurl.com/dy7w8c6* app book for younger students studying light in science includes interactive 3-D holograms while the iOS *The Man in Space http://tinyurl.com/nbn6qob* book app includes 3-D images and videos portraying the history of space travel. For studying literature, the iOS 3-D Classic Literature Collection *http://tinyurl.com/candgsn* contains examples of 3-D illustrations in classical literature. Students can also create their own 3-D e-books; eighth-grade students at Scenic Middle School, Central Point, Oregon, created the *Invertebrates http://tinyurl.com/l625g2o* book that includes 3-D illustrations of different types of invertebrates.

The quality of these interactive books varies in terms of how the interactivity is employed (Itzkovitch, 2012). In some cases, the interactivity is artificial; it is simply done for its own sake. In poorly designed e-books, the interactive media can distract the reader away from important content in the printed text. In contrast, interactivity can effectively engage the reader in learning from a book, as is the case with the Al Gore, *Our Choice http://tinyurl.com/9dw9nym* app book that not only provides the reader with data about climate change, but also actively engages the reader in reflecting about reasons for and consequences of climate change. Students can also participate in interactive activities designed to activate and apply their prior knowledge through responding to questions. And, students can study examples of interactive children's literature published with the Auryn Press iOS *http://tinyurl.com/kpuyxc4* and Android *http://tinyurl.com/q558zn7* Stories Alive apps or app books published by Nosy Crow Press such as the iOS *The Grunts: Beard of Bees http://tinyurl.com/kmel2qj* to then think about creating their own interactive children's literature using literature creation apps that we discuss in the next chapter.

### Hyperlinks to Related Material and Alternative Storylines

In contrast to print texts, e-books include hyperlinks to other related texts so that students can obtain further information about a topic. And, hyperlinks can be employed in interactive fiction to have readers choose and explore alternative storylines in ways that are similar to the *Choose Your Adventure* texts as evident in the iOS *http://tinyurl.com/nho8zyy* and Android *http://tinyurl.com/mdwhd2d Frankenstein* app book. However, hyperlinks can also lead you away from a topic if your navigation isn't planned or you are easily distracted. And, although hyperlinked texts can be rich intertexts that exceed the richness of typical singular, linear print texts, the quality of information found in them can be variable.

### Highlighting and Note-Taking/Annotation Tools for Students and Teachers to Share Notes or Annotations About Specific Sections of Texts

With the Apple iBooks, students can swipe their finger over a section of a text to highlight that section. They can then add notes to those sections, as well as go to a Notes view to review all of their notes in one place; you and/or other students can then access these notes to learn from other readers. These highlights and notes are then published on study cards for review of material from the text. Note-taking tools can be effective as part of an overall study plan that includes a proven note-taking approach and an overall strategy for synthesizing information in notes for studying. But the existence of note-taking tools does not, by themselves, mean that if students use them in some way, their learning will be improved.

### Glossaries or Pop-Up Word Definitions

Students can access glossary definitions in the text and the study cards, as well as click on certain words for pop-up word definitions. The Storia "Enriched eBooks" *http://tinyurl.com/n8bg7lm* include word games, story interactions, and animations, as well as a Smart Dictionary™ providing definitions for words. Many of these "as needed" resources are handy tools that might help students pronounce words or define them as they are used in context. One negative affordance of any pop-up resources is that if someone is reading deeply and critically, in a way that requires complete attention, these resources might distract them by diverting attention to the resource.

### Search Features to Find Certain Topics or Page Numbers

Students can engage in searches of key terms or page numbers to locate relevant information. Rather than a static index as is the case with print books, students can readily locate information on certain topics within a text. This is usually a useful tool to find a specific piece of information. However, keep in mind that when readers read to locate or relocate information they are often reviewing by rereading key pieces of text as they search, which improves their comprehension. Bypassing this process is not always good.

*Adaptive Quizzes to Determine Different Levels of Understanding*

These textbooks also include adaptive quizzes that determine students' levels of understanding. For example, Prep-U *http://www.prep-u.com* has created test-preparation apps based on adaptive technology for use in preparing for Advanced Placement (AP) tests in US History, Chemistry, and Psychology. In using these apps, students' knowledge of topics on these texts is determined by their performance on quizzes. Based on the students' performance as a determination of their level of prior knowledge, students receive material and quiz questions geared for their level. Students who demonstrate higher knowledge receive different material from students who demonstrate lower knowledge. As students progress, the questions become more difficult. Teachers can also monitor students' progress. However, one limitation of these adaptive quiz apps is that they reify a transmission model of acquiring information of teaching as test preparation, as opposed to more constructive modes of learning.

## Apps for Reading Literature

Students in English language arts classes can access online literature from a range of different apps for reading literature.

---

### APPS FOR READING LITERATURE

WattPad *http://tinyurl.com/6pr6wm4*, Narrative Magazine *http://tinyurl.com/8xun46l* (short stories), Shakespeare *http://tinyurl.com/795rmpr* (complete works of Shakespeare), iF Poems *http://tinyurl.com/7zhppr5* (poetry), Top 80 Classic Books *http://tinyurl.com/752damy*, Top Novels Collection *http://tinyurl.com/7c2thk5*, 3D Classic Literature *http://tinyurl.com/86zps8t* (3D versions), The British Library 19th Century Collection *http://tinyurl.com/5r6txrw*, Jane Austen's *Emma http://tinyurl.com/86v3tey*, Dracula *http://tinyurl.com/d7xg9fu*, Eliot's *The Waste Land http://tinyurl.com/6vm94yj*, Alice for the iPad *http://tinyurl.com/y3rffd5*, Kerouac's *On the Road http://tinyurl.com/7xxxsym*, The Fantastic Flying Books of Mr. Morris Lessmore *http://tinyurl.com/7ck6b5t* (301 MG), Twilight, Vol. 1 *http://tinyurl.com/mn5vky6*

---

### Audiobooks

Students can access a wide range of free audiobooks using apps such as iOS *http://tinyurl.com/mp94u4e* or Android *http://tinyurl.com/llgjsob* Audiobooks, iOS *http://tinyurl.com/l3oldbf* and Android *http://tinyurl.com/n4zvomu* LibriVox, iOS Bookmobile Audiobook *http://tinyurl.com/mzh52sg*, iOS Audiobook Player *http://tinyurl.com/khh8257*, iOS Free Audiobooks *http://tinyurl.com/lhbn8sw*, or Android Audiobooks *http://tinyurl.com/n9xcyla*.

They can also access audiobooks from iTunes *http://tinyurl.com/l2xgp84*, Audible.com *http://tinyurl.com/mhfppu6*, or Amazon.com *http://tinyurl.com/6jkzhn5* for downloading, as well as from their local public or school library using the OverDrive Media Console *http://omc.overdrive.com* app.

Hybrid Books *http://tinyurl.com/n46ncua* is an iOS app with audiobooks that have a soundtrack with sound effects and music, so that students experience effects and music consistent with the story. A similar iOS app, Booktrack *http://tinyurl.com/mxh8fjr*, includes soundtracks matched to the actions in the story. And, the iOS BookMovie app *http://tinyurl.com/ldvj3mv* includes multimedia, interactive books that mesh text with images/videos to create a new genre of movie-like books.

One advantage of using audiobooks is that, as previously noted with any audio text, students can listen to them while they are doing other things such as riding on the school bus. For students who have difficulty with reading print, they could listen to the text as they are reading it. In one school that added 400 audiobooks on 50 different iPods, the school organized the audiobooks within playlists according to lexile levels to help students make selections consistent with their reading level; students then took the audiobooks home (Noonoo, 2012). When the students completed the book, they took a quiz and, by passing the quiz, they moved on to a book at a higher difficulty level. Interviews with students indicated that use of the audiobook enhanced their enjoyment of reading; the students' reading scores also improved.

Students could also create their own audiobooks for sharing with peers or family members using recording/podcasting apps noted later in this book. Learning to read a text aloud effectively requires some basic interpretive practices, particularly when students are sharing their texts with their peers or family members. In creating these audiobooks, students could also add their own verbal annotations, commentary, or interpretations, for example, noting how they read aloud characters' dialogue in a manner that served to portray that character's traits, beliefs, or attitudes.

## Digital Comics/Graphic Novels

One important genre for reading across the curriculum is the digital comic or graphic novel. Students are often highly engaged with the visual appeal of comics or print graphic/manga novels such as *Maus: A Survivor's Tale* (Spiegelman, 1993), *American Born Chinese* (Yang, 2007), and *Persepolis: The Story of a Childhood* (Satrapi, 2004), that involve a range of disciplinary literacy practices—interpreting storylines and character development based on images and dialogue, inferring the semiotic and cultural meanings of images, and judging the aesthetic quality of comics or graphic/manga novels (Carter, 2009; Frey & Fisher, 2008).

There are an increasing number of apps for online comics/graphic novels available for students to access.

---

## COMICS APPS

**iOS**: comiXology Comics *http://tinyurl.com/yzx645x*, DC Comics *http://tinyurl.com/34lvk9s*, Dark Horse Comics *http://tinyurl.com/ozw6v94*, Marvel Comics *http://tinyurl.com/yj9ro4j*, Comic Zeal *http://tinyurl.com/3mctuxf*, GoComics *http://tinyurl.com/ksgzo6s*, Image Comics *http://tinyurl.com/34z5lu8*, Boom! Studio comics *http://tinyurl.com/6wv898u*, iOS Comicblendr HD *http://tinyurl.com/7od875z*, ComicBookLover for iPad *http://tinyurl.com/6q85prr*, Heroes Comic Reader *http://tinyurl.com/nvpgmta*, Comics+ *http://tinyurl.com/6pchmzo*, myComics *http://tinyurl.com/726qalk*, IDW Publishing *http://tinyurl.com/pn5wjxk*, Madefire Motion Books *http://tinyurl.com/qchkfdl*

**Android**: DC Comics *http://tinyurl.com/d8z3w8*, Comics *http://tinyurl.com/76hdjhb*, Dark Horse Comics *http://tinyurl.com/odvskpf*, Marvel Comics *http://tinyurl.com/aocs35l*, GoComics *http://tinyurl.com/ah5mm7s*, Comic Zeal *http://tinyurl.com/cnaqtuf*, ComicRack *http://tinyurl.com/l33x22t*, Graphicly *http://tinyurl.com/7pp9tbx*, Perfect Viewer *http://tinyurl.com/7tmauwg*

---

For accessing or reading manga novels, students can use the iOS *http://tinyurl.com/o7wffjsv* or Android *http://tinyurl.com/pbhv77q* Manga Rock app as well as the iOS Manga Storm *http://tinyurl.com/b6wjybd* or Android Manga Searcher *http://tinyurl.com/qzvaa83* apps.

### Producing Comics/Cartoons

Analysis of student learning in projects such as The Comic Book Project in New York City schools finds that students are particularly engaged with reading comics or graphic novels knowing that they can readily produce their own comics/graphic novels (Bitz, 2010). Students can focus on the use of techniques that they may then employ themselves, techniques that parallel digital-movie production. This includes how comic book artists position their readers relative to a character or object through the use of close-ups, medium, or long-shot views, as well as angle-up or angle-down shots. It also includes contrasting variations in the use of panels between different page layouts—that some pages include only one large panel, while other pages include several smaller panels. This also includes how artists use color and images, vary the sizes and sequence of blocks to develop storylines, use dialogue bubbles to portray characters, and use titles or action summaries.

Students can use a number of different apps to create comics or graphic novels (Abel & Madden, 2008 (*http://dw-wp.com*); Hissey, 2011; Kurtz, Straub, Kellett, & Guigar, 2008; McCloud, 2006; Monnin, 2009). One of the most sophisticated apps is the iOS Comic Life *http://tinyurl.com/mebqeh4* app, also available as Comic Life for Mac and Windows *http://tinyurl.com/n3rnnnq* and for iPads *http://tinyurl.com/aff67h7*. (While there is a 30-day free trial, unfortunately, a single license for Comic Life is $19.95 and $4.95 for the iPad app.)

This app provides students with an extensive range of options for creating words in different fonts, font sizes, and font colors; creating and placing speech balloons within a plan; adopting different-size panels; adding captions and titles; importing and resizing photos into panels; and adding drawings. The fact that students can add photos to their comics means that they can create comics building on photos taken on field trips, museum visits, or classroom or social events. Once students have completed their comics, they can share them on Facebook, Twitter, or e-mail, as well as with other iPads in the same vicinity, enhancing collaborative sharing within a classroom.

Based on the idea of engaging students in a multi-genre memoir-writing project created by Beth Frye at Appalachian State University (*http://tinyurl.com/bjh84b7*), Elizabeth Boeser (2012) of Jefferson High School, Bloomington, Minnesota, had her students use Comic Life to create a multi-genre memoir. Students used Comic Life to import their own and others' photos to create a narrative about a memorable event in their lives. Students were given instructions on the uses of a variety of different camera shots and angles, variety essential to designing effective comics. They then added captions, dialogue bubbles, effects, and graphics to tell their stories. (For Elizabeth's conference presentation on this activity: *http://tinyurl.com/b6ugub5*.)

## COMICS/CARTOONS CREATION APPS

**iOS:** MakeBeliefsComix *http://tinyurl.com/6xmkd4*, Toontastic *http://tinyurl.com/m2zh4t*, Strip Designer *http://tinyurl.com/3aekl57*, ComicStrip CSS *http://tinyurl.com/6or7bvz*, Comics Creator *http://tinyurl.com/6ovrdf8*, PhotoComic *http://tinyurl.com/6qxsjz*, Comic Touch Lite *http://tinyurl.com/3ov8mfq*

**Android:** Bitstrips *http://tinyurl.com/mezs7rg*, Comic Strip It! *http://tinyurl.com/8b74w5m*, Comic Book *http://tinyurl.com/k4rza7m*, Comic and Meme Creator *http://tinyurl.com/kaxl9fy*, Comic Maker *http://tinyurl.com/ltbf8h7*

To use these apps, as they would in creating digital videos (see Chapter 9), students first create a script that outlines the different events in their stories, followed by creating storyboards by hand in which they generate a rough sense of the different scenes or actions within these events. Students then select different template options and then import their own digital photos or clip art/images from the program. Drawing on their storyboard, they then create different blocks for specific settings and characters' actions. They then add titles, captions, and dialogue bubbles, along with editing the font size and color for their titles, captions, or dialogue. For example, using photos of different works of art taken on a field trip to a local art museum, students can create a comic book in which they import the images of the artworks and then add dialogue bubbles describing their reactions to the art.

Students can also use comics or cartoons to create narrative visual representations of what they are learning in the classroom. Students in Ohio and California created cartoons about their learning in science classes using the iOS Toontastic app (LaCrosse, 2014). They then shared their cartoons with each other to conduct peer reviews based on the use of effective science inquiry methods; for materials developed to structure the students' interactions and peer reviews: *http://launchpadtoys.com/penpal*.

## Summary

In this chapter, we have described the features of digital texts that require readers to learn practices that differ from those involved in reading print texts, involving an alternative focus to reading instruction. We then demonstrated how apps such as annotation apps can be used to help students synthesize and share their interpretation of texts, for example, in responding to science texts. We also described ways to foster access and response to e-books, as well as audiobooks and comics/graphic novels. Acquiring these reading practices for responding to digital texts is essential for creating their own digital texts, the focus of the next chapter.

## References

Abel, J., & Madden, M. (2008). *Drawing words and writing pictures: Making comics: manga, graphic novels, and beyond*. New York: First Second.

Bitz, M. (2010). *When commas meet kryptonite: Classroom lessons from the comic book project*. New York: Teachers College Press.

Boeser, E. (2012, November 16). Using Comic Life in the classroom. Presentation at the National Council of Teachers of English, Las Vegas.

Carter, J. B. (2009). The comic book show and tell. *ReadWriteThink*. Retrieved from http://tinyurl.com/294xoy8

Castek, J., & Beach, R. (2013a). Using apps to support disciplinary literacy and science learning. *Journal of Adolescent & Adult Literacy*, *56*(7), 554–564. Retrieved from http://tinyurl.com/kzuod4v

Castek, J., & Beach, R. (2013b). Examining middle-school students' uses of iPad annotation apps to engage in collaborative science inquiry purpose. Presentation at the Annual Meeting of the American Educational Research Association, San Franciso, CA.

Coiro, J., Castek, J., & Guzniczak, L. (2011). Uncovering online reading comprehension processes: Two adolescents reading independently and collaboratively on the Internet. In P. L. Dunston, L. B. Gambrell, K. Headley, S. K. Fullerton, P. M. Stecker, V. R. Gilles, & C. C. Bates (Eds.), *60th Yearbook of the Literacy Research Association* (pp. 354–369). Oak Creek, WI: Literacy Research Association.

Council of Chief State School Officers and National Governors' Association. (2010). *Common Core State Standards for English Language Arts & Literacy in History/Social Studies, Science, and Technical Subjects*. Washington, DC: Author. Retrieved from http://www.corestandards.org

Denison, D. C. (2012, January 26). Textbook publishers prep for the e-future. *The Boston Globe*. Retrieved from http://tinyurl.com/7n8z2vy

Eanet, M. G., & Manzo, A. V. (1976). REAP: A strategy for improving reading/writing/study skills. *Journal of Reading, 19*(6), 647–652.

Fisher, M. L., & Cook, N. (2007). Notice, think, and wonder: New pathways to engage critical thinking. *In Transition: Journal of the New York State Middle School Association, 25*(1), 15–18.

Frey, N., & Fisher, D. B. (2008). *Teaching visual literacy: Using comic books, graphic novels, anime, cartoons, and more to develop comprehension and thinking skills*. Los Angeles: Corwin Press.

Hissey, I. (2011). *How to draw digital cartoons: A step-by-step guide with 200 illustrations: from getting started to advanced techniques, with 70 practical exercises and projects*. Lanham, MD: Anness Publishing.

Itzkovitch, A. (2012, April 12). Interactive eBook apps: The reinvention of reading and interactivity. *UX Magazine*. Retrieved from http://tinyurl.com/7m8xaoj

Kelly, K. (2012). *What technology wants*. New York: Citia. Retrieved from http://tinyurl.com/pobwad9

Kress, G. (2003). *Literacy in a new media age*. New York: Routledge.

Kurtz, S., Straub, K., Kellett, D., Guigar, B. (2008). *How to make Webcomics*. New York: Image Comics.

LaCrosse, L. (2014, February 26). Project PenPal: Connecting classrooms through storytelling [Web log post]. Retrieved from http://tinyurl.com/n49sldq

Leu, D. J., Jr., Kinzer, C.K., Coiro, J., Castek, J., & Henry, L. A. (2013). New literacies: A dual-level theory of the changing nature of literacy, instruction, and assessment. In R. B. Ruddell & D. Alvermann (Eds.), *Theoretical models and processes of reading* (6th ed.). Newark, DE: International Reading Association.

McCloud, S. (2006). *Making comics: Storytelling secrets of comics, manga and graphic novels*. New York: Harper Paperbacks.

Monnin, K. (2009). *Teaching graphic novels: Practical strategies for the secondary ELA classroom*. New York: Maupin House Publishing.

Morris, P. (2012). "It's like reading two novels": Using annotation to promote a dialogic community. *Teaching English in Two-Year College, 39*(4), 377–387.

Noonoo, S. (2012, March 7). At one school, iPods help improve reading scores. *THE Journal*. Retrieved from http://tinyurl.com/7hpadaw

Satrapi, M. (2004). *Persepolis: The story of a childhood*. New York: Pantheon.

Shanahan, C., Shanahan, T., & Misischia, C. (2011). Analysis of expert readers in three disciplines: History, mathematics, and chemistry. *Journal of Literacy Research, 43*(4), 393–429. doi:10.1177/1086296X11424071

Spiegelman, M. (1993). *Maus: A survivor's tale*. New York: Pantheon.

Yang, G. (2007). *American born Chinese*. New York: First Second.

Zickuhr, K., & Rainie, L. (2014, January 16). *E-reading rises as device ownership jumps*. Washington, DC: Pew Internet and American Life Project. Retrieved from http://tinyurl.com/nxz78mu

# 6

# USING APPS FOR WRITING

Writing instruction is often perceived as simply learning how to write essays, particularly in preparation for mandated, standardized writing assessment. However, it is useful to think of writing as involving more than just generating essays. Students also use writing as a tool to foster learning. Students use writing to focus their attention on developing a topic in a sustained manner. This sustained attention promotes critical thinking and the written product is a record of students' thoughts and observations through drafting and revising their ideas and communicating to others. Indeed, writing is a strong component of many learning strategies found in the field of content area literacy because writing is part of the process of synthesis of information, which promotes reading comprehension. Indeed, reading and writing are complements in support of strategic learning and, particularly in digital, multimodal environments, reading and composing ideas in various modalities is common.

For example, by taking careful, detailed notes of their observations of a chemistry experiment, students are using their writing to learn to focus on the details of chemical reactions, as well as creating a record of their experience for use in analyzing the results of the experiment. Students also use writing to record their observations as evidence to support or refute claims about certain scientific phenomena. For example, they formulate the claim that the moon changes its shape as it moves across the sky, and then observe the moon or a virtual simulation of the moon, reflecting on how and why their observations support or refute their claim (Castek, Goss, & Tilson, 2011). In observing how the moon is changing its shape, they may then recognize that it is not the moon itself that is changing its shape, but the light shining on it that gives the appearance of its changing its shape.

And, rather than perceiving writing simply as producing texts, writing to learn can also be perceived as a way of experiencing oneself in the world through the act of writing about one's experiences. As Robert Yagelski (2012) notes:

Understanding the experience of writing requires making a key distinction between writing as textual production and writing as a way to experience ourselves in the world; it requires distinguishing between the writer's writing and the *writer writing*—that is, between the text and the act of writing. (p. 191)

## The Common Core State Standards for Writing

Writing to learn, therefore, includes use of different literacy practices contributing to acquiring disciplinary literacies, practices involved in writing integral to learning as captured in the 5–12 English Language Arts Common Core State Standards writing standards (Council of Chief State School Officers and National Governors' Association, 2010).

### Text Types and Purposes

* Write arguments to support claims in an analysis of substantive topics or texts, using valid reasoning and relevant and sufficient evidence.
* Write informative/explanatory texts to examine and convey complex ideas and information clearly and accurately through the effective selection, organization, and analysis of content.
* Write narratives to develop real or imagined experiences or events using effective technique, well-chosen details, and well-structured event sequences.

### Production and Distribution of Writing

* Produce clear and coherent writing in which the development, organization, and style are appropriate to task, purpose, and audience.
* Develop and strengthen writing as needed by planning, revising, editing, rewriting, or trying a new approach.
* Use technology, including the Internet, to produce and publish writing and to interact and collaborate with others. (p. 42)

The writing assessments related to the Common Core will be conducted using computers and will include tasks involving use of the Internet. Having students employ apps for writing will therefore serve to help prepare students for these assessments (Sassi & Gere, 2014).

## Note-Taking Apps

An essential component of writing to learn is the ability to take notes as a way of formulating one's own interpretations of texts, lectures, or presentations, as well as brainstorming ideas as prewriting. Novice note-takers write while the teacher is talking, and rather than listening to organize, reflect on, and retrieve information and encode it to write down important points, students simply write down the text coming from the teacher as it is delivered. The end result is lots of notes, poorly organized and unlikely to cue important information.

And, students need a clear sense of their purpose that serves to focus their attention on formulating notes relevant to that purpose. For example, knowing that they are writing about reasons for the popularity of hip-hop music leads them to focus on identifying those reasons in their reading.

Effective note-taking therefore entails students' ability to organize their notes in a coherent, logical manner. A lecture delivered from a carefully organized text with good signaling is a good start to success. A biology teacher states, "Before we read section 2 in the text, I am going to discuss briefly three key components of cell metabolism . . ." A statement like this, as one of a long series, includes key points and signals what the teacher wants note-takers to write down.

Students may also write notes by simply transcribing verbatim text language as opposed to translating that language into their own words so that they are thinking about what the text is saying relevant to their own schema and purposes. Students also need to recognize that note-taking involves informal versus formal writing—that they are writing notes for themselves using their own shorthand style, as opposed to worrying about others reading their notes. They therefore can use the multimodal features of note-taking apps listed below to include sketches, drawings, or symbols that have meaning only to themselves without concern for audience.

---

## NOTE-TAKING APPS

**iOS**: Notes, Evernote *http://www.evernote.com*, Penultimate *http://www. cocoabox.com/penultimate*, OneNote *http://tinyurl.com/n344lpc*, ePaper *http://tinyurl.com/noh995d*, neu.Notes *http://tinyurl.com/6ds98t2*, PhatPad *http://tinyurl.com/lbcf9pf*, NoteShelf *http://tinyurl.com/48vx2ql*, Notesy *http:// tinyurl.com/3fy5cap*, Notes Plus *http://notesplusapp.com*, PaperDesk Lite *http:// tinyurl.com/86u87vx*, Simplenote *http://simplenoteapp.com*, NyNoteIt *http:// www.mynoteit.com*, Bamboo Paper *http://tinyurl.com/6m7bos6*, SoundNote *http://soundnote.com*, SpringNote *http://springnote.com*, SchoolNotebook *http://tinyurl.com/7366pfg*, Catch *http://tinyurl.com/8yvz6dd*, Springpad *http://tinyurl.com/yaho3xk*, Notability *http://www.gingerlabs.com*

**Android**: Notes *http://tinyurl.com/qae69w3*, OneNote *http://tinyurl.com/ kkgxpay*, Color Note Notepad Notes *http://tinyurl.com/79tlsvl*, PhatPad *http://tinyurl.com/lbcf9pf*, Notepad *http://tinyurl.com/pzjeg44*, Evernote *http://tinyurl.com/7mcj4ph*, Note Everything *http://tinyurl.com/pqmq7su*, Notely *http://tinyurl.com/pcqo4x9*, Catch Notes *http://tinyurl.com/ngwvtna*, Classic Notes Lite *http://tinyurl.com/no8btcp*, Safe Note *http://tinyurl.com/ ovnybax*, mySchoolNotebook *http://tinyurl.com/no7bk3c*, Extensive Notes *http://tinyurl.com/d6shmc3*, Papyrus Natural Note Taking *http://tinyurl.com/ cse2gy4*, and Write *http://tinyurl.com/ntncb6s*

---

Students can use their notes to record specific observations as an important disciplinary literacy in science or social studies using a dual recording system of recording
specific details or talk on the left side of a screen and then their inferences or reflections about those details or talk on the right side of a screen. To scaffold these observations, you can have students use the Critical Response Protocol (CRP) questions:

> What are you noticing? What did you see that makes you say that? What
> does it remind you of? How do you feel? What questions does the "text"
> raise for you? and What did you learn? (Beach, Campano, Edmiston, &
> Borgmann, 2010, p. 35)

Or, you can have students use the Science Writing Heuristic (SWH) set of questions
(Keys, Hand, Prain, & Collins, 1999) related to identifying claims and evidence:

> Beginning ideas—What are my questions? Tests—What did I do?
> Observations—What did I see? Claims—What can I claim? Evidence—
> How do I know? Why am I making these claims? Reading—How do my
> ideas compare with other ideas? Reflection—How have my ideas changed?
> (Norton-Meier, Hand, Hockenberry, & Wise, 2008, p. 26)

## Use of the Evernote App

One of the more popular note-taking apps, Evernote, contains a range of different
features that go beyond simply serving as a note-taking app. Students can organize
their notes in "Notebooks" that can be shared with you and their peers. They can
employ the Web Clipper bookmark for copying, tagging, and describing material
from websites. And they can also share camera shots of whiteboards, websites, or
assignments, as well as use the app, Skitch *http://tinyurl.com/n353duv* for drawing
on images saved in Evernote. Skitch also allows students to add arrows, drawings,
figures, etc., to an image.

Kevin Buran (2011), a middle school teacher in Carmel, CA, describes his uses
of Evernote:

> I put everything my students might need to access—worksheets, articles,
> and labs—into a Shared Notebook that they can access through a link or via
> Moodle, a service that our school district has integrated. I have a Scanscap
> scanner, which I use to shoot worksheets straight into Evernote. Some-
> times, I'll scan student work that I think was particularly impressive. It's a
> great way to acknowledge the work and share it with other students (via
> Shared Notebooks).
>
> Before Evernote, I was bookmarking so many different websites for
> research purposes, or sending emails to myself with links. I found it so

difficult to keep track of things I was reading on the Web. Now, I use Evernote's Web Clipper to simply send things I want to remember to my Evernote account, where it is completely searchable and accessible whenever I need it. I recently had all of my 8th grade students sign up for an Evernote account to help them do research. They clip articles from the Web, take notes and track lab results in Evernote. I put up a daily itinerary on the whiteboard for my students to see what we'll be working on that day. For anyone who isn't in class, I snap a photo of it and put it in Evernote. You can see all of the past daily itineraries in my Shared Notebook. I use JotNot to take those shots, which integrates really well with Evernote.

## Handwriting Apps and Pens

For students who prefer to use handwriting, particularly for taking notes, they can use handwriting apps for both text and sketching or drawing recognizing that, in using these apps, they need to make sure they don't put their palms on the screen, although some apps accommodate for doing so by using a wrist protection feature. And, many of these apps will then convert their handwriting into print text for use in drafting.

---

## HANDWRITING APPS

**iOS:** Penultimate *http://tinyurl.com/myt9a32*, WritePad *http://tinyurl.com/k297tpg*, Inkflow *http://tinyurl.com/ldcnr48*, Paper *http://tinyurl.com/mk59ryo*, Smart Writing Tool *http://tinyurl.com/lbotjr9*, Note Taker HD *http://tinyurl.com/la6f7bk*, Use Your Handwriting *http://tinyurl.com/kg9m2sb*, NoteShelf *http://tinyurl.com/mlq4ybn*, Remarks *http://tinyurl.com/mgcknxf*, neu.Notes+ *http://tinyurl.com/kykxqds*, INKredible *http://tinyurl.com/m3fv7ka*, PaperDesk *http://tinyurl.com/mh3wuco*, PhatPad *http://tinyurl.com/meofhks*

**Android:** Notes Plus *http://tinyurl.com/n4pfwub*, Handwriting *http://tinyurl.com/c2lfunu*, Papyrus *http://tinyurl.com/cse2gy4*, Handrite Note *http://tinyurl.com/kq5eds2*, Write Pad *http://tinyurl.com/kqenq2t*, masec3 *http://tinyurl.com/kgec356*

---

Students can also employ stylus pens such the Adonit Jot Stylus, Just Mobile Alupen, Pogo pens, or oStylus for handwriting as well as drawing on tablets. If they are going to use them for both handwriting and drawing, the pens vary for use in drawing according to how fine they can create lines as well as broader brush strokes. Some pens work well for creating fine lines but not broader brush strokes and other pens work well for broader brush strokes but not fine lines.

## *Using Audio Note-Taking*

Students can also employ audio note-taking apps for both writing notes and recording simultaneously. This means that as students are recording a presentation about a text, they would also be taking notes on that presentation, notes that are then saved as files for sharing or transferring to drafts. Being able to also record audio notes can help students fill in the gaps in their written notes by cueing up and playing the corresponding audio. If their written notes are missing pieces or don't make sense, they click on the text to obtain the audio recording of the oral text on which their notes are based.

---

## AUDIO NOTE-TAKING APPS

Evernote *http://tinyurl.com/cxo6req*, Notepad Pro *http://tinyurl.com/k6zdkyu*, Soundnote *http://tinyurl.com/mnj9fz2*, Word-Cloud Smart Recorder Lite *http://tinyurl.com/7lrozk7*, QuickVoice Recorder *http://tinyurl.com/2amq7x6*, AudioNote Lite *http://tinyurl.com/2akp3ax*, OneNote *http://tinyurl.com/ ys5wou*, Notability *http://www.gingerlabs.com*, Audiotorium *http://tinyurl. com/ydorb68*, Audio Memos *http://tinyurl.com/8xktkye*, SoundCloud *https:// soundcloud.com/mobile*, Audionote *http://tinyurl.com/35jcs3o*, Voice2Note *http://tinyurl.com/p2hh6na*, inClass for iPad/iPhone *http://www.inclassapp. com*, Super Note for iPad/iPhone *http://tinyurl.com/ndzheno*, and Recordium for iPad/iPhone *http://tinyurl.com/q9ynubw*, Remote Dictate *http://tinyurl. com/7x4kqet*

---

Students can also employ audio/video recording note-taking pens such as Livescribe *http://www.livescribe.com* (for a video of the use of Livescribe pens in schools *http:// tinyurl.com/pwr7mlu* and *http://tinyurl.com/ockouou*) that allow students to handwrite their notes as well as drawings that are then synced with a tablet or computer using the Lifescribe+ App *http://tinyurl.com/nwhz93u*, as well as record their own or another's audio that are synced to their written notes. In addition to the Livescribe 3 or Smartpen, there are a number of other note-taking pens: the Mobile Notes Pro, Sky Wifi Smartpen, Echo Smartpen, Staedtler Pen 990, Wacom Inkling, IRISNotes 2 Executive and IRISNotes 1 for Smartphones, LogiPen Notes, Capturx for One-Note, and DigiMemo. These pens have built-in microphones that record audio, as well as video cameras. Some also employ tablet apps or paper that students can use to access audio associated with certain notes when they tap on those notes.

## *Concept-Mapping Apps*

Students can employ concept-mapping apps for brainstorming through visually displaying different concepts and the relationships between these concepts. In using concept-mapping apps, students are identifying different key words or ideas associated with an experience, phenomenon, topic, or issue so they visually define the logical relationships between these words or ideas as nodes. In some cases, they may insert the words into circles or boxes, drawing lines between the circles or boxes with spokes to other boxes or circles in which they insert subtopics or nodes. These lines serve to define the logical relationships between topics, for example, whether a subtopic serves as an illustrative example of a major topic. Doing so helps them organize their thinking for organizing drafts or for recognizing the need to further develop their concepts or ideas.

Students therefore use mapping to visually flesh out and develop information based on certain categories. For example, in responding to a novel, they can use a map to identify traits, feelings, beliefs, and goals for different characters to interpret relationships between these characters.

Concept-mapping also helps students evoke prior knowledge about the topics or categories depicted in their maps. As Harris (2011) notes in describing uses of concept maps in her elementary school science class:

> Concept maps allow students not only to conduct a "memory search" but also to link their understanding in ways that the brain naturally organizes information. Importantly, it provides a visual representation of their thinking, which is key for both students and the teacher. Here is how one-fifth grade student explained the development and importance of a concept map:
>
>> A concept map is like where we write down the main deal, which is energy, and what we are learning about energy, which is light, sound and heat. We have different color writing utensils. The pencil is what we learned first, the red pen is what we learned second, and the black pen is what we learned over the whole unit. It is different than a word Web because it uses connecting words. We write down what we learned to help us remember.
>
> Thus the concept map becomes not only a tool to help both the teacher and the student identify current understanding, but also a tool to help students reflect upon and consolidate their learning. (p. 14)

Employing visual representations of concepts and the relationships between concepts benefits students, particularly students with learning disabilities (Dexter, Park, & Hughes, 2011). Any learner who is having trouble understanding concepts can benefit from the explicit displays of various terms and ways in which these are interrelated. And, clearly, if students understand vocabulary and the concepts represented by the vocabulary, this knowledge enables the comprehension of difficult texts in various subject areas.

Concept-mapping apps also serve to help students collaboratively develop and expand topics. By sharing the same concept maps, a group of students working on the same project can visually represent their thinking for each other so that they are literally and figuratively "on the same page." Students can then pose questions to each other based on their maps; for example, questions about the need to further expand their topics when they perceive the need to further develop topics perceived to be lacking information on their map.

And, as the focus shifts or develops, students use their maps to reflect on changes in their learning. As Harris (2011) notes:

> Students enjoy watching the concept map grow as we progress through the unit. It is a perfect place to show how our ideas change. What they thought they knew at the beginning of the unit sometimes isn't exactly true. At the end of the school year, it was time to erase our class concept map on the human body. This was the first time during my six years that students asked if they could take a picture of it. I said yes, and before I knew it about six students took out their cell phones and started snapping photos. It showed me that they were proud of their learning. (p. 15)

## CONCEPT-MAPPING APPS

**iOS:** MindMeister for Ipad *http://tinyurl.com/7t47atk*, Inspiration Maps Lite *http://tinyurl.com/6p4folr*, Mindjet for iPad *http://tinyurl.com/863dgjy*, iBrainstorm *http://www.universalmind.com/work/ibrainstorm*, Sundry Notes *http://tinyurl.com/6tkesap*, Popplet Lite *http://tinyurl.com/7h64yej*, Idea Sketch *http://tinyurl.com/7nerblt*, Total Recall *http://tinyurl.com/855oj7w*, iMindMap *http://tinyurl.com/87baa2k*, MindNode *http://tinyurl.com/7comdg6*, iThoughtsHD *http://tinyurl.com/37nc6c5*, SimpleMind+ for iPad *http://tinyurl.com/7nerblt*, Maptini *http://tinyurl.com/746bevr*

**Android:** MindMeister *http://tinyurl.com/kylrtcm*, Mindomo *http://www.mindomo.com/googleapps*, SimpleMind Free *http://tinyurl.com/kyeowbu*, MindMap *http://tinyurl.com/k53bl26*

**Chrome OS:** MindMeister *http://tinyurl.com/n26p965*, Mind Map *http://tinyurl.com/k6lxu8n*

These concept-mapping apps include the affordances of color-coding different topics or ideas as a means of visually representing different categories defining these topics. The iOS, Android, and Chrome OS MindMeister apps have a lot of complex features for syncing different maps as well as using it without an online account. Students can also easily add icons, styles, colors, and themes to create visually appealing maps, as well as edit links and nodes, and insert ideas. They can also import text files into their maps as well as export their maps as PDF, image, Word, or PowerPoint files.

Or, students may create hierarchical tree maps with global concepts at the top of their map and subtopics going down from the topic as "roots" to the global topics. These tree maps display the hierarchical relationships between smaller or more specific topics and larger, more global topics. Tree maps could also be horizontal to show how specific topics flow out of larger topics, for example, beginning with the topic of "the US Military" leading to categories of specific branches or units of the military (Army, Air Force, Marines, Coast Guard, Army Reserve, etc.), leading to subcategories within these categories.

For many of these map apps, students can create an outline list of words with subcategories within those words, and the apps will then create different types of maps using these outlines. Once students create a circle or box as a node, they can then create sub-nodes or the "child" of the node associated with the larger node. The app will then create lines as spokes between these nodes or students can then draw lines between the nodes, in some cases, labeling the lines to describe the relationships between the nodes. Some map apps will then transform maps back into outlines for use in writing drafts. Students can also employ icons, images, or symbols into their maps as nodes. They can also color-code their nodes to represent certain types of relationships.

Sixth-grade students in Laura Kretschmar's science class at Lighthouse Community Charter School, Oakland, California were studying the relationships between climate change and weather using the Chrome OS MindMeister app on their Chromebooks to identify different aspects contrasting climate change and weather. By creating two major concepts—climate and weather—as central concepts on their maps, students then created other sub-concepts linked to those central concepts that served to define the differences between climate as involving long-term change and weather involving short-term change. For example, Malik Garcia created a map (see Figure 6.1) in which he uses the images of a news broadcast weekly weather forecast as an example of short-term weather change and the image of earth burning as an example of long-term climate change.

Students can use the free Inspiration Diagrams Lite app for the iPad to create up to five maps; creating additional maps requires an upgrade to the iOS Inspiration Maps *http://tinyurl.com/d3ohxn5* app which is relatively expensive at $9.99. Students can import images, files, and links into their maps, attach notes and hyperlinks, select different templates, and share their maps on Pages, Dropbox, or iTunes. One significant feature of Inspiration for use in writing is the ability to move between maps and an outline. Inspiration provides students with two different ways of perceiving relationships between their concepts and ideas: a "Diagram" (map) and an "Outline" perspective. From the "Diagram" perspective,

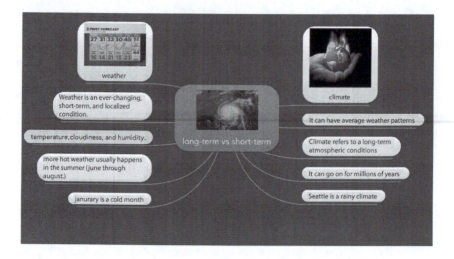

**FIGURE 6.1**   Student's MindMeister Map Contrasting Weather and Climate Change
*Source:* Reprinted with permission from Malik Garcia.

students devise graphic organizers for their material. They start by creating a "Main Idea," which appears in an initial circle. They then create other related ideas around the main idea, drawing connections between those ideas and the main idea, as well as connections between the other related ideas. The "Outline" perspective can therefore serve as a useful resource within the composing process for moving students from developing ideas to drafting.

To brainstorm ideas leading to further development of topics, students can switch at any time to the RapidFire tool. They can then type in material associated with the different topics, in some cases making links to visual icons or symbols. They can also import material from their own digital files or from an extensive collection of symbols, pictures, images, and digital clips including QuickTime movies and MP3 files. And, they can distinguish between their ideas using different colors, fonts, and shapes.

Students can then get an "Outline" view of the material they develop on their maps, allowing them to consider how they would organize their material for writing a paper according to a hierarchical outline with main topics and subtopics. In the "Outline" view, students can also hide subtopics so that they can perceive their overall main topics. They can also move material around if they want to rearrange their topics.

Fifth-grade students in Kretschmar's class employed the free iOS Popplet Lite concept-mapping app on their iPads in a science lesson on rare earth metals to address the question, "What is gold?" (Castek & Beach, 2013). One advantage of using Popplet Lite is that students can pan or zoom in or out on their maps, display maps on a projector using a VGA display, and export their maps as PDFs or JPEGs. In using the free version, students are limited to one free map, while with the full paid version ($4.99), they can create an unlimited number of maps to store on their iPad as well as create online maps on popplet.com or their iPad for sharing and editing with others.

To help students think about ways of categorizing phenomena, students then engaged in categorizing different kinds of sports using post-its on the board, generating categories such as sports they play with their hands, their feet, or with both hands and feet, along with examples of specific sports for these different categories. Students also viewed examples of completed concept maps created by Krestchmar addressing the question: "What is a bird?" The initial map included connections to concepts such as "has two wings," "lays eggs," "can fly," and "has feathers."

Students then learned how to use Popplet Lite for creating different nodes, moving nodes around, and connecting nodes, and using different colors to distinguish between categories. Students then viewed a more elaborate map that added additional information about the concepts in the initial map, as well as making connections between these concepts to demonstrate the relationships between them.

Students then began creating their maps to address the question "What is gold?" Students could use the touch screen to create notes and move around the boxes for their maps. When they needed assistance, they also often sought out peers for help.

The students then revised their maps after sharing their maps in small groups of four students. The map created by one student, Mouzerrat, is shown in Figure 6.2.

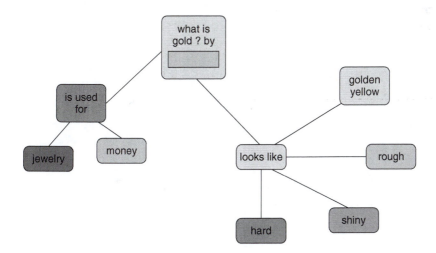

**FIGURE 6.2** Student's Initial Popplet Lite Map on "What Is Gold?"

*Source:* Reprinted with permission from Mouzerrat Camberos.

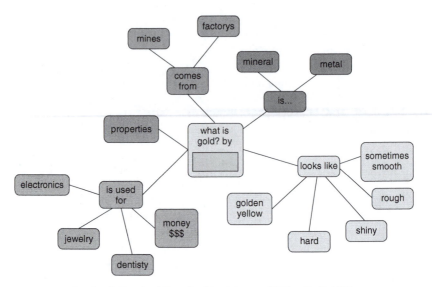

**FIGURE 6.3**   Student's Revised Popplet Lite Map on "What Is Gold?"

*Source:* Reprinted with permission from Mouzerrat Camberos.

They then revised their maps again after watching a two-minute video clip about the different properties of gold and how it is often used in electronics. Based on viewing this clip, Mouzerrat then added more information to her map, as shown in Figure 6.3.

After each revision stage, students took a screenshot of their concept map using their iPads by simultaneously clicking on the power button and the iPad button to create images demonstrating changes in their maps, changes indicating that, over time, students successfully grouped their ideas, reorganized their thinking, and added new ideas as they learned additional content.

This use of concept maps demonstrates how the app affordances of maps apps fostered constructing knowledge over time and through collaboration with peers. In reflecting on their experience of creating maps on exit slips, students noted that revising a map collaboratively with peers "helped me because when we were sharing I got new ideas," "revising made my map better," and "sharing made me get more ideas and check if I got words wrong." They also noted how certain features, such as the color-coding, helped them: "I used the colors to show different categories" and "I just used colors to make it colorful. I used a rainbow."

## Twitter Apps

As we noted in our introduction, much of students' digital writing outside the classroom consists of short textoid messages as evident in their extensive use of texting (Lenhart, 2012), something we discuss in the next chapter on discussion apps. The increased use and ability to craft short, truncated messages is also evident in students' use of Twitter apps for sharing out information in short, 140-character tweets, often including links to useful resources, to their Twitter followers.

For use in the classroom, you can create classroom Twitter accounts so that only students in a class are sharing and receiving tweets. Or, you can create a class hashtag, for example, #GrangerAmericanHistory2, or hashtags related to certain topics being discussed in the class. Students can then share their tweets using hashtags to signal that they are addressing certain topics or issues under discussion in class, particularly for linking to relevant sites, articles, or books, as well as posing questions for others to answer.

---

## TWITTER APPS

**iOS**: Twitter app *http://tinyurl.com/294xxoy*, TweetCaster *http://tinyurl.com/7w83d5w*, Tweetbot *http://tinyurl.com/85nhgq5*, Tweetdeck *http://www.tweetdeck.com*, Twitteriffic *http://tinyurl.com/2ednbrq*, or HootSuite *http://tinyurl.com/22kqxnp*

**Android**: Twitter app *http://tinyurl.com/88ejbmk*, HootSuite *http://tinyurl.com/kfdtdcu*, TweetCaster *http://tinyurl.com/8wrs3pe*, Plume *http://tinyurl.com/7hww6q2*, Tweedle *http://tinyurl.com/7hww6q2*, Echohon *http://tinyurl.com/cpqj7wa*, UbenSocial *http://tinyurl.com/m6qqxm6*, Carbon *http://tinyurl.com/agtzexk*, Seesmic *http://tinyurl.com/9b933rr*

**Chrome OS**: Tweetdeck *http://tinyurl.com/mbnycsb*, Silver Bird *http://tinyurl.com/podqhap*

---

One advantage of apps other than the default Twitter apps is that they provide different formats for organizing tweets. Tweetdeck organizes tweets based on different columns, tools for replying or retweeting tweets, searching tweets, and controlling followers. The TweetCaster app is particularly useful for searching for and clearly organizing tweets as well as simultaneously posting to Facebook. And, there are other related resources for use in supporting Twitter—Twitdoc *http://twitdoc.com* for sharing documents and images on Twitter, TweetWall-Pro *http://www.tweetwallpro.com* for projecting tweets on a screen, GroupTweet *http://www.grouptweet.com* for creating a single Twitter account for members of a group to share their tweets, and TwtPoll *http://twtpoll.com* to create surveys on Twitter.

You can use these Twitter apps to have students share the following:

- links to relevant topics students are studying in a class;
- summaries of or reflections on texts or presentations;
- headline news summaries of events in your school or class;
- one-sentence events in a story that each student builds on to extend the story;
- live coverage of a sports, community, school, or national news event.

To model the use of Twitter, you can show students sites such as the Twitter site *https://twitter.com/cdarwin* on which Charles Darwin "reports" his experiences on the voyage of the *Beagle* to also model ways for students to build on each other's tweets as a form of intertextual communication. Bill Ferriter (2011) notes that Twitter can be used to foster sharing of tweets within a classroom using a classroom hashtag such as #Smith'sScience3. He cites the example of a business teacher, Sarah Bird, whose students tweet the Most Valuable Point for each lesson. Bird then uses the information from these tweets to determine what her students are learning.

Ninth-grade students used Twitter to share their responses to the novel, *The Giver*, using their own fictional hashtag monikers such as #SmartGirlzWorld, #bosslady, and #QuietOne (Hunter & Caraway, 2014). The teacher then shared with the class students' "Tweets of the Day" (p. 18) to initiate small-group discussions. Sharing tweets served to foster students' rereading the novel as well as sharing their critical responses to the novel in discussions or in their journal writing. The fact that students could use anonymous monikers also served to enhance their willingness to voices alternative responses. And, students were also interacting with graduate students on Twitter, which contributed to their sense of the value of their interactions. As one student noted, "Being able to work with graduate students made me feel like a bit more professional, like we were being taken seriously, like young adults and not high school students" (p. 22).

Students can also use Twitter to create parodies of discussions based on how they believe characters from a novel they are reading might tweet each other. For example, Susanne Linder (2011) had her students study the style of characters' dialogue in the Jane Austen novel, *Emma*. Students then created user names on Twitter based on certain characters from the novel and then composed "historical tweets" to each other adopting those characters' language and perspectives, as well as Austen's style, using the Austenbook *http://www.much-ado.net/austenbook* parody retelling of *Pride and Prejudice* as Facebook feeds as a resource. Students then reflected on how their use of language was consistent with Austen's own style (for a description of this activity see *http://tinyurl.com/2bzs4tk*).

## Blogging Apps

Students can use blogging apps to write posts about topics or issues your class is studying or to voice their opinions or ideas, as well as to have peers share comments in response to those topics, issues, opinions, or ideas. One advantage of blogs is that students can readily insert images or hyperlinks to others' blog posts. They can also create RSS feeds to their blogs so that others can subscribe to their blogs.

## BLOGGING APPS

**iOS**: Blogger *http://tinyurl.com/ajpb2se*, BlogPress *http://tinyurl.com/l44k8wj*, WordPress *http://tinyurl.com/8vys584*, Edublogs *http://tinyurl.com/lv949jf*, KidBlog *http://tinyurl.com/msbvo4k*, Tumblr for iPad *http://tinyurl.com/yetg3pl*, or Blogsy *http://tinyurl.com/75p7aqk*

**Android**: Blogger *http://tinyurl.com/mqlycpy*, WordPress *http://tinyurl.com/m3rjp48*, Edublogs *http://tinyurl.com/mnoegct*, Blogger-droid *http://tinyurl.com/lehv8h8*, Tumblr *http://tinyurl.com/6sj9zuc*, Weebly *http://tinyurl.com/n96ayob*, LiveJournal *http://tinyurl.com/laqjtqh*, Bloglovin *http://tinyurl.com/lydu865*

**Chrome OS**: Blogger *http://tinyurl.com/mld7svz*, WordPress *http://tinyurl.com/n427zyd*, Quick Blogcast *http://tinyurl.com/kldqwaz*, JustWriteBlog *http://tinyurl.com/muv43tl*, 24LiveBlog *http://tinyurl.com/mcmkuld*

While these blogging apps are relatively similar, EduBlog and KidBlog are designed primarily for use in schools and therefore have a lot of useful privacy features related to limiting access to only students within your class. Students can also create posts using these apps to then export to Web-based blog platforms such as WordPress, Tumblr, Blogger, Typepad, Posterous, Edmodo, EduBlog, Live Journal, Private Journal, or KidBlog.

It is also the case that course management systems (CMSs) such as Moodle, Blackboard, Edmodo, Schoology, SumTotalSystems, Desire2Learn, or Collaborize Classroom, as well as social networking tools such as Ning, have built-in blogging features. You can also create a classroom blog as an iOS or Android app using the Educators App by emailing the blog's URL to the Educators App's site *http://educatorsapp.com*; you can then distribute the blog as an app for students or parents.

For microblogging of short posts, students can use Tumblr or Blogsy. Blogsy has two "sides" for creating blog posts, a "Write Side" for text editing and a "Rich Side" for importing images, videos, and links, a feature that helps students in importing images, videos, or links; it can also be translated into Spanish, French, Chinese, and Polish.

It is also useful to require specific numbers of entries or posts, as well as to share your own and react to students' entries or posts, posing questions that model certain interpretive strategies/critical approaches to help students extend or elaborate on their thinking. For example, Paul Allison (2009) notes how his students formulate critical inquiry questions for sharing with others on the site, Youth Voices (*http://youthvoices.net*):

> I ask my students to find a question or a set of questions that they develop in their own speculative writing, and eventually they do online research about their questions, connecting with others who have published on the Internet, and critically interpreting the welter of information available to them there. Students grow their blogs over a semester of working with other students and teachers who share their social network, Youth Voices. (p. 98)

In using blogs, students can present their writing in a physically appealing manner and layout, drawing on templates and other design features to readily create attractive, polished layouts, and embedding images or YouTube video clips into their posts to illustrate their ideas. They can also provide and receive comments to blog posts that serve to bolster students' confidence in writing and foster further dialogue about texts. For example, students can create "photologs" that consist of images or photos to which they add their own comments or analysis.

To become familiar with the blogging genre conventions, students should read not only their peers', but also outside experts' blogs by subscribing to both their peers' and these experts' blogs' RSS feeds to automatically receive new posts. You can then ask students to read others' blogs and then link to or add comments to those blogs. To insure students within a class receive comments on each other's posts, you can have students serve as "blog partners." Students will often be motivated to blog about or add comments to others' blog posts with which they may agree or disagree, leading them to engage in formulating arguments and counter-arguments central to addressing the Common Core writing standards focus on argumentative writing.

Based on reading blogs, students can also discuss what constitutes effective blogs in terms of writers' ability to clearly express their opinions or ideas supported by evidence, as well as build on others' blog posts. Essential to effective blogging is for students to connect their posts to their peers' or published blogs' posts as well as websites through hyperlinking as intertextual connections.

Cathy Davidson (2012) describes her uses of blogging in her college courses in ways that foster social interactions. In her class, students blog each week on a WordPress class blog about readings and assignments wherein the students comment on each other's posts. Davidson notes that students are learning from each other as co-learners as they engage in dialogic exchanges:

> By blogging and responding to one another's posts, my students aren't learning how to write for an English professor. They are learning how to

write for the world they are about to enter, in their jobs, in their careers, and they are learning how to improve their active discourse already happening online. They are learning that some of the best thinking (as Socrates would say) is dialogic, and their writing is part of an interactive, vibrant written dialogue.

In making these connections, students are also subscribing to or challenging others' opinions or stances, leading to their formulating their own opinions and stances. In doing so, students need to initially restate these ideas or positions in an objective manner and then raise questions about the ideas or positions, and formulate counter-arguments or examples to refute the ideas or positions.

In creating blog posts, students can readily embed images, videos, or music. In Blogger, they simply need to clip on the relevant icons to add media texts. Troy Hicks (2009) suggests the following activity involving multimodal construction of blog posts:

> Have students write a response to a controversial issue relevant to your course in a blog format. Students should incorporate other online sources to contextualize their own ideas, including hyperlinks to relevant websites, embedded videos, and images. In class, have students then reflect on how the links, videos, and/or images they chose had an impact on the possible meanings and audiences of their post. In the future, you may even ask students to blog multiple times throughout the quarter and respond to their classmates' posts and share other online material that they have found. This provides an additional opportunity for students to read and build upon their classmates' ideas, and to engage in critical conversation with each other. (p. 54)

You can also use blog posts to have students reflect on their learning. For example, at the end of your class, you can ask students to create "exit posts" identifying some things they learned in that class—posts that can provide you with some insights into your own teaching.

## Essay/Report Writing Apps

You can also use different iOS and Android apps for having students write essays or reports that can build on the material developed through uses of note-taking/annotation, concept-mapping, blogging, and Twitter apps. For example, students may be writing lab reports in their chemistry classes, analyses of specific historical events in their history classes, literary interpretations of characters' actions and beliefs in a novel in their English class, or creating a written description of problem-solving strategies to address math problems in their math classes.

As we noted in Chapter 2, engaging in essay or report writing in each of these different classes involves disciplinary literacies constituted by different ways of thinking and knowing. Writing lab reports in a chemistry class requires concise descriptions of specific chemical reactions that might include visual images. Writing historical analyses based on historians' different versions of the same events requires the ability to determine the validity of source data employed by these historians. Writing literacy interpretations of characters' actions and beliefs requires the ability to track consistent patterns in a novel to make reliable inferences about those patterns. And describing one's problem-solving strategies in math class requires the ability to metacognitively reflect on application of different theorems or proofs for solving math problems.

## ESSAY/REPORT WRITING APPS

**iOS**: Pages *http://tinyurl.com/68cv4je*, Word for iPad *http://tinyurl.com/ muascxm*, IA Writer *http://tinyurl.com/22skhdc*, CloudOn *http://site.cloudon. com*, My Writing Spot for iPad *http://tinyurl.com/7eafbfs*, PlainText *http:// tinyurl.com/27wnycg*, Clean Writer *http://tinyurl.com/7uzmk5s*, DraftPad *http://tinyurl.com/6mfq86h*, Heart Writer *http://tinyurl.com/7xz9dzy*, Chapters *http://tinyurl.com/7ekybve*

**Android**: Writer *http://tinyurl.com/k7msl5d*, Google Docs for Android *http:// tinyurl.com/crs5x2w*, Office Mobile for Office 365 *http://tinyurl.com/qbve9lo*, QuickOffice *http://tinyurl.com/mhesykz*, Documents to Go *http://tinyurl.com/ lgl58lo*, Polaris Office *http://tinyurl.com/l22nztl*, Office Suite *http://tinyurl. com/864dxgv*, Olive Office *http://tinyurl.com/cmp2lhu*, Kingsoft Office *http:// tinyurl.com/cpj3d8d*

**Chrome OS**: Writer *http://tinyurl.com/llawgmz*, Writer for Chrome *http:// tinyurl.com/mwhxaah*, ZoHo Writer *http://tinyurl.com/nykn3sa*, MYAccess! *http://tinyurl.com/mtt6j4v*

These apps provide students with many of the features associated with desktop word-processing software programs such as Office Word, Open Office, or Zoho Writing. For essay and report writing on an iPad, they are most likely to use the Pages app. This app has features similar to Word, including templates, formatting features, auto-correcting, spell-check, animations/graphics, compatibility to Word documents, and the ability to export files as a Word, Pages, or PDF file (for a useful book on Pages, see Gary Rosenzweig's *My Pages*, 2012). Pages automatically saves their files on iCloud. And, their files can be saved as Word files, or

Word files can be saved as Pages files. Similar features can be found in iAWriter, as well as touch features unique to the iPad such as the FocusMode for editing sentences using finger swipes, extensive formatting/typography features, and syncing with Dropbox and iCloud.

Because many students will be using desktop Microsoft Office apps such as Word, Excel, or PowerPoint to create documents, they can use Word for iPad *http://tinyurl.com/muascxm*, as well as Excel for iPad *http://tinyurl.com/o48oe7b*, or PowerPoint for iPad *http://tinyurl.com/l7e4mm2*, apps that allows students to read their Word, Excel, or PowerPoint documents on iPads for free. However, students will need to have an Office 365 Education A3 subscription *http://tinyurl.com/mr7gbpg* of $2.50 a month, or $4.50 a month for faculty/staff (there is a 30-day free trial), a fee that poses a challenge for use of Mobile Office in schools. As with iWork documents saved on iCloud, documents created with these apps are saved on their OneDrive *http://tinyurl.com/nyu4rta* cloud account.

Students can use the iOS *http://tinyurl.com/bndyyry* or Android *http://tinyurl.com/mwseqzw* OnLive® Desktop app to add files from their desktop to work on using the iPad. Students can use this app to create and revise Word documents, as well as Adobe Reader for reading PDF files. The Online Desktop includes its own keyboard, which is a useful feature for typing. Students also have access to 2 gigabytes of cloud storage for their files, a bonus for students without access to iCloud.

One challenge for students in composing longer texts as well as collaborating with peers is organizing and sharing files across different platforms. Students may prefer writing on a computer, given the ease of using a desktop keyboard versus an iPad keyboard; but they might want to store their files on an iPad. To move files across different platforms, students can store their files using a number of different cloud-based file storage sites.

---

## CLOUD-BASED FILE STORAGE APPS

Dropbox *https://www.dropbox.com*, Microsoft OneDrive *http://tinyurl.com/nyu4rta*, Wiggio *http://wiggio.com*, Box.net *http://tinyurl.com/6f6csza*, ReaddleDocs for iPad *http://tinyurl.com/39c8uf3*, GoDocs *http://tinyurl.com/d73p5u3*, Documents Free *http://tinyurl.com/2bo7oxz*, GoGoDocs *http://tinyurl.com/7zdgw9l*, Schribblar *http://www.scribblar.com*, Air Sharing *http://tinyurl.com/6hp3zw2*

---

While iCloud is a frequently used cloud service related to use of Pages and Keynote, schools are increasing using Dropbox for file storage. And, with the advent of Office apps such as Word, Excel, and PowerPoint for iPad, there will be increased use of OneDrive *http://tinyurl.com/nyu4rta*.

Students can also employ the iOS CloudOn or Chapters apps to compose Word documents on the iPad; they can also save their files for storage on Dropbox or iBooks. This means that students can compose essays in class using CloudOn and then open them up at home from Dropbox using their tablet or desktop (Gillispie, 2013).

In working with his students, Nicholas Provenzano (2011) uses Dropbox to help his students organize their writing. He notes:

> Dropbox has been a great tool for my students. Signing them up to accounts at the start of the year is one of the best things I did this year. Without pushing, students created their own group shared folders and have been putting all of their work there. Students have been able to upload photos and videos from the app to work on at home. Dropbox has allowed the students to quickly and easily share all of their work. I also noticed that students have created folders for other classes as well, so I know they are really enjoying the program.

Students can also use the iOS Idea Flight *http://tinyurl.com/ky4vdpe* app to share writing across different iPads. The "Pilot" can use the Idea Flight as a whiteboard-like presentation tool to communicate with other students' ("Passengers'") iPads. A Pilot can then present their ideas to Passengers, who can then also add their own material.

## Collaborative Writing

One benefit of use of the affordances of writing apps such as Google Docs or wikis is that they serve to mediate collaborative writing. However, engaging students in collaborative writing can be challenging because it presupposes a culture of sharing versus competition in which members of a community are each willing to contribute to creating the same text.

Effective collaboration also requires contributors to define who is responsible for contributing certain material as well as what they will be contributing. Unless students have a clear understanding of who is responsible for contributing what material, they could experience frustrations, with some members of their group not making adequate contributions, leading to resentment that some members are not contributing their share. But students can learn to work collaboratively with peers to address these challenges by learning to trust themselves and their peers as valued contributors to their group, being open to adopting different perspectives and disagreements, and defining roles and responsibilities to insure that all members contribute equally to the writing.

## Using Google Docs for Collaborative Writing

For engaging in collaborative writing, students are increasing using the Web-based app, Google Docs, as part of the iOS *http://tinyurl.com/ckuvapt* and Android *http://tinyurl.com/crs5x2w* Google Drive suite of tools. Unfortunately, editing using Google Docs on the iPad using the iOS Google Docs Mobile *http://docs.google.com/m* or the Android MyDocs *http://tinyurl.com/mbcbr4l* apps is still limited compared to editing Google Docs on a computer. We recommend that when editing Google Docs files on an iPad, students switch from the Mobile to the Desktop view to obtain access to the Google Docs editing features.

To access Google Docs files, students can add a Google Docs icon to their iPad by following the directions on this YouTube video: *http://tinyurl.com/8pd3z46*. It essentially involves going to Google Docs in Safari on an iPad or Chrome on Android devices and then selecting "Add To Homepage" to add a Google Docs icon. Students can also use the cloud-storage apps for storing or connecting to Google Docs files.

On Google Docs, students can upload Word, RTF, or text documents into these sites as well as download documents as Word, RTF, PDF, zip, or HTML files. And, they can determine with whom they grant permission to edit using the Share feature, as well as which audiences have access to their documents.

By clicking on Revisions, students can perceive changes in the text, just as they would with Track Changes in Office Word. Students then periodically click on "Save" to save revision files, using different file names after major revisions. When their peers go to Google Docs, they then see different versions of their document listed as files. Teachers then access these different versions to determine the nature and extent of the students' revisions. And, because each student's writing appears in a different font color, they can also determine variations in students' contributions as part of their collaboration. To foster peer feedback during drafting, peers and teachers can add comments to foster revision.

## Using Google Drive Forms

Students can also use the iOS *http://tinyurl.com/lfslg5z* or Android *http://tinyurl.com/qyg66f6* Google Drive Forms apps to employ various templates to structure, format, or organize their writing, as well as engage in tasks such as completing surveys, sending out memos, creating rubrics, etc. One advantage of Google Forms is that it creates results in a spreadsheet format for sharing with all students in the class.

To use Google Forms, you include options for students to add information about themselves and then add questions based on different options for answering those questions—multiple choice, checkboxes, drop-down options, scale rating, or grid; drop-down lists with options; or paragraph text. You can therefore use Google Forms to create open-ended questions or prompts for students to write their responses to these questions or prompts. You can then share the form with students using Google+ or via email. Once you've received students' responses, you can then use Forms to provide written feedback.

Brian Turnbaugh (2011) used the Google Drive Forms to create a media survey of his students' uses of media, including questions about how much time they devote to consuming different kinds of media. The survey format allowed him to select certain response options for student responses to his questions: text, paragraph text, multiple choice, checkboxes, choose from a list, scale, and grid. Because he wanted to create bar graphs and pie charts to present his results— not appropriate for text responses—he selected the checkbox and multiple-choice options (go to *http://tiny.cc/SyKoT* for a copy of the survey). Once the survey was completed, he then edited the results by selecting "Edit Form" and then "More Actions" and then "Edit Confirmation" to select the option "Let everyone see response summary" so that he could review the results. He then shared the results with his students for their reflection on their media uses.

In addition to having students employ Google Forms for sharing their responses to questions or prompts, you can also use what are known as "clicker apps" such as the combination iOS *http://tinyurl.com/8fxhxcy* or Android *http://tinyurl.com/c5ettwo* Socrative Teacher Clicker and iOS *http://tinyurl.com/aoxwbug* or Android *http://tinyurl.com/adnuwqy* Socrative Student Clicker. These apps include a short-answer question option, as well as a multiple-choice question option, to acquire students' shared writing about certain topics or issues, writing that can then be displayed to the class. Students' answers are then combined on a spreadsheet that can be shared with all students.

## Wikis

Students can also employ wikis to engage in collaborative writing. In contrast to blogs, which often serve for voicing individuals' opinions, wikis function best as repositories or reports of information that multiple authors collaboratively create based on their knowledge of expertise, as evident in the previously discussed Wikipedia articles.

Because wikis include a revisions history for a document, you can determine which students in a group made what revisions, data that you can use to assess students' collaboration based on which students are contributing what material.

Wikis can also provide a visual organizational structure on their pages for collaborative sharing of information. Students can readily locate the different category links for where to contribute their material or to revise existing text. Then, within those initial category links, they can create further subcategory links to add additional information.

To create wikis, students can use Web-based wiki platforms such as Wikispaces, PBworks, or MediaWiki, as well as a number of iOS or Android apps. One important feature of these apps is that they can sync across different devices so that students can collaborate using different devices, for example, moving their notes taken on a smartphone to a desktop or tablet.

---

## WIKI CREATION TOOLS

**Web-based**: Wikispaces *http://www.wikispaces.com*, PBworks *http://pbworks.com*, MediaWiki *http://www.mediawiki.org*, DokuWiki *https://www.dokuwiki.org*, Wikia *http://www.wikia.com*, PmWiki *http://www.pmwiki.org*

**iOS**: WikiPad *http://tinyurl.com/7egoxa3*, WikiServerPro *http://tinyurl.com/7f256at*, WikiTouch *http://tinyurl.com/7vctfmm*, WikiServerPro *http://tinyurl.com/7f256at*, Wiki Edit *http://tinyurl.com/6pg6tk*

**Android**: Wikidroid *http://www.siriusapplications.com/wikidroid*, Wikia *http://tinyurl.com/khlwlu7*

**Chrome OS**: Zoho Wiki *http://tinyurl.com/mlfe2fj*

---

Students can use the WikiTouch app for sharing of notes between their desktop, iPad, and/or iPhone, as well as attach photos, documents, and video and audio clips. Because WikiTouch employs cloud sharing, students can readily access this material from any of their devices. Students can therefore share their photos from their iPhones to add to their notes on their desktop or iPad. Students can use the Wiki Edit app to move seamlessly to edit on their iPad and on desktop versions of MediaWiki, as well as Wikipedia and Wikia.

Students experience wikis in either read or edit mode. When they read a wiki, they are perusing the text as they would any Web page. However, if they want to edit or revise the text, they then switch to edit mode by clicking on the edit link or button, for example: [edit], or, on Wikipedia, by selecting the "edit this page" option.

As described in Chapter 4, students could also write their own Wikipedia entries, for example, about their school, hometown, or topics that interest them. In studying Wikipedia entries, students can address issues of provided adequate sources, as well as how these sources are vetted by Wikipedia editors.

Students can also use wikis to create study guides for their peers or for students to collaboratively add information in future classes of the same course about a particular text, author, or topic. Students in first-year composition classes at St. Cloud State University each year add new information to a wiki textbook, *Rhetoric and Composition, http://en.wikibooks.org/wiki/Rhetoric_and_Composition,* about different aspects of learning to write.

However, a major challenge in using wikis is that they require students who are willing to actively engage in collaborative writing, which requires that they perceive wikis as serving some purpose that would motivate them to contribute to a wiki. Analysis of wikis created across a large number of different schools found that teachers were typically creating wikis to disseminate information with little evidence of student collaboration (Reich, 2012). This suggests that, rather than using wikis as a website for you to convey information, it is important to have students perceive wikis as a collaborative repository to which they are contributing useful knowledge.

## Literary Writing Apps

Students can also use literary writing apps to create stories or poetry. To foster interest in students writing literature, you can have them access repository sites containing a wide range of different online literary texts: *http://tinyurl.com/meuenra.*

In using these apps, students can create interactive, multimodal stories or poetry that combine text, drawing, photos, and audio recordings as digital storytelling or poetry. These apps provide students with specific story-writing tasks such as creating a setting, characters, story events, sequencing events, developing dialogue, and providing a story ending.

These apps also encourage students to create multimodal versions of their stories through providing them with or encouraging them to make use of their own images, drawings, photos, and/or music to convey additional meanings to their text, something we further describe in Chapter 8 on uses of images to illustrate stories.

These apps are particularly useful for students to create children's books for sharing with younger children. They can create their own stories or use an existing children's literature story to add their own illustrations consisting of images or drawings. Or, they can take literary texts they are reading, add illustrations, and then share their productions with their audience online or in person.

In doing so, they are considering how their illustrations serve to foster their audience's understanding of the written text. This requires going beyond simply using images to literally depict the description of a character, setting, or event as opposed to using the images to interpret or illuminate the character, setting, or event.

In selecting images, students need to reflect on how and why those images serve to illuminate the story meaning for their audiences. They also need to consider whether their readers will readily understand their use of images by anticipating their audiences' prior knowledge or cultural beliefs. To do so, they could first study examples of children's literature, focusing on how authors used images in their books.

## LITERARY WRITING APPS

**iOS**: StoryKit *http://tinyurl.com/6779acy*, Storyrobe *http://tinyurl.com/7zptk7z*, Book Creator *http://tinyurl.com/clkhj52*, Bookemon Mobile *http://tinyurl.com/7r6vz9o*, Picture Books *http://tinyurl.com/79mdlwq*, Writer's Studio *http://tinyurl.com/7l3h8mk*, StoryPatch *http://tinyurl.com/82gvo83*, Demibooks® Composer *http://tinyurl.com/66rpjfd*, StoryBuddy *http://tinyurl.com/7u7kja7*, My Story *http://tinyurl.com/6sldtzf*, MoglueBooks *http://tinyurl.com/8xysqs7*, myebook *http://www.myebook.com*, StoryJumper *http://www.storyjumper.com* (for younger students), i Tell a Story *http://tinyurl.com/kudohpb*, Tikatok *http://www.tikatok.com/create*

**Android**: Writing Challenge *http://tinyurl.com/mmzp3qo*, Writing Prompts *http://tinyurl.com/c55fjxp*, iDeas for Writing *http://tinyurl.com/kn3mrmn*, The Story *http://tinyurl.com/kmj5oku*, My Writing Spot *http://tinyurl.com/lmecm2f*, Story Plot Generator *http://tinyurl.com/n8sod93*

**Chrome OS**: We Write a Story *http://tinyurl.com/n2x9ttg*

Students can also use these apps as well as Google Docs to engage in collaborative fiction writing where groups of students collaboratively construct stories by adding onto or revising each other's stories. For example, participants on The New Worlds Project *http://www.rpgnewworlds.net* site that is based on a science-fiction world grapple with issues of peace in the midst of a world war in 2051. Within this site is a Creative Writing Project in which participants collaborate on stories about their experiences in the world war.

They can also collaboratively create and publish their fiction in online e-zines such as Girls Write Now *http://tinyurl.com/lplvc8m*, Xenith *http://www.xenith.net*, Teen Scene *http://www.teenscene.com*, Teen Mag *http://teammag.free.fr*, Teen Lit *http://www.teenlit.com*, Merlyn's Pen *http://www.merlynspen.org*, Noble Online *http://tinyurl.com/l2s5qz8*, and Zeen *http://www.cyberteens.com/cr* (for lists of e-zines for adolescents *http://tinyurl.com/mljd86j*). In collaboratively constructing e-zines for their peers students were highly engaged in working together to produce their e-zine given their potential audiences (Courtland & Paddington, 2008).

## Fiction Sharing Sites

Students can also share their stories on a number of different sites designed to foster reading and sharing of fiction.

---

### FICTION SHARING SITES

Figment *http://figment.com*, FanFiction.net *http://www.fanfiction.net*, TeenInk *http://www.teenink.com*, iOS *http://tinyurl.com/mqw3mle* and Android *http://tinyurl.com/6pkeg4l* Wattpad, Storywrite *http://storywrite.com*, KidPub *http://www.kidpub.com*, YoungWritersSociety *http://www.youngwriterssociety.com*, WritersCafe *http://www.writerscafe.org*, Pongo Teen Writers *http://www.pongoteenwriting.org*, Mibba *http://www.mibba.com*, Elfwood *http://www.elfwood.com*, iOS Worthy of Publishing *http://tinyurl.com/m9rs778*

---

Students can submit their writing to these sites for feedback from other writers and potential publication. The Figment site contains submitted fiction as well as discussion groups such as a Harry Potter fanfic group *http://tinyurl.com/llpauwy*. Students can also enter their writing in contests based on certain prompts.

Analysis of adolescents' posting fiction and receiving feedback on the Fanfiction site indicated that students valued the collaborative exchange of critical responses to their fiction; female English language learner (ELL) students used creative writing in ways that performed achieved identities that challenged the deficit identities often ascribed to them by their schools (Black, 2008).

## Writing Poetry

In addition to writing fiction, students can employ a number of apps for both reading and creating poems. They can access a wide range of apps for reading poems as inspiration for writing poetry, as well as go to sites such as e-Poetry Center *http://epc.buffalo.edu/e-poetry*, Poets.org *http://tinyurl.com/k3aqc23*, American Poetry *http://tinyurl.com/lzj78dm*, PoetryOutloud *http://www.poetryoutloud.org*, Lit2Go (audio) *http://etc.usf.edu/lit2go*, or AllPoetry *http://allpoetry.com*.

## ONLINE POETRY APPS

**iOS**: Poetry from the Poetry Foundation *http://tinyurl.com/knnhs3q*, The Poetry App *http://tinyurl.com/kjujyc7*, Classic Poetry Aloud *http://tinyurl.com/ mucpwvk*, Poem of the Day *http://tinyurl.com/msysgdw*, American Poetry *http:// tinyurl.com/no2sar8*, iPoetry 101 *http://tinyurl.com/pgu6lj*, Poetry Flow *http:// tinyurl.com/mgpma85*, Poetreat *http://tinyurl.com/lmc2wjw*, Poems by Heart *http://tinyurl.com/ko8plgq*, Writing Poetry: Audio *http://tinyurl.com/mtt6tvq*, Poetry Magazine *http://tinyurl.com/mgfm7m4*

**Android**: Poetry from the Poetry Foundation *http://tinyurl.com/7shcdsy*, Poet's Corner *http://tinyurl.com/lmp7asr*, Famous Poetry *http://tinyurl.com/ mxxszqe*, Poems and Poetry *http://tinyurl.com/l6gh5te*, All Poems *http:// tinyurl.com/kd87sgg*, Best Poems *http://tinyurl.com/lszsnyl*, Thinking and Poems *http://tinyurl.com/lu38s6c*

And, they can employ the poetry writing apps listed below for creating poems, apps that provide assistance in starting poems as well as finding words that rhyme.

## POETRY WRITING APPS

**iOS**: Poet's Pad *http://tinyurl.com/kk2hr9d*, Poetreat *http://tinyurl.com/ n2x7gee*, Poet for iPad *http://tinyurl.com/krdjbjv*, Poet *http://tinyurl.com/ n4gjytg*, Poetics *http://tinyurl.com/m6yajd5*, RhymeNowHD *http://tinyurl. com/kulzuyk*, PortaPoet *http://tinyurl.com/krdjbjv*, Instant Poetry HD *http:// tinyurl.com/lveduwv*, Poetry Creator *http://tinyurl.com/me577lw*, Verses Notebook *http://tinyurl.com/lwj32vx*

**Android**: Poet's Pad *http://tinyurl.com/cqw6k3e*, iPoetry *http://tinyurl.com/ lecwae5*, Digital Poetry *http://tinyurl.com/loanvkb*

For example, students can use the Poetreat app, which helps students in writing poetry by suggesting alternative words that rhyme as they are writing their poems. Or, they can use the Poetics app to write poetry in response to photos or images. And, they can use the Poetica *https://poetica.com* app to receive feedback from peers to foster revision of their poems.

One key motivation for engaging in extensive revision of their poems is to have students perform their poems so that they listen to their own use of language designed to engage their audiences. In working with his students on responding to Romantic poetry as a lead into poetry writing, Matthew Gillispie (2013) had students find a nature image and then write a poem about that image. Students then used the i Tell a Story *http://tinyurl.com/kudohpb* app to record their poems as well as add nature sound effects such as animal noises, thunder, bird calls, etc., and to then share their recordings with the class. He also had students use the iOS Songify *http://tinyurl.com/lwwba2w* app and Autorap *http://tinyurl.com/kp4d5w9* apps to have students record their poem and then add a beat to create a song-like performance.

## Editing Apps

Editing texts involves attempting to enhance audience readability through uses of font size, subheads, layouts, white space, indentation, figures/charts, etc., to achieve a certain unique, visual "look" for blogs, reports, scrapbooks, classroom newspapers, or comic books. Because students perceive their texts as having an attractive format and appearance, they may then be more concerned with editing their texts given the need to make them appear as published texts on the Web. Being able to customize their own texts—for example, selecting a template for their blog that reflects their own interests and personality—helps "students define themselves as individuals, not pupils who use a teacher-sanctioned tool to post work" (Glogowski, 2007, p. 10).

Students can also employ editing apps to focus on issues of readability based on grammar, word choice, or formatting that differ from larger issues of developing or organizing ideas associated with drafting. In doing so, it's important to recognize that relying on readability analyses to guide editing can result in producing less comprehensible texts.

Students can also employ a number of generic writing-skill apps that can assist them with basic writing skills, recognizing that students' writing is most likely to improve through creating engaging writing activities, as opposed to isolated skill instruction.

## WRITING SKILLS APPS

**iOS**: MELS Writing Skills *http://tinyurl.com/myno42x*, Pearson Writer *http://tinyurl.com/mv53wpm*, Essay Czar *http://tinyurl.com/lqtpctu*, How To Improve Your Writing *http://tinyurl.com/me3mng8*

**Android**: IEW Writing Tools *http://tinyurl.com/kx5yltw*, English Writing Skills *http://tinyurl.com/knhv6te*, Pearson Writer *http://tinyurl.com/n26weeh*, Improve Your Writing Skills *http://tinyurl.com/mmvfdw5*

Students can also access editing resources from the Internet Public Library2 (iPL2) *http://tinyurl.com/k24tsl4* or the Purdue University Online Writing Lab *http://tinyurl.com/lb9cfrd*, as well as the Web Writing Style Guide *http://tinyurl.com/lchruan* (Barton, Kalmbach, & Lowe, 2011).

## Dictionary Apps

Students can employ different features of dictionary apps to assist them in editing. They can conduct voice searches using the Merriam-Webster Dictionary HD or Dictionary.com: Dictionary and Thesaurus to find words if they don't know the spelling, as well as audio pronunciations of the words. Or, they can use the Advanced English Dictionary and Thesaurus to search for synonyms connected according to semantic meanings or lexical relations, as well as hyperlinks to different related words.

---

**iOS**: Dictionary! for iPad *http://tinyurl.com/kw3xbse*, Merriam-Webster Dictionary HD *http://tinyurl.com/mmay5gx*, Chambers Dictionary *http://tinyurl.com/n52jjcs*, WordWeb Dictionary, Advanced English Dictionary and Thesaurus *http://tinyurl.com/mybr492*, WordWeb Dictionary *http://tinyurl.com/ka79m9v*, Dictionary.com: Dictionary and Thesaurus *http://tinyurl.com/7dr9b8p*, Dictionary *http://tinyurl.com/mo393ey*

**Android**: Dictionary.com *http://tinyurl.com/ade4bhm*, Dictionary: Merriam-Webster *http://tinyurl.com/cssmhbp*, Oxford Dictionary *http://tinyurl.com/l7hl4as*, English Dictionary *http://tinyurl.com/mbwo757*, Dictionary *http://tinyurl.com/nxulru9*, Chambers Deluxe and Thesaurus *http://tinyurl.com/lry6vsq*

**Chrome OS**: Dictionary Instant *http://tinyurl.com/jw9cgrp*, Dictionary *http://tinyurl.com/lqts45r*

---

The Merriam-Webster Dictionary HD app assists students who are not familiar with the spelling of certain words to use their voice input of words to search for words, as well as the fact that they can hear pronunciations of the words, along with sample uses of words in sentences.

## Grammar Apps

Students can employ grammar apps to acquire knowledge of grammar rules to assist them in editing texts, recognizing that knowledge of these rules does not necessarily improve their writing quality. Practicing the test items in these apps also serves to prepare them for standardized tests such as the SAT that include grammar editing test items.

---

## GRAMMAR APPS

**iOS**: Grammar App HD *http://tinyurl.com/ny3zolz*, Word Study and Grammar Guide *http://tinyurl.com/k2g3j6a*, GE Lite: the Interactive Grammar of English from UCL *http://tinyurl.com/5sar78z*, Practice English Grammar *http://tinyurl.com/ldondnn*, Grammar Up *http://tinyurl.com/7auscfu*, English Grammar *http://tinyurl.com/78v8k2o*, Sentence Builder for iPad *http://tinyurl.com/n6zpkzu*

**Android**: Grammar Guide *http://tinyurl.com/d69r7hz*, English Grammar *http://tinyurl.com/d2pagz5*, Oxford Grammar and Punctuation *http://tinyurl.com/av92gpm*, English Grammar Guru *http://tinyurl.com/m5kbkvv*, Merriam-Webster's Vocabulary Builder *http://tinyurl.com/lj5yaf5*

**Chrome OS**: Grammar Checker *http://tinyurl.com/mof564x*, Road to Grammar *http://tinyurl.com/n6n8zm8*, Spell-Checker and Grammar *http://tinyurl.com/mu2dxds*

---

For editing grammar, students can also employ the free browser app NoRedInk *https://www.noredink.com* designed to help students with specific grammar issues. Many of these grammar apps provide students with quizzes to determine their knowledge of grammar rules and their ability to edit for grammar errors. One limitation of these apps is that the use of multiple-choice test items can presuppose that there are certain "correct" grammatical options, when determining "correctness" can be arbitrary. As indicated by decades of research on the effects of direct instruction in grammar, knowledge of grammar rules does not necessarily result in improvements in students' writing ability (Hillocks, 1984).

### Spell-Checker Apps

Students can use spell-checker apps, which can also help students acquire intuitive rules or strategies that serve to improve their spelling. While they can rely on spell-checking software to assist them in their spelling, they still need to have some knowledge of these rules or strategies to help them learn correct spelling.

## SPELL-CHECKER APPS

**iOS**: Speller *http://tinyurl.com/n2o6c3a*, Spell Better *http://tinyurl.com/ k9u8w8y*, Spell Check *http://tinyurl.com/mjxldyw*, Miss Spell's Class *http:// tinyurl.com/kllyjus*, Mispell or Misspell? *http://tinyurl.com/lblghqs*

**Android**: Spell Checker Editor *http://tinyurl.com/kbg76e2*, Spell Checker *http://tinyurl.com/ldgodrq*, Spell Check and Grammar Keyboard *http://tinyurl. com/mbotvbg*, Miss Spell's Class *http://tinyurl.com/l5h2s4v*

**Chrome OS**: Free Spell Checker *http://tinyurl.com/moyw86f*, Spell-Checker and Grammar *http://tinyurl.com/mu2dxds*

For students who have difficulty with spelling, the Mispell or Misspell? *http:// tinyurl.com/lblghqs* app employs a game-like approach to assist students in spelling, which includes examples of commonly misspelled words and strategies to help students correct their spelling of those words. At the same time, it's important to recognize that grammar and spell-checker apps can note errors based on dated or erroneous grammar or spelling rules, rules that confuse syntax with usage that can vary according to dialect/language differences.

## Citation/Reference Style Apps

There are also apps designed to help students employ appropriate bibliographic styles consistent with the APA, MLA, or Chicago style manuals. To do so, they can employ citation apps such as those listed below.

## CITATION/REFERENCE APPS

**iOS**: EasyBib *http://tinyurl.com/mk6d9nb*, iSource APA *http://tinyurl.com/ mkncqpc*, iSource MLA *http://tinyurl.com/luylfwk*, ReferenceMe *http://tinyurl. com/m84n865*, MY MLA *http://tinyurl.com/ktfqjs3*, MyBib *http://tinyurl.com/ k43t32f*

**Android**: EasyBib *http://tinyurl.com/knghmbv*, MLA Generator *http://tinyurl. com/k6h465z*, APA Generator Reference *http://tinyurl.com/mtv3b66*, Bibliog-raphy Helper *http://tinyurl.com/mksqhde*, Reference Me *http://tinyurl.com/ lf3r9u3*, i-Cite APA *http://tinyurl.com/ltycll3*

**Chrome OS**: EasyBib *http://tinyurl.com/m645jg4*, OttoBib *http://tinyurl.com/ l9pwg6v*

Students can use these apps to put in titles or scan ISBN numbers of books to obtain reference lists consistent with APA, MLA, Chicago, or other styles.

## Publishing E-books

Both you and your students can publish e-books as multimodal texts either just for distribution to a class or that can be published free or for purchase on the Amazon *http://tinyurl.com/puauzqy*, iBooks Store *http://tinyurl.com/cb9olpf*, Barnes & Noble *http://tinyurl.com/7yley3d*, or other e-book publishers' sites (Luke, 2012; Rice, 2012). Rather than think of these texts as extended "books," students could then create shorter reports or digital stories as "books" for sharing with their class or parents. Or, as did seventh-grade students at Woodlawn Beach Middle School, Woodlawn Beach, Florida, they can create an iBook that was converted into an app entitled *Creatures, Plants, and More! http://tinyurl.com/kfyv5v5*, describing animals and plants in Northern Florida that became a best-seller book on the Apple bookstore. And, teachers are increasingly creating their own e-textbooks that can be tailored to a school's specific curriculum, as well as be continually updated with new information and materials.

The fact that they can publish these books for free as either a PDF or as an iBook means that students can store these books on their devices to read them as well as add notes or create flash cards for later reading without having to be connected to the Internet, something that could benefit students who may lack Internet access in their homes. In contrast to print textbooks, these e-books are highly interactive and multimodal in that they can include links to websites, presentations, interactive images, or videos.

### *Using ePub and iBooks Author Apps*

You or your students can create books simply as PDF files converted from Word or Pages. They can then be read using the iBooks *http://tinyurl.com/cb9olpf* app (for reading on iPads) or iOS *http://tinyurl.com/k6qbmlu* or Android *http://tinyurl.com/k3h8xk8* Kindle app for reading on different devices. However, for distribution on Amazon, the iBooks Store, or Barnes & Noble, it is necessary to publish an e-book as either an ePub or Mobi file (for Amazon). To open up a PDF or ePub text in iBooks or Kindle on their iPad or iPhone, students connect their iOS device to iTunes on a computer, drag the PDF or ePub file to Books (under iTunes Library), and sync their device with iTunes to obtain the ePub file on their iPad or iPhone.

The e-book publication standard, ePub, includes a set of features that add metadata to files and enabling features like embedded links/videos, word searches, images, page display options, etc., associated with e-books. To create ePub files, students employ Pages; they can also import Word files into Pages. When they have completed their writing, they select Export in Pages to publish that writing as an ePub book published on iTunes or iBooks for peers, teachers, and parents to read.

Students can also use ePub software programs such as the desktop 2epub *http://www.2epub.com* or dotEPUB *http://dotepub.com* that also works on an iPad or on Chromebooks with the Chrome OS app *http://tinyurl.com/mv4ho46*. Students install a dotEPUB extension to their browsers to create ePub publications from their Word documents, PDF files, or Web pages. Or, for creating ePub files using a Mac, students can employ the Mac apps, Easy ePub Creator *http://tinyurl.com/mg5nnqp* or Mac PDF to ePub converter *http://tinyurl.com/mx8caqu*. Or, they can submit their files to CloudConvert *http://tinyurl.com/nh4rejk*, which will create ePub files.

Because there is a difference between the appearance of their Pages and their ePub documents, students should format their Pages files using paragraph styles in Pages consistent with an ePub file format. Exporting to ePub automatically creates a table of contents based on the original Pages subheads that allows readers to move easily within a text; for assistance on using Pages to create ePubs, see Apple Support: *http://support.apple.com/kb/HT4168*. Another option involves use of the desktop software, Calibre *http://calibre-ebook.com* to convert Word files into Mobi for Kindle e-readers or ePub, for formatting, previewing, and then saving a file to an e-reader.

Students can then add images, videos, or links to enhance the multimodal aspect of their texts. When they are done, they can choose to export their files as ePubs or as PDFs, recognizing that they should use ePubs when the text *content* is most important, for example, when creating a children's book, and PDF when the text *layout* is most important, for example, when creating a flyer or manual.

You and your students can also use the Mac iBooks Author *http://tinyurl.com/875lxud* app (for support: Apple: iBooks Author Support *http://www.apple.com/support/ibooksauthor*) to create e-books from Pages or Word files for a range of different purposes (Lo & Wood, 2012; McKesson & Witwer, 2012). The iBooks Author app does require more expertise than creating ePub text from Pages but is much more powerful. It can be used to collect and curate articles, news clippings, spreadsheets, and video clips within a published, interactive book format that includes hyperlinks, presentations, photo galleries, or 3-D images.

## Apps for Creating E-books

There are also a number of different apps listed below that you or your students can use for creating e-books. These apps provide students with structured formats or templates that serve to scaffold their design decisions, although in some cases, these format structures can be limiting. Students can readily upload images, videos, or presentations, as well as add their audio recording.

---

## APPS FOR CREATING E-BOOKS

**iOS**: Book Creator *http://tinyurl.com/cxcyoby*, Book Writer *http://goodeffect. com*, eBook Creator *http://tinyurl.com/n6ot87b*, eBook Magic *http:// tinyurl.com/lx52b9s*, Scribble Press *http://tinyurl.com/axj4wqz*, Creative Book Builder *http://tinyurl.com/cyx578e*, Writer's Studio *http://tinyurl.com/ mwjx8m5*, Storyteller Deluxe *http://tinyurl.com/mvccnkk*, eBook Maker *http://tinyurl.com/l4vhlb3*, DemibooksComposer *http://tinyurl.com/ksojlee*, StoryBuddy 2 Lite *http://tinyurl.com/kkw454n*, eBooks Journal *http://tinyurl. com/mzejpkm*, Mooklet *http://tinyurl.com/ltfxefe*, Simplebooklet *http:// tinyurl.com/aegh4rr*

**Android**: BONZOI *http://tinyurl.com/lh6ayc9*, BookWriter *http://tinyurl.com/ lceu5xq*, I Write A Book 2 *http://tinyurl.com/lxhtewr*, My Story Builder *http:// tinyurl.com/mjlykk5*, BookWriterLite *http://tinyurl.com/lay899z*, Creative Book Builder *http://tinyurl.com/kla3red*, eBookMaker *http://tinyurl.com/lz4kud2*, Epub Generator *http://tinyurl.com/meraf4g*, Ebook Convertor *http://tinyurl. com/l6b5yu2*

---

One of the easier, popular apps for creating e-books is the iOS Book Creator. In Book Creator, the Pages button on the top left of a screen provides options to use text, images, or sound; format texts using different fonts; import images or video from Photo library; record a voice-over; align and position material on a page; and reorder pages (Gliksman, 2013). Some of these apps, such as ScribblePress, include drawing features so that students can create their own illustrations. Other apps such as Mooklet are designed to create photo stories that revolve around writing about imported photos.

## Apps for Learning to Code

There has recently been an increased interest in having students learn coding for the purpose of creating software, games, or apps. One argument for having students learn coding is that it provides them with a tool that will become increasingly important in the future as people create their own software or apps (see the TED Talks video, Reading, Writing, and Programming *http://tinyurl. com/qfd8lqf* by Mitch Resnick, creator of Scratch, on the value of learning to program). And, providing students with coding experiences can lead them to consider future careers in computer programming given the future need for programmers.

While learning to code in previous years required extensive training and knowledge given the complexity of different coding languages, more recently, a number of apps listed below have been developed that students can use to learn coding using Python, Java, C, C++, Objective-C, MacRuby, PyObjC, MonoTouch, coding that can be used to create iOS or Android apps.

---

### APPS FOR LEARNING TO CODE

**iOS**: Hopscotch *http://tinyurl.com/lgxhvt2*, L2Code CSS—Learn to Code! *http://tinyurl.com/mzj2mwy*, Codea *http://tinyurl.com/k2uh726*, Codeacademy: Hour of Code *http://tinyurl.com/obxpqwm*, Kodable *http://tinyurl.com/ n67zuhn*, Move the Turtle *http://tinyurl.com/k4z6u68*, Tynker *http://tinyurl. com/khrll5d*, Lightbot: Programming Puzzles *http://tinyurl.com/kfmfp2h*, Daisy the Dinosaur *http://tinyurl.com/okdnmth*

**Android Apps (Code Editing for Java/C++ Script)**
AIDE—Android IDE—Java, C++ *http://tinyurl.com/6wceb9u*, Android Script Programming *http://tinyurl.com/k65a2sl*, Droidedit *http://tinyurl.com/ lexvf92*, DroidDevelop *http://tinyurl.com/ljxs6b7*, JavaIDEdroid *http://tinyurl. com/mmjpd4j*

**Other Coding Tools/Sites**
Scratch *http://scratch.mit.edu* (Scratched for teachers: *http://scratched.media. mit.edu*), Treehouse *http://tinyurl.com/mjduvnz*, Alice *http://www.alice.org/ index.php*, Hackety Hack *http://hackety.com*, Codeconquest *http://www. codeconquest.com*, Code.org *http://code.org/learn*, Pluralsight *http://tinyurl. com/lycxa2e*, CodeMonster *http://tinyurl.com/bcjktgs*, KidsRuby *http://www. kidsruby.com*

---

Many of the iOS apps, as well as Scratch, Codeconquest, Code.org, CodeMonster, or KidsRuby can be used by younger students to create code for creating commands for moving objects. For example, students can use the Hopscotch *http://tinyurl.com/lgxhvt2* app to learn to code for iOS devices, beginning with creating simple directions that then leads into creating games (Fryer, 2013). The Android apps involving code editing for Java or C++ require that students have more advanced knowledge of coding.

## Students Creating Their Own Apps

Students can also use apps listed below that require limited or no coding to create their own apps.

## APPS FOR CREATING APPS

**iOS apps**: AppToolz *http://tinyurl.com/k8yc52s*, TouchAppCreator *http://tinyurl.com/cwfdmop*, iBuildApp *http://tinyurl.com/lphorxa*

**Android apps**: App Inventor 2 *http://tinyurl.com/mf3cqkq*, TouchApp Creator *http://tinyurl.com/kewhpfh*, Android App Development *http://tinyurl.com/lr8m5ct*, Android Mobile Application Development *http://tinyurl.com/l6ha8ge*, Maker *http://tinyurl.com/n2t5ow9*

**Web-based apps**: appsbar *http://www.appsbar.com*, AppMakr *http://appmakr.com*, iGenapps *http://igenapps.com*, Andromo *http://www.andromo.com*, Appy Pie *http://www.appypie.com*, AppGeyser *http://www.appsgeyser.com*, Appery *http://appery.io*, The App Builder *http://www.theappbuilder.com*, Mozilla Hackasaurus *http://tinyurl.com/km2cupd*, MobileRoadie *http://mobileroadie.com*, Good Barber *http://www.goodbarber.com*, Mobile *http://tinyurl.com/ldwhgl4*, AppArchitect *http://apparchitect.com*, appsme *http://www.appsme.com*, appery.io *http://appery.io*

For creating iOS apps, the AppToolz *http://tinyurl.com/k8yc52s* app is relatively easy to use. For creating Android apps, the most frequently used app is the App Inventor 2 app; for books on use of App Inventor: Kloss, 2012; Tyler, 2011; Wolber, Abelson, Spertus, & Looney, 2011.

Creating iOS apps using Apple's own coding language involves use of Apple's iOS Software Development Kit (SDK) and Xcode using a Mac 10.8 or later (for tutorials from Apple *http://tinyurl.com/nlm2a6g*; for books on creating iOS apps: Harris, 2014; Feiler, 2014; Warren, 2013; White, 2013). Developing Android apps involves use of Java or C++; the Android Development Tools *http://tinyurl.com/8goqong* or the more recent (as of Spring, 2014) Android Studio *http://tinyurl.com/cvjq35v* include use of Java.

Students may develop apps that can address issues or challenges in their school or community. For example, students in the Mobile Action Lab at Youth Radio in Oakland, California, devised the iOS Forage City: *http://www.foragecity.com* app designed to share information about gathering excess food grown in trees in Oakland for redistributing to people through food banks or homeless shelters (Soep, 2014). Using the App Inventor app, they also designed the Android All Day Play *http://tinyurl.com/lz82nrp* app for streaming hip-hop/eclectic music to publicize the work of certain young musicians in Oakland. And, students in the Youth Speaks spoken word organization created the Android VoxPop *http://tinyurl.com/msjy4yh* app for use in sharing news stories for certain areas of the world where such stories may not receive impartial coverage.

## Summary

In this chapter, we discussed a range of different writing apps for creating different kinds of digital texts. Central to generating engaging digital texts is the effective use of visual rhetoric through uses of formatting, images, color, white space, and font. While it could be argued that these writing apps have certain affordances based on effective design principles, as we have argued in regards to affordances, your own instructional activities contribute much to fostering students' use of effective design, aspects of design that also inform the use of audio, images, and video-creation apps discussed later in this book. This includes creating opportunities for students to share their digital texts with peers and parents so that they have some sense of a potential audience guiding their design decisions.

## References

Allison, P. (2009). Be a blogger: Social networking in the classroom. In A. Herrington, K. Hodgson, & C. Moran (Eds.), *The new writing: Technology, change, and assessment* (pp. 93–110). New York: Teachers College Press.

Barton, M., Kalmbach, J., & Lowe, C. (2011). *Writing spaces: Web writing style guide.* Anderson, SC: Parlor Press. Retrieved from http://tinyurl.com/lchruan

Beach, R., Campano, G., Edmiston, B., & Borgmann, M. (2010). *Literacy tools in the classroom: Teaching through critical inquiry, Grades 5–12.* New York: Teachers College Press.

Black, R. (2008). *Adolescents and online fan fiction.* New York: Peter Lang.

Buran, K. (2011, June 25). Teaching with Evernote: A 6th and 8th grade science teacher shares his top tips [Web log post]. Retrieved from http://blog.evernote.com/2009/06/25/notebook-sharing-phase-1

Castek, J., & Beach, R. (2013a). Using apps to support disciplinary literacy and science learning. *Journal of Adolescent & Adult Literacy, 56*(7), 554–564. Retrieved from http://tinyurl.com/kzuod4v

Castek, J., Goss, M., & Tilson, J. (2011). *Writing scientific explanations: Practice strategies for success.* The Lawrence Hall of Science, University of California, Berkeley.

Council of Chief State School Officers and National Governors' Association. (2010). *Common Core State Standards for English Language Arts & Literacy in History/Social Studies, Science, and Technical Subjects.* Washington, DC: Author. Retrieved from http://www.corestandards.org

Courtland, M. C., & Paddington, D. (2008). Digital literacy in a grade 8 classroom: An E-zine WebQuest. *Language & Literacy, 10*(1). Retrieved from http://tinyurl.com/ln8rq27

Davidson, C. (2012, January 21). Should we really ABOLISH the term paper? A response to the NY Times [Web log post]. Retrieved from http://tinyurl.com/7s8lon5

Dexter, D. D., Park, Y. J., & Hughes, C. A. (2011). A meta-analytic review of graphic organizers and science instruction for adolescents with learning disabilities: Implications for the intermediate and secondary classroom. *Learning Disabilities Research and Practice, 26*(4), 204–213.

Feiler, J. (2014). *iOS app development for dummies.* Hoboken, NJ: Wiley.

Ferriter, B. (2011, December 13). Using Twitter in high school classrooms. *Teacher Magazine.* Retrieved from http://tinyurl.com/77m9p37

Fryer, W. (2013). *Hopscotch challenges: Learn to code on an iPad!* [Amazon Kindle Edition] Speed of Creativity Learning LLC. Retrieved from http://tinyurl.com/n8sr84q

Gillispie, M. D. (2013). *From notepad to iPad: Using apps and Web tools to engage a new generation of students.* New York: Routledge.

Gliksman, S. (2013). *iPad in education for dummies.* Hoboken, NJ: John Wiley & Sons.

Glogowski, K. (2007, August 16). Creating learning experiences [Web log post]. Retrieved from http://www.teachandlearn.ca/blog/2007/08/16/creating-learning-experiences

Harris, M. (2011). Negotiation: Why letting students talk is essential. In B. Hand & L. Norton-Meier (Eds.), *Voices from the classroom: Elementary teachers' experience with argument-based inquiry, 1–12* (pp. 13–24). Rotterdam, Netherlands: Sense Publishers.

Harris, N. (2014). *Beginning iOS programming: Building and deploying iOS applications.* Hoboken, NJ: Wiley.

Hicks, T. (2009). *The digital writing workshop.* Portsmouth, NH: Heinemann.

Hillocks, G. (1984). What works in teaching composition: A meta-analysis of experimental studies. *American Journal of Education, 93*(1), 133–170.

Hunter, J. D., & Caraway, H. J. (2014). Urban youth use Twitter to transform learning and engagement. *English Journal, 103*(4), 18–24.

Keys, C. W., Hand, B., Prain, V., & Collins, S. (1999). Using the Science Writing Heuristic as a tool for learning from laboratory investigations in secondary science. *Journal of Research in Science Teaching, 36*(10), 1065–1084.

Kloss, J. H. (2012). *Android apps with App Inventor.* Boston, MA: Addison-Wesley

Lenhart, A. (2012, March 19). *Teens, smartphones & texting.* Washington, DC: Pew Research Center's Internet and American Life Project. Retrieved from http://pewinternet.org/Reports/2012/Teens-and-smartphones.aspx

Linder, S. (2011). Dear Emma, just tweet me: Using microblogging to explore characterization and style. In M. T. Christel & S. Sullivan (Eds.), *Lesson plans for developing digital literacies* (pp. 228–236). Urbana, IL: National Council of Teachers of English.

Lo, B., & Wood, J. (2012, April 11). 7 reasons to learn Apple iBooks Author now. *THE Journal.* Retrieved from http://tinyurl.com/7o8xm6n

Luke, A. (2012). *Publishing e-books for dummies.* Hoboken, NJ: John Wiley & Sons.

McKesson, N., & Witwer, A. (2012). *Publishing with iBooks Author.* Sebastopol, CA: O'Reilly Media.

Norton-Meier, L., Hand, B., Hockenberry, L., & Wise, K. (2008). *Questions, claims, and evidence: The important place of argument in children's science writing.* Portsmouth, NH: Heinemann.

Provenzano, N. (2011, December 9). Update 2: iP@ds in my classroom [Web log post]. Retrieved from http://tinyurl.com/7d3dq99

Reich, J. (2012). The state of wiki usage in U.S. K-12 schools: Leveraging Web 2.0 data warehouses to assess quality and equity in U.S. K-12 schools. *Educational Researcher, 41*(1), 7–15. Retrieved from http://www.edtechresearcher.com/2012/02/the-state-of-wiki-usage-in-u-s-k-12-schools

Rice, W. (2012). *How to publish your own iBook in 4 hours or less, Kindle too.* William Rice. Retrieved from http://tinyurl.com/lvxz2jy

Rosenzweig, G. (2012). *My Pages.* Indianapolis, IN: Que Publishing

Sassi, K., & Gere, A. (2014). *Writing on demand for the Common Core State Standards assessments.* Portsmouth, NH: Heinemann.

Soep, E. (2014, February 25). Youth productions in digital-age civics. Presentation at the Learning Technologies Media Lab, University of Minnesota, Twin Cities. Retrieved from http://new.livestream.com/ltmedialab/soep

Turnbaugh, B. (2011). Survey says! Using Google Forms to evaluate media trends and habits. In M. T. Christel & S. Sullivan (Eds.), *Lesson plans for developing digital literacies* (pp. 53–60). Urbana, IL: National Council of Teachers of English.

Tyler, J. (2011). *App Inventor for Android*. Hoboken, NJ: Wiley.

Warren, R. (2013). *Creating iOS apps: Develop and design* (2nd ed). San Francisco, CA: Peachpit Press.

White, C. (2013). *Idea to iPhone: The essential guide to creating your first app for the iPhone and iPad*. Hoboken, NJ: Wiley.

Wolber, D., Abelson, H., Spertus, E., & Looney, L. (2011). *App Inventor*. Sebastopol, CA: O'Reilly Media.

Yagelski, R. P. (2012). Writing as praxis. *English Education, 44*(2), 188–204.

# 7

# USING APPS TO FOSTER DISCUSSION

One of the more important literacies involves students' ability to collaboratively discuss topics, issues, and texts in small or large groups. Engaging in discussions allows students to share their ideas, questions, concerns, engagements, and perceptions related to learning across the curriculum. For example, in a math class, students can collaboratively work through a math problem by each sharing their own particular expertise. In a social studies class, students can debate competing explanations for historical events. In a science class, students can collaboratively entertain alternative hypotheses to account for why fish are dying in a lake. In a literature class, students can share their responses to a literary text. Through discussion, students are collaboratively voicing their opinions, formulating arguments and counter-arguments, adopting alternative perspectives, and synthesizing shared ideas.

## Common Core State Standards Related to Speaking and Listening

One category of the 5–12 English Language Arts Common Core State Standards is devoted to these *Speaking and Listening* standards (Council of Chief State School Officers and National Governors' Association, 2010).

### Comprehension and Collaboration

1. Participate effectively in a range of interactions (one-on-one and in groups), exchanging information to advance a discussion and to build on the input of others.

2. Integrate and evaluate information from multiple oral, visual, or multimodal sources in order to answer questions, solve problems, or build knowledge.
3. Evaluate the speaker's point of view, reasoning, and use of evidence and rhetoric.

### Presentation of Knowledge and Ideas

4. Present information, evidence, and reasoning in a clear and well-structured way appropriate to purpose and audience.
5. Make strategic use of digital media and visual displays of data to express information and enhance understanding.
6. Adapt speech to a variety of contexts and communicative tasks, demonstrating a command of formal English when indicated or appropriate. (p. 49)

In this chapter, we describe how the app affordances of social interaction and online sharing of ideas serves to address these standards. Again, how you employ these apps to effectively achieve the standards depends on your ability to create engaging discussion contexts that foster active student participation. While it is often assumed that face-to-face discussions provide for richer learning opportunities, a comparison of learning in face-to-face versus online hybrid classes found no difference between college students' learning in six different colleges (Bowen, Chingos, Lack, & Nygren, 2012). Well-designed online discussions can therefore be equally productive as face-to-face discussions.

## Tools for Hosting Discussion

Teachers employ a number of different types of tools for hosting online discussions: course management systems (CMSs), social networking sites, or online discussion apps, tools that support use of both asynchronous and synchronous discussions.

### Course Management Systems (CMSs)

While this chapter focuses on apps for discussions, it is useful to be familiar with the desktop versions of course management systems (CMSs) such as the commercial CMSs: Desire2Learn, WebCT/Vista, Angel, Brainhoney, Blackboard Mobile Learn, Blackboard Illuminate, Pearson's PowerTeacher 2.0, LanSchool, or iTALC; and the open-source CMSs: Moodle *https://moodle.org*, Collaborize Classroom *http://www.collaborizeclassroom.com*, Schoology *https://www.schoology.com/home.php*, Edmodo *https://www.edmodo.com*, and Canvas *http://www.instructure.com*, because a number of these systems also have apps.

These CMSs include forums for having students engage in asynchronous and synchronous discussions, as well as video/podcast sharing, blogs, document upload/download, presentation tools, quizzes, evaluation rubrics, and student records. Some of these sites are typically operated and managed at the district or school-wide level, although teachers can set up some of these themselves, particularly Collaborize Classroom, Schoology, Edmodo, and Canvas.

## Social Networking/Discussion Sites

You can also employ social networking sites such as Ning *http://tinyurl. com/6vo7bet*, NeatChat *http://www.neatchat.com*, Grou.ps *https://grou.ps/home*, Tapatalk *http://tapatalk.com*, Mixxt *http://smallcommunities.mixxt.com*, Zoho Discussions *https://discussions.zoho.com*, AnswerGarden *http://answergarden. ch*, Lefora *http://www.lefora.com*, Qlubb *http://tinyurl.com/mkxk3m*, Google Groups *http://tinyurl.com/3emlc8*, Yahoo Groups *https://groups.yahoo.com/ neo*, Vialogues *https://vialogues.com*, as well as Facebook or Google+ to foster discussions.

One popular reason for twinning social networking sites with CMSs is that CMS sites are strong in organizing and presenting content and managing some types of assessments, but are lacking in flexible and appealing interactive features. An advantage of using a social networking or discussion platform is that, given their participation on Facebook, students are relatively familiar with the features of social networking sites. One advantage of using CMSs is that they are more geared for supporting instruction in that they include a lot of instructional tools not included in social networking sites.

Ning is a popular social networking browser app for fostering discussions with a threaded asynchronous forum feature as well as a synchronous chat feature on the Premium version. Even though there is a monthly charge of $20.00 for the basic classroom option, it is relatively easy to set up and is visually attractive. You can also control the membership of your class Ning so that only your students have access to the site. Students can also use the Vialogues *https://vialogues.com* site for posting a video and then inviting their peers to engage in an asynchronous discussion or just comment on the video.

## Apps for Engaging Students in Online Discussions

For engaging students in discussions on their devices, we recommend a number of different online discussion apps, some of which are linked to the previously cited desktop platforms.

## ONLINE DISCUSSION APPS

**iOS**: iOS Collaborize Classroom *http://tinyurl.com/mctdhkr/*Collaborize Classroom Pro *http://tinyurl.com/mk4t36w*, Blackboard Mobile Learn for iPad *http://tinyurl.com/nq3frtt*, Canvas *http://tinyurl.com/mvkmc8p*, GoClass *http://tinyurl.com/kyglmaz*, Tapatalk *http://tinyurl.com/kyd5pwc*, Stick Pick *http://tinyurl.com/q9a4j44*, Communication for Groups *http://tinyurl.com/llbuu8j*, Subtext *http://tinyurl.com/9ykogpm*

**Android**: Tapatalk *http://tinyurl.com/d628yj5*, GoClass *http://tinyurl.com/kh6q2ra*, Discussions *http://tinyurl.com/ltp2esl*, Pearson Open Discussion *http://tinyurl.com/ljg6u79*, Mixable *http://tinyurl.com/ljmzkua*, Forum Runner *http://tinyurl.com/bq7ulyp*

One of the more useful of the free classroom management apps is the Collaborize Classroom and Collaborize Classroom Pro apps that are especially designed for fostering discussions. You can create small groups based on differences in students' ability, along with scaffolding features for facilitating large and small group discussions, including tips on leading discussions. For example, there is information on the differences between assuming the roles of "silent moderator," who poses questions without participating in the discussion or responds to students' contributions, and the "involved participant" who facilitates and directs the discussion via a focus on certain topics or issues and models ways of responding to and clarifying certain ideas without dominating the discussion.

Students can employ the Discussion Prompts feature in the Collaborize Classroom site that provides them with prompts along with images to foster discussions. For example, math or science teachers could use the following prompts (Briner, 2011):

- Explain a concept to a five-year-old.
- Provide real-life examples of concepts for peers.
- Find examples from their own life that demonstrate concepts.
- Use real objects they interact with everyday (textbook) to teach concepts.
- Connect their lives, personalities, interests, etc. to concepts (e.g. periodic table).

Or, you can use the Subtext app to have students share their responses to books within your own class, as well as have students share links to topics related to a book. As noted in Chapter 1, Sara Speicher and Julie Walthour (2013) use

Subtext to foster discussions of literary texts at West Junior High School, Hopkins, Minnesota, to organize book club discussion groups where students in the groups select their own books or texts for discussions. And, students in these groups can then share their highlights and annotations in response to books or texts with each other.

One advantage of using these apps for discussions is that you have a written record of students' contributions that you can use for assessing the degree and quality of those contributions.

### Synchronous Audio or Video Chat Discussions

Synchronous forms of online discussion are described as "real-time" written, audio, or video, or written chat discussions, meaning that discussion participants are on the computer at the same time and are typing messages or speaking to one another via the Internet. When participants type messages to one another synchronously, the resulting discussion appears as a written transcript, with contributions labeled according to participant names.

Students can engage in written, audio, or video chat discussions using Skype, Google+ Hangouts, or FaceTime, as well as the apps listed below; for more on videoconferencing tools see *http://tinyurl.com/lyem98y*.

---

### AUDIO AND VIDEO DISCUSSIONS

**iOS**: Share Board *http://tinyurl.com/mdgjt27*, Fring: Video Calls + Chat *http://tinyurl.com/au8we3a*, Spin *http://tinyurl.com/me5to*, BT Chat HD *http://tinyurl.com/mnt7dvf*, ooVoo Video Chat *http://tinyurl.com/bfy4pd6*, Vtok: Google Talk Video *http://tinyurl.com/lefb2lo*, Chat for GoogleTalk *http://tinyurl.com/kd7bcdx*, ClickMe Online Meetings *http://tinyurl.com/kutxq3w*, GoToMeeting *http://tinyurl.com/n34h4n2*, Adobe Connect Mobile for iOS *http://tinyurl.com/avpvm88*

**Android**: fring: Free Calls, Video + Text *http://tinyurl.com/ct7bu6z*, Adobe Connect Mobile *http://tinyurl.com/bbmylsf*, ooVoo Video Text & Voice *http://tinyurl.com/kuabd9f*, Video Calling *http://tinyurl.com/qxfqmgr*, Tango Messenger Video & Calls *http://tinyurl.com/8nswhdw*, Android Face Video Calling *http://tinyurl.com/lpn4mb2*, imo Free Video Calls and Text *http://tinyurl.com/c2drkng*, Random Video Chat *http://tinyurl.com/lr6ebtx*

---

Consistent with the flipped classroom concept, you can use these apps to hold virtual office hours with students to address issues or respond to questions. You can also arrange with experts, authors, parents, or community officials to present and interact with your students using videoconferencing tools. For example, if students are reading a young adult novel in an English class, you can arrange for young adult authors to discuss their novel with your class.

And, students can use the iOS Flipgrid *http://tinyurl.com/m52e9ck* app to create video clip responses limited to 90 seconds from students as grids of collections of questions addressing a topic or theme. Collections of these students' responses along with photo images of each student can then be posted on class blogs or websites.

## FaceTime

Built into the iOS platform is the FaceTime app for use with iPad, iPhone, and Mac OS. FaceTime allows for live video chats using the forward-facing camera on the iPad and the Camera app on the iPhone. Students will need to enter their Apple ID to use FaceTime and then connect with other Contacts, ideally employing Wi-Fi. The person being called will appear on the large screen and the caller will appear on a small screen in the upper-left corner of the screen.

You can also use FaceTime to connect different users with iOS devices to create collaborative exchanges, as well as for presentations by guest speakers. For example, students can use FaceTime to provide peer feedback for other students' drafts. One advantage of FaceTime is that it requires minimal set-up and its video streaming can be superior to Skype.

## Skype

You can use the iOS Skype for iPhone and iPad app *http://tinyurl.com/keouzfn* as well as the Skype for iPad *http://tinyurl.com/ogt4adx* app and the Android Skype *http://tinyurl.com/83evxo2* app for use with videoconferencing. Skype is a free service that includes both audio and video options. Skype Video is particularly useful for having guest speakers do presentations given its ease of use. Speakers can also show their PowerPoint or Keynote slides using the Share Screen feature.

In using Skype, students should not use their actual names, location, or the "SkypeMe" feature; rather, they should put their online setting to "invisible" to protect their privacy and avoid letting strangers know that they are online (Berger & Trexler, 2010).

For large-group conference calls (up to 24 users), you and/or your students select the Conference Call option and then select students who will be participating in the call. For one-to-one videoconferencing, students need to set up their webcam and then select the video call option. You can also set up Skype for group videoconferencing for up to ten students using Skype group video calling; however, that requires setting up a Skype Premium Account ($4.49 per month for a year).

Skype initiated Skype for Educators *http://www.skypeforeducators.com/educators.htm*, designed to help students match up with other students from throughout the world to interact using Skype. Teachers can arrange with other teachers to work on collaborative projects that can involve different cultural perspectives on a topic or issue. Or, students in world or second-language classes can practice their language with speakers of different languages.

## Google+ Hangouts

The iOS *http://tinyurl.com/b8weyja*, Android *http://tinyurl.com/dy2uuns*, and Chrome OS *http://tinyurl.com/o3bkgdh* Google+ Hangouts apps allows up to 15 students over age 13 to participate simultaneously, with up to ten of their faces appearing at the bottom of the screen, making it ideal for small group discussions. This means that Hangouts can be consistently used for small seminar classes or small group discussions of ten or less. When each person speaks, their face then appears on the large screen.

Teachers are using Google+ Hangouts to bring their classes behind the scenes at national laboratories and to teach students about careers in STEM. For example, students at a high school in Jackson Hole, Wyoming, were addressing the question of "How does dark matter interact with regular matter?" To interact with physicists at a lab, students went on a virtual field trip using both the Hangouts and the Google Education Connected Classrooms program to engage in a virtual visit to the SLAC National Accelerator Laboratory, demonstrating the use of the lab's two-mile-long linear accelerator, a chamber that uses an X-ray laser, and use of a space telescope (Freeberg, 2014). These virtual trips are also recorded for sharing on YouTube, as illustrated with a subsequent video. Teachers who are interested in signing up for a virtual field trip with their own class can visit the Connected Classrooms homepage for more information on joining the Connected Classrooms community: Google+ Connected Classrooms *http://connectedclassrooms.withgoogle.com*.

## Texting Apps

One major tool students now use for communicating is texting. A survey of teens ages 12 to 17 found that 63% of them text daily; 39% of them use cell phones; 35% use face-to-face socializing; 29% use social networking messages; 22% use IMing; and 6% use email (Lenhart, 2012). In this survey, one in four teens said that they own smartphones.

The median number of texts these teens sent daily was 60 in 2011. The heaviest texters (more than 100 texts a day) were also the heaviest talkers; 69% of heavy texters reported talking daily on their cell phones versus 46% of medium texters (those exchanging 21–100 texts a day) and compared to 43% of light texters (those exchanging 0–20 texts a day). A Nielsen survey (2010) found that teens send an average of 3,339 texts a month, about 130 texts a day.

More recently, there has been a slight decline in the number of written text messages with an increase in the use of photo messages using the iOS *http://tinyurl.com/ar63ctm* and Android *http://tinyurl.com/auxg993* Snapchat, iOS *http://tinyurl.com/b4ytl47* and Android *http://tinyurl.com/bov5nq2* Instagram, iOS *http://tinyurl.com/ou8z7mj* and Android *http://tinyurl.com/c7sooe9* Kik Messanger, and iOS *http://tinyurl.com/kcl8jvh* and Android *http://tinyurl.com/nkumcb2* Wickr apps (Luckerson, 2013). Users may perceive photos as more intimate or personal than a text message.

Clearly, texting, whether through written or photo messages, has become one preferred means by which students write to communicate. When 444 high school and middle school students were asked what motivated them to write, both in and out of school, researchers found that the students' primary motivation to write was dominated by social communication uses ("texting," Facebook, instant messaging) (Dredger, Woods, Beach, & Sagstetter, 2010).

Students can use a wide range of different texting apps listed below.

## TEXTING APPS

**iOS**: iMessage app *http://tinyurl.com/4yp53b6* for the iPad or iPhone, Messages *http://tinyurl.com/73llr2b* app on a Mac, Whatsapp for iPhone, iPad, Android, and Windows *http://www.whatsapp.com*, Text Me! *http://tinyurl.com/7zx7ypw*, AK Messenger! *http://tinyurl.com/bwduf5g*, Facebook Messenger *http://tinyurl.com/3jz2cnx*, textPlus Free Texting + Group Text *http://tinyurl.com/crx6cr6*, Cel.ly *http://cel.ly/school*, Textie™ Messaging *http://tinyurl.com/7oz83cz*, Textfree *http://tinyurl.com/cr8sn2m*, TextNow + Voice —Free Texting and Calling *http://tinyurl.com/86b2beu*, iPushIt *http://tinyurl.com/c7kletj*, gText *http://www.gtext.com*

**Android**: HeyWire *http://tinyurl.com/ctoenah*, Text Me! *http://tinyurl.com/bxhvv4d*, WhatsApp Messenger *http://tinyurl.com/84erglx*, Text+ *http://tinyurl.com/8x24e8m*, Text Free *http://tinyurl.com/cpbegyz*, TextNow *http://tinyurl.com/lk23zlj*, Pinger *http://tinyurl.com/nxncw3b*, SMS Text Messaging *http://tinyurl.com/7gbgn54*, TextSecure *http://tinyurl.com/9pyr3kw*, Tango *http://tinyurl.com/8nswhdw*

**School-based messaging systems**: Kikutext *http://kikutext.com*, WeTxt *http://www.wetxt.com*, Remind101 *https://www.remind101.com*, Sendhub *https://www.sendhub.com*, Class Pager *https://www.classpager.com*

Most of these apps provide free texting that save students money compared to their cell phone texting plans. You or your students can also use these apps to send texts to groups created within the app, which is particularly helpful when you want to send a text to all students in your class. The free Text Me! app provides free, unlimited texting in the US, Canada, and 40 counties, as well as the ability to send and receive pictures, voice, and video messages, as well as phone calls into one's voicemail. At the same time, one limitation of some of these apps is that everyone in one's audience needs to also have the same app in order to receive a message.

There are also school-based messaging systems such as Kikutext, WeTxt, Remind101, Sendhub, and Class Pager for teachers, administrators, counselors, parents, and/or students to communicate with students and parents. You can also use apps such as Google Voice to send audio messages or iOS *http://tinyurl.com/7v7klxw* and Android *http://tinyurl.com/lemoepk* Tom's Messenger to record audio messages that appear as talking animation characters speaking the message. For sending messages to his students or parents, Richard Byrne (2012) describes how teachers use Class Pager *https://www.classpager.com* to send text messages to students without revealing cell phone numbers. Teachers obtain a code to give to students and parents so that when they text the code, they are then added to the class roster so that they then receive the teacher's texts.

Because many students rely primarily on texting to communicate, you may find that texting may be the most effective way to communicate with students about academic matters. And, students may be more comfortable texting you as their teacher rather than calling or e-mailing regarding questions they have about completing assignments or scheduling issues.

Students can use texting/IMing apps to pose questions to their peers or teachers, as well as provide summaries of their readings, viewings, or discussions. For example, at the end of a class, students can text to you what they learned in the class, providing you with a sense of what students gained from your class.

You can also have students use texting itself as a means of playing with language and reflecting on these playful uses of language. Students can create texts that involve inventive uses of language and words, for example, creating novel acronyms or abbreviations for longer words (Trubek, 2012). Students can also use texting as a form of note-taking and sharing notes; they can also imagine how characters would text each other (Trubek, 2012).

### Concerns About Texting

When students first began to employ texting there was a lot of concern that texting would undermine the quality of their writing—that their use of texting acronyms would adversely influence their spelling and syntax. However, more recent research disproves these potentially negative effects, finding that texting may actually improve students' literacy practices associated with traditional reading and writing practices (Trubek, 2012). One study of younger children found a positive correlation between their texting and their reading, spelling, and phonological processing (Wood, Jackson, Hart, Plester, & Wilde, 2011).

On the other hand, another study of 228 sixth-to-eighth-graders found a negative relationship between the students' use of techspeak in text messages and scores on a grammar assessment (Cingel & Sundar, 2012). "Word adaptations" were negatively related to grammar scores, while "structural adaptations" were found to not be negatively related to grammar scores, suggesting that it is the use of shortened words/acronyms that may have a negative influence on grammar use.

One related concern is that students would use texting conventions in their writing in school. However, a study conducted at City University, London found that students are able to code-switch between use of texting for informal social purposes and their formal, academic writing (Rowan, 2011). That is, they were able to switch between texting conventions and more formal writing conventions. To highlight the importance of code-switching between informal and formal contexts, you can discuss with students how they use different types of language for different purposes and audiences.

## Apps for Written Chat Discussions

While synchronous discussions can be appealing in terms of engaging in real-time chat, there are a number of advantages for use of asynchronous written chat versus synchronous discussions. A survey of students who employed both preferred the asynchronous because it gave them more time to reflect on their contributions or conduct research on a topic before responding so that they could participate at their own pace (Bali & Meier, 2014). As one student noted:

> I like not feeling pressured to communicate right away—I like to have processing time and feel as though I can come back to the conversation later and still participate. It helps me to be more thoughtful. (p. 212)

And, students who are not fluent in English perceive synchronous discussions as more constraining. Also, it is often less difficult to obtain transcripts from asynchronous discussions to create a written record of students' discussions for use in formative assessment of students' discussion practices as well as having them use these records for their own e-portfolio self-assessing.

### Micro-blogging and Twitter

As also noted in Chapter 6, students can use micro-blogging apps such as Edmodo, Tumblr, Posterous, or Plurk as well as Twitter apps: Twitter,

TweetCaster, Tweetbot, Tweetdeck, Twitteriffic, or HootSuite to engage students in asynchronous discussions. These micro-blogs include features designed to foster this dialogic interaction. For example, Tumblr includes the Submissions feature that allows student writers to invite readers to contribute their own material, so that the writer becomes more of a curator of material based on these reader contributions. Students can also use Tumblr to "re-blog" material from others' Tumblr's posts, fostering intertextual connections between posts. Posterous is particularly useful for sharing images on iPhone or Android phones.

## Facebook

Given students' familiarity with Facebook, you can use the iOS *http://tinyurl. com/cww4omf*, Android *http://tinyurl.com/6qzn4y4*, or Chrome OS *http://tinyurl. com/kv6v2e4* Facebook apps for conducting discussions. To avoid students' access to your own personal Facebook account, it is important to distinguish between academic and personal uses of Facebook. We recommend setting up a separate account in your role as teacher and then "friending" only students in your current classes to have them join your classroom account. You should also make sure that students know how to limit your access to their personal pages so that you are not accessing their personal information or photos. Students can then post their responses to discussion prompts and react to each other's posts.

In responding to novels or historical events, students can adopt the roles of characters or historical figures and create profiles based on these characters or historical figures, creating what James Gee (2007) defines as a "projective identity." Students can then conduct discussions adopting these profiles. You can have students reflect on how their postings differ in terms of their uses of language, persona, purpose, and sense of audience in postings on their Inbox, Status updates, Wall posting, and Live chats (Hawley & Golden, 2011). They can also reflect on differences between their postings on Facebook and how they communicate via phone, e-mail, texting, Twitter, or face-to-face communication, as well as differences in how they communicate with different Facebook friends (Hawley & Golden, 2011).

A survey of teachers' attitudes on uses of social media in the classroom found that while 47% believed that participation in social media can enhance learning, 80% expressed concerns about conflicts in using it in terms of potential conflicts with parents, in that 69% believed that parents use social media to monitor students' lives (Hendee, 2014).

Currently, four out of five teachers report using social media on a personal level, yet 55% of those surveyed said they have not integrated social media into their classroom and have no plans to do so.

## Setting Guidelines for Participating in Online Discussions

In using discussion apps, it is important to set some guidelines for students' participating in discussions in ways that are supportive versus detrimental to open, safe exchange of ideas. Most districts have established guidelines for responsible use of online social media that include "netiquette" norms for engaging in respectful online discussions. For example, the New York City Department of Education (2013) released a social media code of conduct *http://tinyurl.com/n343e5o* that recommends that students consider the impact of their digital footprint on their perceived reputation, assuming responsibility for their posted content, gaining advice from others on the difference between public versus private posting, applying classroom norms to academic uses of social media, reflecting on posts prior to posting, accepting only posts from people they know, adjusting their privacy settings, and recognizing and reporting instances of cyberbullying. For example, the Guidelines note the need for students to reflect on their online posts in terms of any potential impact of those posts on their peers:

- When you use social media for academic purposes, such as for a school assignment, treat the platform as a digital extension of your classroom—the same rules apply online as they do at school. For example, if you would not make fun of a classmate in English class, do not do it online either.
- Once a comment is posted online, you cannot later say, "never mind." It may seem funny or harmless when you post it, but it could hurt or offend someone. As guidance, take a few extra minutes to think about whether a post will be hurtful or embarrassing or whether it could negatively affect a future opportunity. (p. 5)

And, for further information about responsible use of the Internet related to digital literacy, Common Sense Media has issued iBooks: *Digital Literacy & Citizenship Student Workbook: Grades 6–8* and *Digital Literacy & Citizenship Student Workbook: Grades 9–12*: *https://itunes.com/commonsensemedia*.

## Apps Combining Face-to-Face and Online Discussions

There are a number of useful apps that can combine face-to-face and online discussions so that students can view their written chat contributions on a screen, whiteboard, or their own device.

### Interactive Whiteboards

You and/or your students can also actively share thoughts and ideas as well as images, texts, or videos using interactive whiteboard apps listed below that allow you and your students to use their tablets as whiteboards in any place in the class-room for sharing of images/Flash media or texts. The fact that you or your students can move around in the classroom using their tablets enhances the tablets' affordances in terms of mobility and interactivity, mitigating the limitations of the traditional classroom physical setting.

---

## INTERACTIVE WHITEBOARD APPS

**iOS**: Splashtop Whiteboard *http://tinyurl.com/mly9zar*, Study Hall *http://tinyurl.com/kynjltr*, Doceri Interactive Whiteboard *http://tinyurl.com/kmmnkyw*, Groupboard Collaborative Whiteboard *http://tinyurl.com/m6a8cyh*, SyncPad *http://tinyurl.com/kdphbk2*

**Android**: Splashtop Whiteboard *http://tinyurl.com/mxm262u*, Groupboard *http://tinyurl.com/lv9t3xf*, Share Your Board *http://tinyurl.com/mgdhnhx*, Whiteboard *http://tinyurl.com/mamcdef*, LiveBoard Lite *http://tinyurl.com/m6a8cyh*, Study Hall *http://tinyurl.com/l65moo6*

---

You can also project your desktop computer's window for students, for example, using the Splashtop Streamer feature of Splashtop Whiteboard. Then you or your students can use these apps to add annotations or draw on images or texts using different colors, further fostering interactions with images or texts. For example, as you are walking around the room with your iPad, you can draw on an image as you are talking about that image.

You can also use the iPad bundled app, Air Display, or Splashtop Remote Desktop 2 *http://tinyurl.com/l3erh2o* app to project your iPad screen to the entire class using an LCD projector (Fryer, 2011) as well as the Android *http://tinyurl.com/mq5ghe8* Splashtop Remote Desktop 2 app for use with Android devices. You can also use the iOS Ask3 app that transforms students' individual iPads into recordable whiteboards so that they can interact with you and peers through sharing their thoughts and drawings using their iPads.

### Interactive Presentation Apps

To foster student interaction with your presentation material, you can employ the interactive whiteboard apps noted above as well as interactive presentation browser apps so that students are actively responding to presentations projected to their devices or a whiteboard using annotations or drawing.

## INTERACTIVE PRESENTATION APPS

**iOS**: Ask3 *http://tinyurl.com/d45ovze*, Doceri *http://tinyurl.com/kmmnkyw*, Celly *http://tinyurl.com/mnsh8mk*, Socrative *http://tinyurl.com/n4vgbym*, MimeoMobile *http://tinyurl.com/lj2zom2*, InkToGo *http://tinyurl.com/l6dhn9j*, Presentation Link *http://tinyurl.com/n2qcq6d*, Xaxier Presentations *http://tinyurl.com/n67eybe*, Slideidea *http://tinyurl.com/mnuzay4*, Display-Note *http://tinyurl.com/k34psxs*, NearPod *http://tinyurl.com/bjuh45l*

**Android**: Celly *http://tinyurl.com/mjjuuqq*, Socrative *http://tinyurl.com/c5ettwo*, DisplayNote *http://tinyurl.com/lz2jjr2*, IncStagePresenter *http://tinyurl.com/m9facnh*, NearPod *http://tinyurl.com/lk8qrth*

These apps let you include questions or prompts for discussion in your Keynote/PowerPoint presentations or your videos, images, or texts so that students can respond to these questions or prompts. With these apps, students can take notes linked to certain slides or pose questions to you. These apps therefore position students to adopt an active rather than passive role in responding to your presentations, so that you go beyond just presenting information to building in activities designed to foster students adopting an active role in a discussion. Some of these apps such as the iOS InkToGo app let you record your presentations to create a video for students to view outside of class.

### Clicker Apps

You can also employ clicker apps including Socrative Teacher Clicker and Socrative Student Clicker, eClicker, eClicker Client, QuestionPress, iClicker, or Turning Point Response Card to have students share their open-ended responses to questions by using their phones or devices. You can use these apps to have students provide answers to open-ended questions, respond to multiple-choice questions, or engage in games involving responses to questions; these apps then generate summary reports for your use.

### Opinion Survey/Polling Apps

To foster discussions based on sharing students' attitudes or beliefs about certain topics or issues, you can employ opinion survey or polling apps. Given some limitations to the clicker apps noted above, particularly the cost, one alternative to buying a clicker system is to simply use one of the free opinion survey/response apps listed below to create your own set of choices for students to select.

## OPINION SURVEY/POLLING APPS

**iOS**: Polldaddy *http://tinyurl.com/kc5noss*, Show of Hands *http://tinyurl.com/qdt85tu*, Vote Kiosk *http://tinyurl.com/maw45el*, QuickTapSurvey *http://tinyurl.com/nwox7hh*, Toluna *http://tinyurl.com/kbsz6px*, Survey Pocket *http://tinyurl.com/mnwzl2m*, Survey.com Mobile *http://tinyurl.com/lbk6d9s*

**Android**: Smart Poll *http://tinyurl.com/ma4ypxe*, Polling *http://tinyurl.com/ltwvugd*, Push Poll *http://tinyurl.com/kbk3679*, Poll It! *http://tinyurl.com/mdj97y5*, Poll App *http://tinyurl.com/mgv82ef*, Lets Poll *http://tinyurl.com/k3ttfa2*, Pollion Survey App *http://tinyurl.com/k4vcdk8*, Survey.com Mobile *http://tinyurl.com/lxgubcz*, Survey *http://tinyurl.com/mmvvslh*

By asking students their opinions about certain positions or provocative statements, you can then project the results to the class and have students discuss reasons for those results. For example, you may ask students in a social studies class to indicate on a scale from 1 to 6 whether they agree with the statement, "negative attack ads serve to provide useful information for voters," resulting in students viewing results as a bar graph. You can also use Google Moderator *http://tinyurl.com/27e7tta* to have students pose questions or topics and then determine which questions or topics most interest them for further discussion, something that can be particularly useful for guest speakers in a class.

### Backchannel Interactions

You can also have students use backchannel Web apps such as TodaysMeet *https://todaysmeet.com*, GoSoapBox *http://www.gosoapbox.com*, or BackChannel *http://backchannel.us*, as well as the iOS Backchannel Chat *http://tinyurl.com/kg5z9pf* or Android Backchannel *http://tinyurl.com/m7z55jx* apps, as well as micro-blogs or Twitter to post responses to presentations, discussions, viewings, debates, or activities that are then projected to the entire class (Atkinson, 2009). Backchannel responses provide students who may be reluctant to publicly voice their responses to share those responses to the class. They also provide students with some sense of the variety of alternative responses given differences in students' beliefs, knowledge, and experiences, leading students to appreciate their peers' ability as learners.

### Using Apps to Foster Discussions of Shared Images

You can stimulate discussions by having students share discussion response to images or photos, something we discuss in more detail in the next chapter on using images to learn. Students can use the iOS *http://tinyurl.com/b4ytl47* or Android *http://tinyurl.com/bov5nq2* Instagram as well as the iOS *http://tinyurl.com/dycxr59* or Android *http://tinyurl.com/7r3mla7* Flickr apps to share their photos along with comments or annotations/drawings on their images. Focusing students' attention on discussing the same images encourages collaborative reactions to images, leading them to compare and contrast their perspectives on those images.

## VoiceThread

One of the more popular iOS apps is the *http://tinyurl.com/lujk7fs* VoiceThread app, as well as the Ed.VoiceThread *http://tinyurl.com/meprxqq* browser education version of VoiceThread for use in schools (the cost is $15.00 a month for up to 50 students or $60.00 a year). One advantage of using Ed.VoiceThread is that students' individual accounts can be retained throughout the students' academic careers.

Students use VoiceThread to engage in collaborative audio discussions or text annotations to a slideshow of images or video for posting on the Web. Students can import images or video into VoiceThread directly from Flickr or from an iPad or desktop. They can then click on the audio button to record annotations or write their annotations. Students can also draw on the image or video as they are commenting. Peers, parents, and/or teachers can comment on the same image. Hence, VoiceThread serves to foster collaborative discussion by focusing different students', parents', and or teachers' comments on a specific image or video, resulting in multiple, often quite different perspectives on the same visual artifact. When students are exposed to a range of alternative interpretations, this can lead them to rethink their own interpretations.

To illustrate the use of VoiceThread to foster discussions, we cite the example of students (identified with pseudonyms; students gave permission to use their work) in Laura Kretschmar's fifth-grade classes at Lighthouse Community Charter School, Oakland, California, who created VoiceThread productions on their iPads on the extinction of the dinosaurs. Laura describes this four-day activity:

> These projects were framed as Scientific Arguments that address the question: What caused the extinction of the dinosaurs 50 million years ago? Students read three different articles from which they framed their claims. The three focus areas were: (1) supernova, (2) volcanic eruption, and (3) asteroid. Students viewed each others' VoiceThreads and offered critiques through the comments feature (most used either text or voice comments).

Students in Laura's class used their VoiceThread productions to collect images related to alternative causes of the dinosaur extinction—whether the extinction was caused by an exploding supernova star, a volcanic eruption, or an asteroid. As Laura has described, they viewed each other's VoiceThreads and offered critique through the comments feature. They also put their VoiceThreads up on a website that was shared with parents during their Fall open house to showcase students' projects.

In this activity, based on their reading about one of these three causes, students then created their VoiceThreads to argue for that cause as being the primary cause. And, they could also challenge claims by their peers advocating for alternative causes. So, in defending their claim that the supernova was the primary cause, they could refute claims that a volcano or asteroid were the primary causes. Being aware of their peers' alternative, competing claims served to motivate students to provide evidence supporting the validity of their particular claim. The fact that students were working collaboratively in creating their VoiceThreads served to benefit individual students. Each student brought their own perspectives, ideas, and knowledge to their work, resulting in the students playing off of each other's perspectives, ideas, and knowledge.

## Students' VoiceThread Discussions

The following are examples of students' VoiceThread discussions illustrating how they were using literacy practices associated with discussion to learn. We provide you some of the key images they included in the presentations, along with descriptions of those images.

We also note how the students argued their positions for certain causes of the dinosaur extinction—the asteroids, supernova, and/or volcanoes—as well as refuting claims for certain causes made by their peers. In doing so, students were employing the disciplinary literacy of thinking like scientists who weigh evidence and counter-evidence to support their claims. (Note: Viewing these students' VoiceTheads requires that VoiceThread is downloaded on an iPad or computer with a VoiceThread account; to view specific VoiceThreads, sign into that account.)

Jessica and Katherine *http://voicethread.com/share/2454743* posited that volcanoes were the primary cause of the dinosaurs' extinction, using the image of a volcano (Figure 7.1) to illustrate their position:

> Volcanic eruptions caused dinosaur extinction because dust and ash went to the atmosphere which made the temperatures go down and the dinosaurs couldn't survive, further evidence that a volcanic eruption happened 65 million years ago. What caused extinction was a layer of iridium. The iridium came from the dust and air.

Miguel and German *http://voicethread.com/#q.b2545650.i13501639* posited that the cause of the dinosaurs extinction was a supernova; they included an image of an exploding supernova (Figure 7.2): "The supernova caused the dinosaur extinction because when a supernova happens, iridium dust and radiation goes

**FIGURE 7.1**    Students' VoiceThread: Volcanoes as the Cause of Dinosaur Extinction

*Source:* Reprinted with permission from Katherine Carreon and Jessica Chavarria.

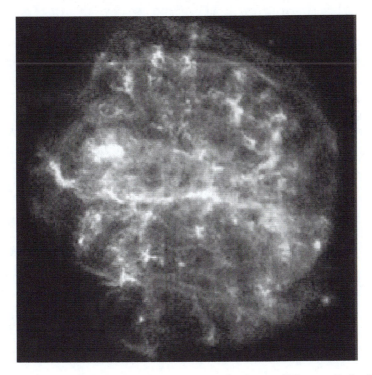

**FIGURE 7.2**    Students' VoiceThread: Supernova as the Cause of Dinosaur Extinction

*Source:* Reprinted with permission from Miguel Cuevas and German Romero.

out to space. The radiation then made it to the earth's atmosphere and so did the iridium."

Melanie and Cassandra *http://voicethread.com/share/2454752* (Figure 7.3) made their argument for an asteroid as the primary cause of the extinction. They noted that "our evidence is that when the asteroid hit the earth it caused high waves and destroyed plants and trees. This contact killed dinosaurs. Other evidence is the iridium layer because the asteroid carries a lot of iridium."

Given the fact that students were viewing each others' VoiceThreads, they were exposed to competing claims regarding explanations for the dinosaur extinction, leading them to formulate counter-arguments, as reflected in Anthony and Martina's critique of the claim for the supernova as the primary cause: "that other species on the earth would have died."

## Second/World Language Learning

One challenge for engaging students in online discussion is that a sizable number of students are English language learners (ELLs) who may be struggling with their use of English to contribute to discussions. These students often need highly individualized assistance in learning English, particularly to engage in meaningful practice in using English. Rather than simply learning vocabulary, students also need opportunities to employ English in contexts in which they are using language to achieve a certain goal, for example, requesting or sharing information on how to do something. To assist these students, you can provide them with instruction or work with ESL/ELL instructors using English

**FIGURE 7.3** Students' VoiceThread: Asteroid as the Cause of Dinosaur Extinction

*Source:* Reprinted with permission from Melanie Solano and Cassandra Becerra.

language learning apps designed to help students learn English or other world languages through English vocabulary/syntax instruction, as well as activities involving students in use of English.

### Apps for Second Language Learners

For working with second language learners, there are a variety of different apps designed for use in ELL/ESL instruction; for other resources see *http://tinyurl. com/lldfxb7*. These apps provide students with activities for practicing language proficiency, as well as teacher resources. One advantage of these apps is that they scaffold students' language practice within social conversational contexts so that students practice their language use on their own, but within a meaningful context facilitating language use.

---

## APPS TO ASSIST ELL STUDENTS

**iOS**: HGP 2.0 *http://tinyurl.com/kt2a447*, Hello English *http://tinyurl.com/ lltwuc3*, Basic Pronunciation: Clear Speech from the Start *http://tinyurl.com/ lltwuc3*, Beginner English *http://tinyurl.com/lewebvp*, Everyday English *http:// tinyurl.com/lghnmwh*, English is Easy *http://tinyurl.com/n67en92*, MyWord-Book2 *http://tinyurl.com/meznzuf*, Speaking Pal English Tutor *http://tinyurl. com/ptn3q5t*, Learn English Grammar *http://tinyurl.com/lhxs3dq*, Pocket English (ESL) *http://tinyurl.com/n7p9bo9*, Learn American English *http://tinyurl. com/lkb72js*

**Android**: English Training *http://tinyurl.com/lja5qs7*, Speak English *http:// tinyurl.com/kbtchrx*, Fluent English *http://tinyurl.com/kvswf2k*, Learn English Speaking *http://tinyurl.com/lg59cg5*, Learn English *http://tinyurl.com/ ms2rty7*, MyWordBook2 *http://tinyurl.com/meybvdg*, Learning English Speaking *http://tinyurl.com/lucd47l*, Learn and Play English *http://tinyurl.com/ lsotsxa*, English Lessons *http://tinyurl.com/kbpxcfp*, American English *http:// tinyurl.com/le3y32w*

**Chrome OS**: English Vocabulary *http://tinyurl.com/lh3l9kp*, Learn English *http://tinyurl.com/mvxdmza*, Language Games: English *http://tinyurl.com/ ku8mzg2*

---

The iOS HGPlus app includes the ability to create a personalized dictionary for storing vocabulary; personalized flashcards for practicing vocabulary; access to podcasts, websites, and worksheets with language learning activities, as well as a handwriting and notes feature for practice writing English (go to *http://www.*

*hagipod.com* for these resources). And, students can record their own or others' presentations for listening to English language use.

Also, ELL/ESL students can employ translation apps listed below to assist them in acquiring English. The fact that they can dictate their thoughts in their primary language and then read or hear the translation of that language supports their translation learning. While it could be argued that students need to learn to translate on their own, use of translation apps serves to support them by providing examples of translations. Because they can test out their language proficiency by dictating in English and reviewing the audio or written English translation, students can then self-assess their translation abilities. Students can also use translation apps in studying world languages to determine their translation abilities.

---

## TRANSLATION APPS

**iOS:** Google Translate *http://tinyurl.com/3gspfvf*, Translator with Voice *http://tinyurl.com/yautdfx*, Communilator Free *http://tinyurl.com/mmbnfon*, Odyssey Translator *http://odysseytranslator.com*, iTranslate *http://tinyurl.com/kp6trxy*, Vocre Translate *http://tinyurl.com/mr7kts7*, Vocal Interpreter Pro *http://tinyurl.com/lten62d*, Universal Translator *http://tinyurl.com/kcoovuv*, Lonely Planet FastTalk *http://tinyurl.com/ls5neqn*, gTranslate *http://tinyurl.com/kqvcd6x*, Ultralingua *http://tinyurl.com/kz8dgy*, Jibbigo Voice Translator *http://tinyurl.com/kc7fd45*

**Android:** Google Translate *http://tinyurl.com/bhkkcnw*, Jibbigo Translator 2.0 *http://tinyurl.com/kdrh2tw*, Translator Speak & Translate *http://tinyurl.com/mcnjy3s*, Voice Translator *http://tinyurl.com/klbhzlw*, Universal Translator *http://tinyurl.com/kkaleqt*, Free Translator *http://tinyurl.com/mul8fln*, MacDroid Translator *http://tinyurl.com/kpclfno*, Talking Translator *http://tinyurl.com/lpj57m9*, Voice Interpreter *http://tinyurl.com/kd483k8*

**Chrome OS:** Translator *http://tinyurl.com/bhkkcnw*

---

These apps can therefore help ELL students by assisting them in translating their native language into English. Students can also translate their overall documents into a different language, for example, writing in Spanish and then translating that document into English. In using Google Translate, students select one of 58 languages for both their own language and the language for which they want a translation. They can then record or type in their own language, also using Word or PDF files (to save a plain text files), and then they receive a written translation; for most languages, they can also listen to an audio translation. Students can also use this app to translate their own or others' written documents. Once their document is uploaded to Google Docs, students can select the Translate Document from the Tools menu, identify the name of the document, choose the language that the document will be translated into, and then the document will be translated. From the File menu, they then select Download and select PDF to download the file to their computer. They then use Google Docs to translate and save that file as a PDF file (as opposed to just a plain text file in Google Translate) (Eswarlu, 2011).

## World Language Learning Apps

There are also numerous world language learning apps for learning world languages, for example, the Learn Languages for Free: English, French, Spanish, German, Italian, Portuguese, Polish, Russian, Turkish, Japanese, Chinese *http://tinyurl.com/kxv65b3* app. We list apps for learning Spanish and Chinese below.

---

## WORLD LANGUAGE LEARNING APPS

### Spanish

**iOS**: iSpeak Spanish *http://tinyurl.com/lvfltbc*, Learn Spanish *http://tinyurl.com/lpwzcgg*, Spanish Living Language *http://tinyurl.com/mpppz5k*, Learning Spanish Free *http://tinyurl.com/nyg9xha*, Learn Spanish Quick *http://tinyurl.com/lsbu9nz*, Spanish Conversation HD *http://tinyurl.com/mpqtxpd*, Learn Spanish 24/7 *http://tinyurl.com/mmjemra*

**Android**: Learning Spanish *http://tinyurl.com/k2rutn9*, Learn Spanish with Babbel *http://tinyurl.com/lnwswjh*, Learn Spanish Easy Talk *http://tinyurl.com/k89e29e*, Interactive Spanish *http://tinyurl.com/n46lol9*, RightNow Spanish Conversation *http://tinyurl.com/k4ezxyj*

### Chinese (Mandarin)

**iOS**: Learn Chinese (Mandarin) *http://tinyurl.com/lubvwrk*, Chinese Mandarin Course *http://tinyurl.com/msx3wym*, uTalk Classic Learn Chinese *http://tinyurl.com/k3oowar*, Learn Chinese Free *http://tinyurl.com/mul7n8t*

**Android**: Learn Chinese *http://tinyurl.com/knhcebb*, Learn Chinese Phrases *http://tinyurl.com/mbtseqa*, Learn Chinese Mandarin Madness *http://tinyurl.com/n88xkwh*, RightNow Chinese Conversation *http://tinyurl.com/kklpc73*, Free Mandarin Chinese *http://tinyurl.com/lrys7f9*

---

For example, students can use the iSpeak Spanish app for translating audio and written texts from English to Spanish as well as Spanish to English using Google

Translate. Students can cut and paste materials from documents to enter into the app, a feature that is useful for writing papers. Students can enter in text to the app, select Translate, then hear the translation, and then save the translation to their device.

## Summary

In this chapter, we described the use of a range of different kinds of apps for fostering online discussions, including ways of sharing responses to images or presentations, as well as apps for supporting language learning. We provided an example of students' use of the VoiceThread app for engaging in collaborative science inquiry in response to images. In the next chapter, we provide some other examples of the use of image apps for engaging students in learning.

## References

Atkinson, C. (2009). *The backchannel: How audiences are using Twitter and social media and changing presentations forever.* Berkeley, CA: New Riders Press.

Bali, B., & Meier, B. (2014, March 4). An affinity for asynchronous learning. *Hybrid Pedagogy*. Retrieved from http://tinyurl.com/og8lmq7

Berger, P., & Trexler, S. (2010). *Choosing Web 2.0 tools for learning and teaching in a digital world.* Santa Barbara, CA: Libraries Unlimited.

Bowen, W. G., Chingos, M. M., Lack, K. A., & Nygren, T. I. (2012, May 22). Interactive learning online at public universities: Evidence from randomized trials. New York: Ithaka S+R. Retrieved from http://tinyurl.com/7j79rls

Briner, C. (2011, December 10). Making math and science relevant with online discussions. Presentation at the TIES Conference, Minneapolis, Minnesota. Retrieved from http://www.collaborizeclassroom.com/blog/bringing-math-and-science-to-life-with-blended-learning

Byrne, R. (2012, December 29). 7 ways to send group texts to parents and students [Web log post]. Retrieved from http://tinyurl.com/d37vxb2

Cingel, D. P., & Sundar, S. (2012). Texting, techspeak, and tweens: The relationship between text messaging and English grammar skills. *New Media & Society, 14*(8), 1304–1320.

Council of Chief State School Officers and National Governors' Association. (2010). *Common Core State Standards for English Language Arts & Literacy in History/Social Studies, Science, and Technical Subjects.* Washington, DC: Author. Retrieved from http://www.corestandards.org

Dredger, K., Woods, D., Beach, C., & Sagstetter, V. (2010). Engage me: Using new literacies to create third space classrooms that engage student writers. *Journal of Media Literacy Education, 2*(2), 85–101.

Eswarlu, V. (2011, September 11). Translate PDF files & Word documents with Google Docs [Web log post]. Retrieved from http://tinyurl.com/3ch53cn

Freeberg, A. (2014, February 6). Virtual field trips take students into the labs [Web log post]. Retrieved from http://tinyurl.com/mbya9vo

Fryer, W. (2011, March 24). iPad as an interactive white board for $5 or $10 [Web log post]. Retrieved from http://tinyurl.com/6zbypjc

Gee, J. P. (2007). *What video games have to teach us about learning and literacy*. New York: Palgrave MacMillan.

Hawley, M., & Golden, J. (2011). How did that get on my Facebook page? Understanding voice, audience, and purpose on social networking sites. In M. T. Christel & S. Sullivan (Eds.), *Lesson plans for developing digital literacies* (pp. 21–31). Urbana, IL: National Council of Teachers of English.

Hendee, C. (2014, February 11). Teachers have mixed feelings on using social media in classrooms. *Denver Business Journal*. Retrieved from http://tinyurl.com/kelxd7y

Lenhart, A. (2012, March 19). *Teens, smartphones & texting*. Washington, DC: Pew Research Center Internet and American Life Project. Retrieved from http://pewinternet.org/Reports/2012/Teens-and-smartphones.aspx

Luckerson, V. (2013, December 30). Oh, snap! How photo messages would make texting obsolete. *Time Magazine*, 18, 19. Retrieved from http://tinyurl.com/kgtpo64

New York City Department of Education (2013, Fall). *Social media use guidelines*. Author. Retrieved from http://tinyurl.com/n343e5o

Nielsen Survey. (2010, October 14). US teen mobile report: Calling yesterday, texting today, using apps tomorrow. Author. Retrieved from http://tinyurl.com/32h5go6

Rowan, A. (2011, July 1). How texting helps pupils with their textbooks. *The Telegraph*. Retrieved from http://www.telegraph.co.uk/education/expateducation/8596454/How-texting-helps-pupils-with-their-textbooks.html

Speicher, S., & Walthour, J. (2013, May 11). Subtext iPad app: Collaborative reading made easy. Edina, MN: Minnesota Google Summit. Retrieved from https://docs.google.com/document/d/1ebYMFGWcJh3YrwjucirQe00DrsK62Gwq9J7aAgEAW-w/pub

Trubek, A. (2012). Txting 2 lrn. *Instructor*, Spring issue, 49–51.

Wood, C., Jackson, E., Hart, L., Plester, B., & Wilde, L. (2011). The effect of text messaging on 9- and 10-year-old children's reading, spelling and phonological processing skills. *Journal of Computer Assisted Learning*, 27(1), 28–36.

# 8

# USING APPS TO RESPOND TO AND PRODUCE IMAGES

In this chapter, we describe the uses of photo/image apps to foster learning in the classroom. Students are already using digital images to engage in multimodal learning that integrates the images with print text, audio, and music; they commonly use drawing or photo-editing apps to represent and communicate meaning. They also use their iOS and Android devices to take and display brilliant photos and other images, and then edit, share, and comment on them using a range of different apps.

Using images in the class can serve to enhance learning. Students are more likely to understand concepts or ideas if they have visual representations of those concepts or ideas; we can also assume that sometimes images are more engaging than print text. For example, in studying cell mutations in biology, when students see visual images of those cell mutations, the students are more likely to understand the concept of mutations with high-quality images used in conjunction with a well-designed lesson.

Students can use images to:

- communicate concepts or ideas to engage their audiences through visual rhetoric;
- create a visual record of classroom/athletic events, field trips, experiments, or their work for sharing with peers and parents on websites, blogs, or digital newsletters; they can enhance audience engagement with their presentations by embedding images;
- present images as graphs or charts for presenting empirical data in all disciplines involving data analysis;
- embed images in the blog posts, websites, or e-books to illustrate their ideas and experiences.

There are an almost infinite number of ways images can be used in learning across the curriculum. For example, students can respond to a research report that includes graphs showing the linear relationship between adolescents' uses of cell phones/ texting and automobile accidents. To interpret these graphs, students need to know how to focus on the graphs' lines relative to the idea of these relationships. And, in creating their own images to communicate information or ideas, students need to know how to translate information or ideas into nonlinguistic representations.

This transformation into nonlinguistic representations requires that students first specify and clarify the meanings of the information or ideas they want to communicate to determine what images will best represent these meanings. For example, in creating a slide presentation on the relationships between poor urban neighborhoods and murder rates in their city, students decided to employ a map showing circles indicating high murder rates that also happen to occur in the poorest neighborhoods of their city. And, when students used images to convey information or ideas, they also needed to be able to explain how and why they chose particular images to convey that information or those ideas. Students created a children's e-book, searching for an appropriate image for the book cover that would convey the overall storyline and theme. Having to explain how and why they selected a particular image required that they inferred their book's storyline and theme.

In addition to using images to communicate, students also need to know how to analyze and respond critically to images of advertising, flyers, posters, CD/ book covers, billboards, and brand icons, which are increasingly used as forms of visual rhetoric to appeal to audiences to promote certain products, ideas, or people; for more on visual rhetoric see *http://tinyurl.com/c5ott4f*.

All of this reflects the importance of students understanding the meaning of images as central to students' lives. Semiotics theory shows that multimodal meaning is leaning increasingly toward the visual and away from print (Kress & Van Leeuwen, 2006). Semiotics is concerned with signs and how they are used to convey meaning within a social system or culture (social semiotics)—not only specific intended, everyday signs, but things that can be taken for signs, things that represent meaning within our social lives (Chandler, 2007). Included within this general category are not only intentionally constructed signs like road signs but also a range of objects like print, images, architecture, dress, and even enactments like performances.

## English Language Arts Common Core State Standards Related to Using Images to Learn

There are a number of different Common Core State Standards (Council of Chief State Schools Officers and National Governors' Association, 2010) that involve the ability to employ images to learn:

* Synthesize and apply information presented in diverse ways (e.g., through words, images, graphs, and video) via print and digital sources in order to answer questions, solve problems, or compare modes of presentation (reading standard). (p. 39)

- Integrate and evaluate information from multiple oral, visual, or multimodal sources in order to answer questions, solve problems, or build knowledge (speaking and listening standard). (p. 49)
- Use technology, including the Internet, to produce, publish, and interact with others about writing (writing standard). (p. 42)
- Gather relevant information from multiple print and digital sources, assess the credibility and accuracy of each source, and integrate and cite the information while avoiding plagiarism (writing standard). (p. 42)
- Make strategic use of digital media and visual displays of data to express information and enhance understanding (speaking and listening standard). (p. 49)

Addressing these standards through the use of images involves students knowing how to identify the specific, relevant information or ideas represented by images (Marzano, 2010).

## Fostering Visual Literacies Through App Affordances

There are many apps that include collections of images designed to enhance learning in all subjects. Students in science classes can use apps to analyze images of chemical reactions, outer space, frogs for dissection, and water pollution. Students in social studies can use apps to capture and analyze historical photography and maps. Students in math can use apps to create and analyze graphs and figures presenting data. Students in English language arts can use apps to create and analyze images in their writing, graphic novels/comics, literature, and media.

Students in art classes draw or paint images or take and edit photos as well as analyze artwork; for more on activities employing images to foster learning see *http://tinyurl.com/7v7kdv9*.

To exploit the visual affordances of apps, students need to be able to employ visual literacies associated with understanding and producing images. A primary visual literacy involves multimodal production that transforms print-based communication through the use of visual or aural digital tools to create multimodal texts. Understanding these visual literacies involves understanding how an image of an object, artifact, or phenomenon conveys meaning differently than a verbal description of an object, artifact, or phenomena. Gunther Kress notes that an image conveys meaning through:

> limited potential of space, which is very different from the chronology and sequence of speech. For example, a science teacher talks about, say, a simple thing like a cell, and she asks the child, "Tell me something about a cell." This child may say, "Oh, ah, Miss, the cell has a nucleus." Then if she says to the child, "Well, go and draw it on the board," we have a very different question. Now the child has to say, "How big is the nucleus? Where in the cell is the nucleus? Is it a dot? Is it a circle?" (Harste & Kress, 2012, p. 209)

Kress (2009) also notes that students are now much more focused on responding to and producing multimodal texts

> that are no longer simply written and that are not necessarily linear, but are modular. For example, children visit a website to *do*—to enter it as she or he would like—and they have very different practices of engaging. (p. 211)

The fact that they are more engaged in multimodal texts outside of the classroom means that learning in the classroom also needs to be multimodal, while, at the same time, fostering critical responses to images.

In responding to and producing websites or multimodal texts, students therefore need to attend to their design and how images in these texts are designed to evoke certain meanings. All of this points to the importance of students understanding visual design—how images are designed to engage and communicate information and ideas to audiences. Effective visual design considers how images are selected, combined, organized, arranged, and presented in ways that appeal to audiences. For example, a well-designed magazine ad may place an appealing image on the left side of the page to attract an audience's attention and then a product or brand icon on the right side of the page so that the audience shifts their initial focus to that product or brand icon; for more on visual design see *http://tinyurl.com/d275xl6*.

## Image Collection Sites

Students can access an extensive number of images on image collection sites listed below; for more on image collections see *http://tinyurl.com/7xbb8d4*.

---

### ACCESSING IMAGES

**iOS**: Flickr *http://tinyurl.com/2bnbazn*, Google Images *http://www.google.com/images*, Picasa *http://picasa.google.com* and Picasa Webalbums *https://picasaweb.google.com/home*, Photobucket *http://www.photobucket.com*, Expono *http://www.expono.com*, Fotolog *http://www.fotolog.com*, Shutterfly *http://www.shutterfly.com*, Flickstackr *http://tinyurl.com/6ux9poe*, Darkslide *http://tinyurl.com/7vcyu8j*, FlickrHD *http://tinyurl.com/8yha7r6*, Photo Pad: Flickr *http://tinyurl.com/88d22bx*, Flickpack *http://tinyurl.com/6sx68ee*, Mobile Photos *http://tinyurl.com/6vdlbn3*, Flockrstudio *http://flickrstudioapp.com*

**Android**: Flickr *http://tinyurl.com/7r3mla7*, Google Search by Image *http://tinyurl.com/mqdn9fx*, Photobucket Mobile *http://tinyurl.com/7tphurq*, Shutterfly for Android *http://tinyurl.com/n3osgzs*, SuperImage Search *http://tinyurl.com/ldcm63v*, Image Search *http://tinyurl.com/cga8vyn*, Internet Image Search *http://tinyurl.com/n5wu5ol*, Quick Image Search *http://tinyurl.com/luu7oee*, Picasa: Flickr Image Search *http://tinyurl.com/kbjdpc8*

---

Students can search on these apps according to topic or genre, recognizing that, unlike language-based searches, categorizing images is far less precise. They can also use Web apps to find free images at morgueFile *http://www.morguefile. com*, imageafter *http://www.imageafter.com*, stock.xchig *http://www.sxc.hu*, or everystockphoto *http://www.everystockphoto.com* (Hicks, 2013).

Once they have acquired images, they can select those images that are relevant to their own project topic or issue. They can then add comments or annotations to those images and export them as a slideshow to share with peers and yourself. They can then use these images to add to their blog posts, wikis, websites, reports, literary texts, etc. And, they can import these images into screencasting apps such as ShowMe, Explain Everything, or VoiceThread to create audio or written responses to the images to share with others, something we describe later in this chapter.

Flickr is particularly interesting because the images are tagged using the bottom-up "folksomony" tagging system we discussed previously and also use geo-tagging by location. And, searches can be conducted using a number of different types of categories to obtain not only images but also video clips using RSS feeds. Users can also search by Groups—people who share a common interest in certain topics or phenomena as portrayed in their images or video clips. And, on The Commons link, users can access images from archives of The Library of Congress, The Smithsonian, The New York Public Library, and The U.S. National Archives.

One app for sharing images is the iOS *http://tinyurl.com/b4ytl47* and Android *http://tinyurl.com/bov5nq2* Instagram app. This app is both an editing app to add filters and borders to photos, particularly those that provide a vintage, traditional appearance for photos, as well as an app for sharing photos created by both peers and up to 15 million users. As with Flickr, students can rate photos as well as add their own comments.

## Apps for Acquiring Images for Learning Across the Curriculum

There are numerous apps that provide students with images for learning across the curriculum.

### Literature

In studying literature, students can go on Web Google Lit Trips *http://tinyurl. com/ycdt62l* that consist of files portraying famous characters' journeys with pop-up windows with images associated with these characters' journeys in different locations. You and/or your students can create their own Lit Trips as well as virtual travelogues using placemarks with images or videos. You can also have your students access the Cambridge University Press Explore Shakespeare *http:// tinyurl.com/kl9q3n6* app which includes multimodal materials for responding to six Skakespeare plays—photos of productions, maps portraying characters' relationships, word clouds of each scene, a "Themeline" capturing thematic shifts in the plays, and tools for highlighting passages.

## Chemistry

For use of images in chemistry, students could use the iOS The Elements: A Visual Exploration *http://tinyurl.com/n8kdrwh*, Element Matching *http://tinyurl.com/o4n8kjq*, The Chemical Touch *http://tinyurl.com/o23dsmw*, or the K12 Periodic Table of the Elements *http://tinyurl.com/metekfq* and Android Periodic Table *http://tinyurl.com/kpo27n7*, or Elements *http://tinyurl.com/jvomqrn* for identifying different chemical elements. They can also use the iOS MolSim *http://tinyurl.com/p9uc5zp*, Ball & Stick *http://tinyurl.com/ol7keeo*, or Molecules *http://tinyurl.com/cxaxbtl* or Android Molecule Viewer 3D *http://tinyurl.com/d6r7zzx* or Jmol Molecular Viewer *http://tinyurl.com/ov6pbn4* to visualize molecules by zooming in and out to analyze molecular structures.

## Geometry

For studying the design of alternative shapes in geometry, students can use Google SketchUp *http://sketchup.google.com*, which allows students to create virtual 3D models or designs of buildings, places, or objects (for training videos: *http://go-2-school.com/media*). Students could use this app to create different buildings based on their geometric shapes. For an illustration of the use of 3D Modeling with Google SketchUp on MacBreak, see podcast by Alex Oliver: *http://twit.tv/show/macbreak/37*. For examples of students' projects: *http://tinyurl.com/l4v7nmw* and *http://tinyurl.com/6rqdndg*. You and or/your students can also insert 3D illustrations into e-books using iBooks Author; you and/or your students can search the 3d Warehouse *http://sketchup.google.com/3dwarehouse* for examples to download as .skp (open in Sketchup) or .dae files to then export as a Collada (.dae) file. Then in iBooks Author, select Widgets, select the 3D Object, and insert into the text.

## Biology

For use of images in biology, students could use the iOS Leafsnap *http://tinyurl.com/nuh46t7* or Android Mister Smarty Plants *http://tinyurl.com/mrslw55* to identify different tree species based on photographs of their leaves, flowers, fruit, petiole, seeds, or bark. To identify wildflowers on field trips, they could use the iOS *http://tinyurl.com/kugzjlg* or Android *http://tinyurl.com/n8ahdpc* GSM Wildflowers; for identifying birds they can use the iOS Audubon Birds or Butterflies *http://tinyurl.com/kdzad7r* or iBird Yard and Guide to Birds *http://tinyurl.com/mftlklc* or the Android Audubon Bird Pro *http://tinyurl.com/laxy7y4* or Birdwatching *http://tinyurl.com/kh83mu8* apps.

In studying cells, they could use the iOS 3D Cell Simulation and Stain Tool *http://tinyurl.com/mvevfde*, Mitosis *http://tinyurl.com/msxpqrs*, or Cell and Cell Structure *http://tinyurl.com/mgbabcq* apps as well as the Android Cell Imaging *http://tinyurl.com/kq8ne5c* or iCell *http://tinyurl.com/mahx3yn* apps for analyzing cell growth. For observing DNA structures and composition, they could use the iOS OnScreen DNA Model *http://tinyurl.com/lhodmpz*. And, for observing the human genome, they could employ the iOS GeneIndexHD *http://tinyurl.com/mw6w3tg* to identify genes and find research about those genes.

## Astronomy

For studying astronomy, students can employ a number of different apps for viewing images of the sky, for example, the iOS *http://tinyurl.com/cqjryr7* and Android *http://tinyurl.com/mln8kmo* Star Walk, the iOS GoSkyWatch Planetarium *http://tinyurl.com/bch286r* or Solar Walk *http://tinyurl.com/cqjryr7* apps, or the Android SkEyd *http://tinyurl.com/bskydmx*, Star Chart *http://tinyurl.com/peav4vt*, and Sky Map *http://tinyurl.com/d8vtwq3* apps.

Brian Cox's Wonders of the Universe *http://tinyurl.com/b6xlsst* provides students with views of the universe that includes 200 interactive articles, two-and-a-half hours of video from the BBC TV series *Wonders of the Solar System* and *Wonders of the Universe*, and hundreds of infographics and images of space objects supplied by astronomy experts, NASA, and other space researchers.

## Social Studies

In social studies classes, students can use the:

- Interactive Historical Atlas *http://tinyurl.com/lef57jr* to obtain images of maps associated with certain historical events;
- iOS ReadWriteThink Timeline app *http://tinyurl.com/l37kor6* to create a visual timeline to represent different historical events that occurred during certain historical periods;
- US States *http://tinyurl.com/lwlmmf7* app or the American Presidents *http://tinyurl.com/dyt3zmp* app that includes essays about the Presidents;
- iOS US Geography *http://tinyurl.com/kxemlkb* app or the Android Geography Learning Game *http://tinyurl.com/lo7nq52* app;
- bundled iOS Apple Maps or iOS *http://tinyurl.com/cuwn8wk* and Android *http://tinyurl.com/7lsev67* Google Maps to acquire maps of specific cities, towns, neighborhoods, or places, as well as the Apple Maps and iOS *http://tinyurl.com/bvesxlq* and Android *http://tinyurl.com/pve5nt9* Google Earth "flyover" feature that allows students to zoom in for virtual visits of those cities, towns, neighborhoods, or places.

## Fair Use Of Copyrighted Online Images

In searching for images for use in their presentations, reports, blogs, or websites, students need to be aware of issues of use of copyrighted images. If they upload copyrighted material they need to obtain permission from owners who have copyrighted that material.

They should therefore seek out material for which owners have granted Creative Commons copyright permission to use their material with some attribution. To find Creative Commons copyrighted images, in using Flickr, students can select the option of only Creative Commons images.

However, students may use copyrighted material under the fair use provision of copyright law. Fair use allows you and/or your students to use a copyrighted image according to a set of purposes for use of that material (Hobbs, 2011); see also the Code of Best Practices in Fair Use for Media Literacy Education.

These fair use purposes include whether or not the copyrighted images are being used for educational purposes in ways that transform the original image to create a new, creative work for the purpose of parody or critique; if you use material in way that transforms it for educational use, it falls under fair use. For example, if students are satirizing an image by remixing or altering that image in ways that are similar to an *Adbusters* Magazine parody of advertising images, then this is an instance of fair use. However, if the image was being used for the same original intent or for commercial purposes, for example, using the same, unaltered image to put on a t-shirt to sell the t-shirt, then this use represents a violation of copyright.

These technical points of copyright mean that students need to clearly understand the purposes for using material. They need to ask if the use is of a commercial nature or is for nonprofit educational purposes; they also need to understand whether the copyrighted image is being transformed for the purpose of critique or parody and know the amount and substantiality of the portion used in relation to the copyrighted work as a whole. Finally, they need to understand the effect of the use upon the potential market for, or value of, the copyrighted work. When in doubt, please refer to the sources we just cited.

## Responding to Images Using Screencasting Apps

There are a number of screencasting apps that you can use to have students share their responses to images. By screencasting, we mean the ability to record a video copy of an image or video on a computer or tablet screen by adding audio or written comments. This means that you or your students can import an image or video into a screencasting app and then add audio or written comments about the image or video to create a new video. You can also use these apps for creating training videos for use by students on how to employ certain digital tools or for giving feedback to students' work, something we describe in more detail in Chapter 11.

## SCREENCASTING APPS

**iOS**: VoiceThread *http://tinyurl.com/lujk7fs,* ShowMe *http://tinyurl.com/ ohwh3ed,* Explain Everything *http://tinyurl.com/a6z4tsu,* Screenchomp *http:// tinyurl.com/ajhlf8j,* Educreations Interactive Whiteboard *http://tinyurl.com/ adx58ep,* Skitch *http://skitch.com,* Blurb Mobile *http://tinyurl.com/77stp8k*

**Android**: Explain Everything *http://tinyurl.com/mk3jw39,* Whiteboard Cast *http://tinyurl.com/kgjbtwd,* Splashtop Whiteboard *http://tinyurl.com/ mxm262u,* Skitch *http://tinyurl.com/kknfmkk,* Screencast Video Recorder *http://tinyurl.com/lgl83gb,* Screencast *http://tinyurl.com/mewrjec*

### *ShowMe*

One previously described popular screencasting app is the iOS ShowMe, particularly for use with upper elementary/middle school students. You or your students can import an image and then draw on the image as they record their audio. They can then share a URL for their productions via e-mail or on a website. You can also determine whether your screencast will be private or public, something that's useful when you want to provide students with some feedback, in which case you'll select the private options, versus create a training video, in which case you select public. This means that you or your students can use ShowMe for creating presentations for use in sharing information.

Seventh-grade students at Valley View Middle School, Pleasant Hill, California, who were students in two of Ms. Linda Wilhelm's science classes, were studying Mendelian genetics in a four-day unit. Because the teacher wanted students to collaboratively generate a final product to demonstrate their application of what they learned about genetics to a specific example, the students were asked to work in groups to use ShowMe to create a presentation.

Students read one of four articles about genetics on a website, DNA from the Beginning: (1) Some genes are dominant, (2) Mendelian laws apply to human beings, (3) All cells arise from pre-existing cells, and (4) Sex cells have one set of chromosomes; body cells have two. Students then met with a partner who read the same article to discuss the content and write a summary of what they read. Students also viewed an example of a ShowMe presentation, acquiring a rubric that would be used to assess their own final ShowMe project designed to explain the ideas in each article and discuss how the ideas were related. All of this served to provide students with a sense of purpose and audience for their presentations.

To plan their ShowMe presentations in which they created doodle drawings to illustrate their voice-over recordings about certain examples of genetics, students used a storyboard (paper folded into four parts). However, the students discovered that they could just use the ShowMe for planning and drafting their presentation. They therefore created some temporary doodle images of cells, plants, birds, human stick figures, etc., as well as changes in these images, to illustrate their verbal recordings about genetics. Because they could easily erase their doodles on ShowMe, they could then revise their images to make them more consistent with their ideas. In this revision process, students were testing out alternative ways to visually convey their ideas to determine which visual representation best captured their intended meanings. Many students also went back to the articles as well as their textbook to clarify their thinking about their presentation.

At the same time, because these images were perceived as highly temporary and easy to erase/revise, the affordance of the temporal, unfolding images themselves fostered students' own verbal revisions. Once students recognized that their doodles didn't quite capture their ideas and they erased and generated a revised version, this revision of their doodles also helped them clarify their voice-over description. For example, in creating a drawing of a cell mutation, one student noted that the drawing wasn't clearly conveying the process of cell mutation, so the student noted, "let's do it this way," and created a revised drawing, which then served to help both students clarify what they wanted to say about cell mutations.

One important disciplinary literacy in science is the use of images, graphs, figures, or charts to visually illustrate certain scientific phenomena. In their presentations, the students were also employing concepts related to genetics—traits, genes, chromosomes, dominant, recessive, sexual reproduction, mitosis, meiosis, allele, and spindle fibers. The students used their drawings to not only illustrate their ideas about genetics, but to also develop, revise, and clarify those unfolding ideas. And, because the students could both share the same images and readily revise those images, these shared images themselves served to scaffold and focus this collaboration.

Andrea Draper and Dominic Kazda *http://www.showme.com/sh/?h=RNKspgu* created a ShowMe presentation describing the process of meiosis related to Mendel's experiments on the role of dominant versus recessive genetic make-up in a male versus female bird related to the color of their offspring's feathers and eyes. In their presentation (see Figure 8.1), they created doodle images representing the mother and father birds' feather and eye colors to illustrate their description:

**FIGURE 8.1**   Students' ShowMe Presentation on Genetics

*Source:* Reprinted with permission from Andrea Draper and Dominic Kazda.

This is the mother bird and it has blue feathers which is dominant and green eyes which is dominant also. This is the dad. He has grey feathers which are recessive. He has green eyes which are dominant. Mendel's experiments shows that if a dominant allele is present, the recessive doesn't show up. The adult birds have 69 chromosomes and 34 chromosomes from each bird go into the offspring. The offspring has blue feathers since blue is dominant. It has green eyes since both green eyes are dominant on both parents. And that's the process of meiosis.

Andrea and Dominic were therefore using their doodling of the color of the father and mother's feathers and eyes to illustrate their description of how the offspring had blue feathers and green eyes.

These students are employing another disciplinary literacy associated with science—drawing on previous scientific work to empirically confirm or refute that work.

The following are some other student ShowMe presentations.

Alyssa and Jessica *http://www.showme.com/sh/?h=ibbycYS*
Lauren and Marley *http://www.showme.com/sh/?h=njmyNU0*
Emily and Roselyn *http://www.showme.com/sh/?h=216Fw2q*
Marcos and Alison *http://www.showme.com/sh/?h=hn2cnJo*
Nikilar and Conrad *http://www.showme.com/sh/?h=GC6q3nM*
Salma and Ryan *http://www.showme.com/sh/?h=pW36aKO*

## Other Screencasting Apps

Another screencasting app for use in drawing and adding audio commentary to images is the iOS and Android Explain Everything. This app, which has more features than ShowMe, is particularly useful, as suggested by the title, for creating tutorials for showing on an interactive whiteboard using video display. You can import images, photos, notes, or presentation slides to record your drawings and annotations along with audio commentary and then export your file as video podcasts as MP4 or PNG files. Explain Everything also includes a lot of geometric tools for use in math or science demonstrations.

The iOS Screenchomp app can also be used to import images to then record audio or doodles. These screencasts can then be uploaded to Screenchomp.com or downloaded as mp4 video files for sharing with students.

The iOS Educreations Interactive Whiteboard app allows students to record their commentary across different screens, as opposed to just one screen, as is the case with Screenchomp and ShowMe. Students can write doodles using a pen with ten different ink colors. Students can also import images from their camera, as well as share their screencast using email, Facebook, or Twitter.

The iOS and Android Skitch apps can be used for drawing of graphics over images as well as superimposing other arrows, circles, or squares and then sharing that image with others on Twitter or Apple TV using AirPlay. Skitch includes 25 different graphic organizers for different ways to organize thinking for responding to texts based on cause/effect, main idea/detail, sequence of events, pro/con, story elements, characterization, etc. Students can use Skitch to take screenshots of any image on their iPad to add annotations, as well as exporting their drawings or graphics into Evernote for sharing with others. As with VoiceThread and ShowMe, this app can be used to generate tutorial videos for your students.

## Charts and Graphs Apps

The use of charts or graphs to present numerical data is a primary focus in math, science, and social sciences. In these disciplines, students need to be able to comprehend and create visual representations of empirical or geographical data by taking raw data, often from Excel spreadsheets, and presenting the data to illustrate certain ideas or findings in a manner that readers can readily comprehend. This involves learning to read and produce Venn diagrams/plots, bar graphs/charts, pie plots, stack plots, and axis plots to visually communicate data, particularly in math and science classes (Siebert & Hendrickson, 2010).

---

### CHARTS AND GRAPHS CREATION APPS

**Web apps:** Google Charts *http://tinyurl.com/728sggd*, Many Eyes *http://tinyurl.com/9wpg7tt*, Hohli *http://tinyurl.com/3xas8co*, JS Charts *http://www.jscharts.com*, ChartGizmo *http://chartgizmo.com*, Map Tools *http://www.maptools.org/owtchart/chartgen.phtml*, ChartTools *http://www.onlinecharttool.com*, DIYChart *http://www.diychart.com/Default.aspx*

**iOS:** Numbers *http://tinyurl.com/b9qteu8*, iMathematics *http://tinyurl.com/lwk567h*, Math Studio *http://tinyurl.com/m9b4plg*, Graphing Calculator HD *http://tinyurl.com/m2o932e*, Chart Maker *http://tinyurl.com/mt65aw4*, iChart Maker *http://tinyurl.com/kv8g6wr*, Graphs *http://tinyurl.com/km66d72*, Pie Chart Maker *http://tinyurl.com/mmzg6pv*, Lovely Charts *http://tinyurl.com/l97o4pz*, Bar Chart Maker *http://tinyurl.com/lo4m4wy*

**Android:** Chart Creator *http://tinyurl.com/mfhk7j8*, 3D Charts *http://tinyurl.com/mb8fluy*, Statistics Graph Maker Creator *http://tinyurl.com/kydb8f8*, Pie Chart Maker *http://tinyurl.com/kbpvqbg*, Graph Maker *http://tinyurl.com/m7ztlvc*, Graph It *http://tinyurl.com/lxy42vh*, Graph Draw *http://tinyurl.com/mzwb8wh*

---

One basic app to create charts and graphs that is part of the Apple iWork Suite is Numbers. Students can use Numbers to read Excel files from Dropbox, e-mail, iTunes, or iCloud and then export those files as a PDF, Excel, or Numbers file. Students can choose from 30 different templates for creating their charts or graphs, for example, circle or bar graphs. Given the relatively high cost of Numbers ($9.99), a free option is the Calc Lite Spreadsheet for iPad *http://tinyurl.com/kxoahod* to read and edit Excel files; users can also choose from templates for creating graphs or charts. Students can also employ the browser app, Google Charts, as well as the other chart creation apps listed above for creating a range of different types of charts.

Students are also using calculators to engage in analysis using different formulas that then generate graphs. The iOS iMathematics and Math Studio apps include calculator and graph outputs, as well as a lot of instructional support for students including examples of how to use the calculators, links to topics on Wikipedia, and quizzes. Similarly, the Graphing Calculator HD or Graphs apps let students view their graph results from their calculations; they can take screen shots of their graphs to email to themselves as well as create videos to show on a screen.

## Infographics Apps

Students can also acquire and display empirical information using infographics apps that include numerous graphs and charts about certain topics or issues. Newspapers such as the *New York Times* have increasingly used infographics to communicate complex data in visually appealing ways.

Students can access infographics using the iOS Infographic Hub *http://tinyurl.com/mngprn4*, Lemonly Infographics *http://tinyurl.com/mnjsvpo*, Android Infography *http://tinyurl.com/lb52g2j*, The Best Infographics *http://tinyurl.com/mw6fsen*, Infographics Hub *http://tinyurl.com/kmc7ksv*, or the Daily Infographic *http://tinyurl.com/mvj8dzt*.

To obtain data for creating infographics, students can also use the iOS *http://tinyurl.com/bp37ytn* or Android *http://tinyurl.com/c5fe6d2* WolframAlpha apps, the iOS The Economist World in Figures *http://tinyurl.com/l95325v* app, or the iOS Stats of the Union *http://tinyurl.com/lmng7a9* apps that provide extensive empirical data and charts/graphs for all different disciplinary areas. They can then use infographic creation apps, most of which are Web apps, to create their own infographics.

---

### INFOGRAPHIC CREATION TOOLS

**Web apps**: Visual.ly *http://create.visual.ly*, Easel.ly *http://www.easel.ly*, Infogr.am *http://infogr.am*, Venngage *https://venngage.com*, Google Developers *https://developers.google.com/chart*, Tableau Public *http://www.tableausoftware.com/public/community*, Piktochart *http://tinyurl.com/my7xps5*, Dipity *http://www.dipity.com*, Infoactive *https://infoactive.co*, Pearltrees *http://tinyurl.com/lhjhu22*

**iOS**: Easy Charts *http://tinyurl.com/lp7gal8*, i Visual info Touch *http://tinyurl.com/kmgyx89*

**Android**: Photo Infographic Gen Lite *http://tinyurl.com/l7ymj42*

---

## Collage-Creation Apps

In collecting and responding to images, it is important that students respond critically to these images, for example, media images representing gender, race, or class differences that reflect certain cultural messages or ideological assumptions.

While we may assume that students can generate critical responses to images, it is often helpful to provide them with specific prompts to have them attend to both the aesthetic aspects of images, as well as the emotional, social, and cultural content of the images. To help students focus on specific aspects of images, you can have them learn to ask questions based on the Critical Response Protocol (Beach, Campano, Edmiston, & Borgmann, 2010): "What are you noticing?" "What did you see that makes you say that?" "What does it remind you of?" "How do you feel?" "What questions does the image raise for you?" and "What did you learn?" (p. 27).

Other questions based on the Visual Thinking Strategies model (Housen, 2007) include "What's going on in this image?" "What emotions do you associate with this image?" "What in the image made you think X?" "What are you seeing that suggests X?" and "What's missing or left out of this picture?" For example, in having her students respond to photos, Delainia Haug, a teacher at Roosevelt High School in Minneapolis, has students respond to their photographs using the following prompts:

1.  What do you see? Start with the literal. List only tangible things—not ideas, feelings or conclusions. (For example, you can see a smile, but you cannot see happiness.)
2.  Make three supported inferences from the photo. I think _____ because I see _____.
3.  Do some analysis and make predictions. If you were in the photo, what would you be thinking, hoping and wondering? If you asked a person in the photo a question, what would they answer? Support your analysis with photographic evidence and background knowledge.
4.  What does the photo tell you about the time and place, and these people?
5.  What is missing from the photo? What do you think has been cropped out of the image? What questions do you have about what's outside the frame? (Beach et al., 2010, p. 48)

To engage in critical analysis of media representations, students can employ collage-creation apps listed below that combine photos or images together to create collages.

---

## COLLAGE-CREATION APPS

**iOS**: Glogster *http://tinyurl.com/l8ltysw*, Mixel *http://tinyurl.com/kznttg5*, Photo Wall Pro *http://tinyurl.com/lderx8p*, Collage Creator Lite *http://tinyurl.com/larpky4*, PicMix *http://tinyurl.com/kb32jab*, Diptic *http://tinyurl.com/mbtbpdt*, Picture Collage Creator *http://tinyurl.com/mm7nc5h*, Photo Collage Creator *http://tinyurl.com/klkptpx*, Photo Grid *http://tinyurl.com/mbvbdtn*

**Android**: PicMix *http://tinyurl.com/ln5yw8z*, Photo Grid Collage Maker *http://tinyurl.com/923v2mw*, PhotoMix *http://tinyurl.com/kja9wlt*, PicCollage *http://tinyurl.com/kf38nrc*

---

By combining images in these collages, students begin to discern certain consistent patterns in the images reflecting certain underlying meanings. For example, by collecting images of women in advertising, they can critique how women are often portrayed primarily in terms of their appearance or as physically thin and compliant based on assumptions about femininity—representations driven by the commercial interests of the beauty industry. To critique these images, students could pose the questions:

- Where do these representations come from?
- Who produces these representations?
- Why are they producing these representations?
- How is complexity limited by these representations?
- What is missing or silenced in these representations?

Students in Richard's media studies class at the University of Minnesota examined gender representations in magazine and online advertising. By selecting a range of different images, they identified consistent groupings or patterns reflecting common signified meanings. For images of masculinity, they found that the images involved the projection of physical prowess or toughness portrayed by muscular professional athletes engaged in competitive sports activities. They also observed how the men in the ads are portrayed as autonomous—as operating on their own without displaying affection for others or being constrained by social relationships.

## Photo Apps

In addition to using apps for responding to images for learning across the curriculum, students can also use the hundreds of photo apps for taking and editing photos with their iPhones, iPads, and Android devices. The iPhone camera is a high-quality camera used to create photos that equal the quality of some digital cameras. Students can also take photos on digital cameras to load into their iPads or iPhones for editing using Apple's Camera Connection Kit. And, if they have access to both devices, they can upload their iPhone photos to their iPads for editing on their iPads.

## Taking Photos

To take photos, students use the bundled iOS Camera app that comes with iPads or iPhones or Android camera apps for Android devices listed below.

---

### APPS FOR TAKING PHOTOS

**iOS**: Camera (bundled), Camera+ *http://tinyurl.com/7awwxbw*, Picture Show *http://tinyurl.com/26rm9jn*, ProCamera *http://tinyurl.com/y9kytv3*, Gigapan *http://www.gigapan.org*, Photosynth *http://tinyurl.com/3q4zwxv*, 360 Panorama *http://tinyurl.com/2b2qyr5*, AutoStitch Panorama *http://tinyurl.com/29a9wmu*, or Pano *http://tinyurl.com/27e73tq*, You Gotta See This *http://tinyurl.com/755lsz8* (3D-like photo), Quick Pix *http://tinyurl.com/6nyxn7w*, FotoBabble *http://tinyurl.com/3u7so4y*

**Android**: Camera360 Ultimate *http://tinyurl.com/7oyo5nq*, Cymera *http://tinyurl.com/d97ptx3*, Line Camera *http://tinyurl.com/7sry67e*, Camera MX *http://tinyurl.com/anofaqh*, HD Camera Ultra *http://tinyurl.com/n8nywun*

---

The iOS Camera app allows them to take front-facing and rear-facing shots by changing the Switch Cameras icon. They can also switch between still and video shots. Once they open up the Camera app, they can then open up the zoom slider by tapping on the screen.

Students can also take what are described as high dynamic range (HDR) shots that take three quick shots of the same area at different exposures and then combine these three shots into one shot that improves the quality of that shot (Hart-Davis, 2012). To activate the HDR feature, they turn on the HRD switch within Options. They then take the photo and create the HRD shot that is typically superior to the original single shot—the original is also saved.

Students can also take panorama shots that provide more of a 360-degree portrait of a site or event. They can use apps such as iOS Photosynth *http://tinyurl.com/bhj7zfs*, iOS *http://tinyurl.com/l56zz8x* and Android *http://tinyurl.com/7dsgrpd* 360 Panorama, iOS *http://tinyurl.com/mht3b4m* and Android *http://tinyurl.com/kj59wx7* AutoStitch Panorama to take an initial photo, move the camera to an area that overlaps with the area in the original photo, and the app continues to take additional photos that are then stitched together to create a panorama photo.

## Photo Editing

Students can then edit their photos using a number of different photo-editing apps listed below; for further discussion of these apps, see Hoffman (2011) and Muchmore (2012).

## PHOTO-EDITING APPS

**iOS**: Adobe® Photoshop® Express *http://tinyurl.com/6mp34fh*, Snapseed *http://tinyurl.com/3clobca*, Instagram *http://tinyurl.com/36c3exb*, 3D Camera *http://tinyurl.com/24z8lpo*, 3D Photo Maker *http://tinyurl.com/3bzpaku*, PhotoSpeak: 3D Talking Photo *http://tinyurl.com/7s23k7p*, Pixlr-o-matic *http://tinyurl.com/43fljot*, Picture Effect Magic *http://tinyurl.com/68juhst*, Filterstorm *http://tinyurl.com/362lgk7*, Luminance *http://tinyurl.com/7qnfw6v*, Neon Image App *http://tinyurl.com/7g9c3t8*, Photogene for iPad *http://tinyurl.com/33603s9*

**Android**: Snapseed *http://tinyurl.com/akq5rt8*, Photo Editor Aviary *http://tinyurl.com/bn2w6jh*, Photo Editor *http://tinyurl.com/73c9edx*, Photo Editor Pro *http://tinyurl.com/n7e2g68*, PhotoEffectsPro *http://tinyurl.com/l89kbkj*, Photo Editor for Android *http://tinyurl.com/mrx8mwt*

One of the primary editing apps is Adobe® Photoshop® Express, an app that is familiar to users of the desktop Adobe Photoshop photo sharing, editing, and hosting site. Students can use it to rotate, crop, flip, or straighten their photos; change or alter colors, including black and white or tint; add filters of Soft Focus, Sharpen, or Sketch; add special effects such as Border, Rainbow, Vibrant, or White Glow; and add borders. Other popular editing apps include the iOS and Android Snapseed and iOS Instagram that includes filters for altering photos. For example, Instagram includes a filter to make photos appear as if they were taken with an Instant Polaroid camera or Lomography lens.

The photo app, Snapseed, can be used to automatically enhance their photos to improve the quality of their images. They can also use swiping gestures to manually edit their images in terms of brightness, contrast, color, and cropping. They can also add special effects using filters such as Vintage Films for use in making photos appear as vintage color film photos, Drama to add artistic effects, Details to sharper specific features, Grunge to add a hip appearance, or Tilt-Shift to highlight depth of field by choosing an elliptical or linear focus. Students then share their photos via email or to the Photos library, Flickr, Twitter, or Facebook.

Students can also use the iOS *http://tinyurl.com/nxx3aau* and Android *http://tinyurl.com/bqu98gy* Geotag Photos Lite apps that, when location identification is turned on, logs their photos' location. They can also use the iOS *http://tinyurl.com/lvj89wk* and Android *http://tinyurl.com/n7vjj8y* EveryTrail apps to create a trip map that includes images portraying the different sites on their trips, as well as view 400,000 examples of trips. Or, students can use the iOS *http://tinyurl.com/b7ocne4* and Android *http://tinyurl.com/l3rmayo* Trip Journal app to add images and notes to Places on a map to describe their experiences on a trip; they can also use the Record Your Trip app using GPS tracking to add certain Places.

Students can use photos to create productions about historical events or sites through use of the iOS WhatWasThere *http://tinyurl.com/k5nr9lj* app designed for users to add historical photos to specific locations on a Google Map (Brustein, 2011). This app is designed to mesh together students' own photos of sites or places from institutional archives or from people's own family collections. People can then use their iPhones to shoot the present location, site, or building, and then overlay the historical photo of that same location, site, or building, creating a fusion of the past and the present.

### Photo Presentation Apps

Once they have edited their photos, students can then share their photos using photologs (blogs for photos)/e-portfolio and album/gallery apps with their peers and family members.

## PHOTOLOG/E-PORTFOLIO APPS

**iOS**: PhotoLog *http://tinyurl.com/84qped2*, ShoZu *http://tinyurl.com/6v4x38o*, 500px *http://tinyurl.com/dxoas5x*, SmugMug *http://tinyurl.com/7mp2mth*, FolioBook *http://tinyurl.com/6w3wa32*, Flexfolios *http://tinyurl.com/254erhd*, Portfolio to Go for Flickr *http://tinyurl.com/77uos6m*, Project 365 *http://tinyurl.com/mmm8rwb*, PadPort for iPad Portfolio *http://tinyurl.com/7pdvo3l*

**Android**: Photo Log Lite *http://tinyurl.com/l7fd6we*, PhotoBlog.pl *http://tinyurl.com/jvn5o7v*, Blogger for Android *http://tinyurl.com/jvn5o7v*, FlickFolio for Flickr *http://tinyurl.com/jvn5o7v*, Quickpic *http://tinyurl.com/82jtwdv*

## ALBUM/GALLERY APPS

**iOS**: Albums FX *http://tinyurl.com/7fx2nor*, Albums FX Lite *http://tinyurl.com/7dt95t6*, Web Albums for iPad *http://tinyurl.com/8736lf6*, Album App *http://tinyurl.com/7mzqo2v*, ScrapPad *http://tinyurl.com/7svqc8z*, Coolibah *http://tinyurl.com/7573uth*, Skrappy *http://tinyurl.com/7w8jljo*

**Android**: PhotoGallery *http://tinyurl.com/ofdpj75*, PhotoGallery Easy Album *http://tinyurl.com/mmklxf8*, PhotoAlbum *http://tinyurl.com/kft29yw*, Infinity Photo Album *http://tinyurl.com/lryspw6*, Android Photo Album *http://tinyurl.com/kln57ma*

Based on comparisons of current and past images, students can then discuss or write about the nature of the changes that have occurred over time and speculate on reasons for these changes. For example, students may note that, in some cases, urban neighborhoods have been gentrified with the negative effects of dislocating people; in other cases, neighborhoods have deteriorated due to urban blight and lack of economic development.

Students can also take photos of themselves at different times of the year, post them to their photolog, and write about changes in themselves and reasons for those changes. For examples of such photos, they can draw on the Project 365 app to create a photo for each day of the year to add to a photo album. They can create their own visual autobiographies combined with writing or poetry to portray changes in their identities over time. In one project entitled "Sistahs," female students of color created Web-based visual autobiographies for sharing with others (Wissman, 2008).

### Presentation Apps

There are a range of different presentation apps you or your students can employ to create and share presentations; for more on presentation tools see *http://tinyurl.com/6ogfrn7*.

---

## PRESENTATION APPS

**iOS:** Keynote *http://tinyurl.com/yzctrzu*, PowerPoint (use OnLive Desktop for iPad) *http://tinyurl.com/6tzvxgw*, Documents2Go *http://tinyurl.com/3e9pczu*, Haiku Deck *http://tinyurl.com/k8bh2mk*, SlideShark *http://tinyurl.com/8yowb6a*, CloudOn *http://tinyurl.com/6thj3b3*, Prezi *http://prezi.com* (viewed or edits on an iPad using Prezi Viewer *http://tinyurl.com/843gkjm*)

**Android:** Android Deck Slideshow *http://tinyurl.com/ny8znt6*, Office Presentations *http://tinyurl.com/kxhd8tl*, QuickOffice (for use with PowerPoint) *http://tinyurl.com/mhesykz*

---

The most commonly used iOS presentation app for the iPad is Keynote, which includes the same features found on PowerPoint—the ability to import images from Photos, video links, create transitions between slides, edit fonts, create charts and tables, and add animations.

Keynote, like PowerPoint, provides students with themes for creating a consistent appearance across their slides. For making presentations, Keynote includes thumbnails of slides in the left column and the primary slides in the right viewer window.

You or your students can also use Apple's Keynote Remote app that enables the use of an iPhone to remotely control a Keynote presentation on an iPad using a Wi-Fi or Bluetooth connection. They can also employ the Presenter display to view the current and subsequent slides and notes during their presentation.

In contrast to PowerPoint and Keynote, Prezi is a cloud-based tool created on a desktop and stored at Prezi. Presentations can then be viewed or edited on an iPad using the Prezi Viewer *http://tinyurl.com/bz95szk* app (for a useful introduction to Prezi see *http://tinyurl.com/lhwqrnq*). The Prezi Viewer app enables you to have iPads with Prezi presentations going automatically at different stations in a classroom or science lab to convey information or to demonstrate certain procedures. Students can also import their PowerPoint slides into Prezi.

In Prezi, students use toolbar options to insert images, shapes, links, and files to place onto a blank canvas. They can structure this material using shapes or brackets to create a path for navigating through these shapes or brackets. Audiences then zoom in and out in their focus on the content as they move along this path. The Prezi site provides instructions for how to create a Prezi presentation under the "learn" tab. Students can also work collaboratively on creating a presentation using the "Prezi Meeting" link to "edit with others."

Denise Stuart (2012) notes how Prezi enhances audience engagement to a greater degree than PowerPoint or Keynote through zooming in on images and animation as a virtual journey. She cites the example of students using Prezi to present poems through images and music. For example, in one production, "the lines of the poem took form as in a concrete poem and then when clicked and zoomed in were horizontal for reading before flipping and turning back to shape" (p. 4).

Creating effective presentations involves knowing how to employ images, charts, graphs, images and websites, in place of, or in conjunction with, print. You or your students can use the image apps previously described in this chapter to convey their ideas or concepts.

Making effective presentations also involves the ability to engage audiences interactively by having them respond to these images, charts, graphs, websites, or videos, as well as through questions posed to the audience. You or your students can add question prompts or clicker surveys to slides that serve to elicit audience participation.

The use of images in presentations enhances the visual rhetoric for persuading audiences to consider certain beliefs or ideas. For example, four African American eighth-grade girls constructed a multimodal PowerPoint presentation that portrayed different images about the poverty in their community with music (Mahiri, 2006). They created presentations using images of homeless people in their neighborhood, including some digital photos. To add music to their photos, they went to some singers' sites, including *http://www.aaliyah.com* and *http://www.kirkfranklin.com*, where they found some background music such as the song, "I Care 4 U" by Aaliyah, as well as gospel music, which, as one student noted, provided a spiritual perspective on issues of poverty (p. 59).

One app that encourages students to focus on the use of images for their presentations is the iOS Haiku Deck app. Within the app, students can readily access a range of different images. And, they are limited to using only a certain number of words so that they will not be overly reliant on too much language.

One limitation of presentations is that they perpetuate a transmission model of learning with little audience engagement. To foster audience interactions with presentations you or your students can embed prompts involving smartphone or clicker polling or voting options using the Socrative Teacher Clicker or Student Clicker, ResponseWare (subscription service), eClicker, iResponse, or SRN Response apps. These apps include polling questions and text message options, as well as presentations of results. Audience members can also directly communicate reactions or questions to you or your students during a presentation.

You and/or your students can also upload your presentations to Google Docs, VoiceThread, YouTube, Spresent, Google Presenter (within Google Docs), Zoho Show, or Slideshare to create a URL link to then embed presentations in a website, blog, e-book, Facebook, or a Tweet. (Given the fact that Slideshare contains a large number of education presentations, you can use the Slide by Slide app to search for presentations on Slideshare and then view those presentations on an iPad.)

## Drawing and Painting Apps

There are also numerous drawing and painting apps that are particularly relevant for art courses, but which can also be employed to create illustrations for use in any discipline. Many of these apps involve the use of finger painting, while others involve the use of virtual brushes.

---

### APPS FOR CREATING DRAWINGS

**iOS**: Paper *http://tinyurl.com/d793uvt*, ArtStudio *http://tinyurl.com/6ed9y7q*, iDraw *http://tinyurl.com/6pujdkb*, ArtRage *http://tinyurl.com/3oerbbv*, Adobe® Ideas *http://tinyurl.com/2beomdv*, Adobe® Eazel for Photoshop® *http://tinyurl.com/3zogy7l*, WURM *http://tinyurl.com/72lbzv2*, Paintbook 2 *http://tinyurl.com/89usywg*, Draw Free for iPad *http://tinyurl.com/875svsh*, Draw *http://tinyurl.com/6va2dff*

**Android**: Picasso: Paint, Draw, Doodle! *http://tinyurl.com/kfuuxqj*, Drawing Pad *http://tinyurl.com/kvcshma*, Sketcher Free *http://tinyurl.com/mba894c*, How To Draw: Easy Lessons *http://tinyurl.com/mgan7wu*, Sketchbook Pro *http://tinyurl.com/lqaoj4w*, Paperless: Draw, Sketch, Tablet *http://tinyurl.com/p9zwnzb*, Draw! *http://tinyurl.com/k3js42x*

---

One popular drawing app is the Paper app that involves drawing using a free drawing tool; other in-app tools can be purchased. The Paper app is a well-designed app to employ for drawing with the free drawing tool so that students can create high-quality drawings, although to engage in writing, outlining, or painting, they need to purchase additional tools.

The Brushes app provides for a range of 19 different brush selections that vary according to brush size, five different blend modes, the use of four different layers, and the capacity to import photos as well as export the drawing or painting to Flickr or other photo apps. The Brushes iPad Edition app contains 19 different "brushes," the use of different layers, and the capacity to import photos and export to Flickr. Students can zoom in and out, as well as use the undo or redo feature in case they want to erase a mistake. For demonstrating the use of different techniques to students, you can use the playback feature that shows how different Brushes tools can be employed to create a drawing or painting.

Another popular app for drawing/painting is Doodle Buddy, which contains brushes, chalk, smudges, glitter, and image stamps, along with 44,000 color options. Doodle Buddy is particularly useful for finger painting because students can easily use their fingers to select colors and paint, while being able to quickly erase mistakes. The ArtStudio app draws on mathematical formulas to foster high-quality results, as well as the use of lessons on drawing different types of images (for results, see their Flickr group's drawings/painting). And, the ArtRage app determines the amount of paint that has been applied to a canvas so that students can blend different colors as well as flatten or smear the paint with a Palette Knife tool. Given the variations in degrees of wetness, they can also use their brushes to create different textured effects. There are also apps that combine iPad or iPhone photos with painting, such as the ArtStudio app that allows students to add photo effects to their paintings.

## Museum/Gallery Apps

In preparation for or as part of their drawing and painting, students could study examples of drawing/painting techniques by accessing examples of great artists or drawings/paintings using museum/gallery apps such as Art Authority for iPad *http://tinyurl.com/3xov4h2* or Art Envi *http://tinyurl.com/7topokr*. They could also go on virtual trips using museum/gallery apps listed below.

---

**Museum/gallery apps**: Museum of Modern Art (MOMA), New York *http://tinyurl.com/32sfzz6*; Metropolitan Museum, New York *http://tinyurl.com/763z9hx*; Brooklyn Museum of Art *http://tinyurl.com/7aokaxl*; Los Angeles County Museum, Los Angeles *http://tinyurl.com/7sdv4sd*; DeYoung Museum, San Francisco *http://tinyurl.com/lfhqlox*; Chicago Art Institute *http://tinyurl.com/25bv4sg*; National Portrait Gallery, Washington, DC *http://tinyurl.com/7nb4tsm*; Musee de Lourve, Paris, France *http://tinyurl.com/39jhqrji*; Museum Musée d'Orsay, Paris, France *http://tinyurl.com/858y2t7*; Centre Pompidou, Paris, France *http://tinyurl.com/7zr4fz3*; Guggenheim Museum Bilbao, Spain *http://tinyurl.com/7rgeoy3*; or the Uffizi Gallery, Florence, Italy *http://tinyurl.com/843wb6s*

---

Students can also employ the CultureNOW: Guidebook for the Museum Without Walls *http://tinyurl.com/8x7d5af* app to access 55 public art collections from museums throughout the United States, including 15,000 photos and 400 podcasts by artists, architects, planners, historians, and curators. They can also use the CultureNOW: A Guidebook for the Museum Without Walls, Lower Manhattan *http://tinyurl.com/6uaubjg* app to access 2000 pictures housed in Manhattan museums along with 70 podcasts about these pictures

Students could use note-taking apps to share their specific responses to these drawings/paintings based on the questions in the beginning of this chapter, as well as their analyses of the aesthetic qualities of these drawings/paintings having to do with use of techniques related to color, design, perspectives, juxtaposition/remix of different materials, etc. You can ask students to reflect on how they can then use some techniques in creating their own art.

## Summary

In this chapter, we described the use of apps for responding to and creating images for use in different subject matter areas. The uses of these apps reflect the increasing importance of the visual in communications, suggesting the need for students to acquire visual literacies to effectively understand and create images. In the next chapter, we describe the use of audio and video apps that are also essential for multimodal communication.

## References

Beach, R., Campano, G., Edmiston, B., & Borgmann, M. (2010). *Literacy tools in the classroom: Teaching through critical inquiry, grades 5–12*. New York: Teachers College Press.

Brustein, J. (2011, July 8). Bringing past, present and future into focus. *The New York Times*. Retrieved from http://tinyurl.com/7ybfhn6

Chandler, D. (2007). *Semiotics: The basics* (2nd ed.). New York: Routledge.

Council of Chief State Schools Officers and National Governors' Association. (2010). *Common Core State Standards for English Language Arts & Literacy in History/Social Studies, Science, and Technical Subjects*. Washington, DC: Author. Retrieved from http://www.corestandards.org

Harste, J. C., & Kress, G. (2012). Image, identity, and insights into language. *Language Arts, 89*(3), 205–212.

Hart-Davis, G. (2012). *Teach yourself visually: iPhone 4S*. Indianapolis, IN: John Wiley.

Hicks, T. (2013). *Crafting digital writing: Composing texts across media and genres*. Portsmouth, NH: Heinemann.

Hobbs, R. (2011). *Copyright clarity: How fair use supports digital learning*. Los Angeles: Corwin Press.

Hoffman, A. (2011). *Create great iPhone photos: Apps, tips, tricks, and effects*. San Francisco, CA: No Starch Press.

Housen, A. (2007). Art viewing and aesthetic development: Designing for the viewer. In P. Villeneuve (Ed.), *From periphery to center: Art museum education in the 21st century* (pp. 102–134). Reston, VA: the National Art Education Association.

Kress, G. (2009). *Multimodality: A social semiotic approach to contemporary communication*. New York: Routledge.

Kress, G., & Van Leeuwen, T. (2006). *Reading images: The grammar of visual design* (2nd ed.). New York: Routledge.

Mahiri, J. (2006). Digital DJ-ing: Rhythms of learning in an urban school. *Language Arts*, *84*(1), 55–62.

Marzano, R. (2010). Representing knowledge nonlinguistically. *Educational Leadership*, *67*(8), 84–86.

Muchmore, M. (2012, January 24). 9 great iPhone camera apps. *PC Magazine*. Retrieved from http://tinyurl.com/74cap3n

Siebert, D., & Hendrickson, S. (2010). (Re)Imagining literacies for mathematics classrooms. In R. Draper (Ed.), *(Re)Imagining content-area literacy instruction* (pp. 40–53). New York: Teachers College Press.

Stuart, D. H. (2012). Razzle dazzle of the Prezi adventure: Beyond the slide show. *Technology in Literacy Education Special Interest Group Newsletter*, *5*(2), 2–3, 5–6.

Wissman, K. K. (2008). "This is what I see": (Re)envisioning photography as a social practice. In M. L. Hill & L. Vasudevan (Eds.), *Media, learning, and sites of possibility* (pp. 13–46). New York: Peter Lang

# 9

# USING APPS FOR AUDIO AND VIDEO PRODUCTIONS

In addition to the use of apps to respond to and create images, students also use apps to create audio and video productions. We have organized this chapter into two sections: apps to foster the use of audio to support learning and apps to foster the use of video to support learning. Students use audio apps to listen to podcasts, presentations, music, and audiobooks, as well as to create their own podcasts and audiobooks, add audio comments to images and texts, and produce music. And students view online videos for learning and entertainment, as well as for creating their own videos to share experience and communicate information and ideas.

The English Language Arts Standards (Council of Chief State Schools Officers and National Governors' Association, 2010) listed below show how we are in a transitional period of moving from primarily print to visual and audio forms to support learning in school. The references to presenting information in "diverse ways" using technologies and "digital sources" indicates progress, but also shows that the standards have not caught up with research and theories from social semiotics and multimodality. But they do alert us to the fact that we need to be considering multiple sources of information and representation other than print. And the references to "strategic uses" and critical positions on various media represent a crucial step forward in consuming and producing ideas via a range of audio and video media.

## English Language Arts Common Core State Standards Related to Using Audio and Video to Learn

- Synthesize and apply information presented in diverse ways (e.g., through words, images, graphs, and video) in print and digital sources in order to answer questions, solve problems, or compare modes of presentation (reading standard). (p. 39)

- Use technology, including the Internet, to produce, publish, and interact with others about writing (writing standard). (p. 42)
- Gather relevant information from multiple print and digital sources, assess the credibility and accuracy of each source, and integrate and cite the information while avoiding plagiarism (writing standard). (p. 42)
- Integrate and evaluate information from multiple oral, visual, or multimodal sources in order to answer questions, solve problems, or build knowledge (speaking and listening standard). (p. 49)
- Make strategic use of digital media and visual displays of data to express information and enhance understanding (speaking and listening standard). (p. 49)

Addressing these standards through responding to and producing audio and video productions builds on students' strong interest in audio and video as tools for learning about the world. Knowing how to effectively employ these apps to enhance learning involves helping students understand the technical aspects of audio and video production, as well as their ability to critically analyze the quality and content of these productions.

## Using Audio

Audio can be a powerful medium for learning, as evident in the increased use of podcasts, audiobooks, and music designed to enhance students' learning across the curriculum. One advantage of digital audio files is that they can be readily created and shared. You can also listen to audio files while engaged in other activities. Hence, the popularity of listening to audiobooks while out walking, working out in the gym, or commuting in traffic.

Educators ask about the benefits and drawbacks of audio renditions of print text in place of reading. For example, teachers and parents wonder if listening to audio versions of print text might be detrimental in that listeners are not practicing reading when listening. This topic is extensive and controversial, but in this limited space, we return to our *accessibility* argument. Especially in the case of students with learning disabilities and others who struggle with reading, audio versions of texts can make previously inaccessible content accessible.

Our recommendation is to have students who struggle with reading fluency and word recognition listen to audio versions of texts they struggle with. Having an audio file of a difficult history or physics chapter, while the students read the text, is a useful online reading support in that students can read with a supportive voice giving them some fluency and word recognition support in places in the text where they might get stuck or slow down. We even have a couple of strategies in which some of your really good readers can ham it up, read like radio announcers and commentators, and insert some engaging jokes or other humor in making audio texts or podcasts that go with print informational texts that can be accessed by their peers. One trusted strategy we adapted from "Radio Reading" (Searfoss, 1975) includes the following steps:

1. Find some volunteers who like the sounds of their voices and have played with the idea of being announcers, sportscasters, or TV anchors.
2. Let them practice oral "announcer" reading with informational text from your textbook or other learning materials.
3. Have them script out the text and mark places in which radio readers insert text into the main text like jokes, fun questions, or commentaries on the text. These should be designed to keep their audience engaged and ideally connect to the original text.
4. When the radio-reading students have planned and practiced their scripts, have them use an audio editor like GarageBand or Audacity to create audio texts. These can be done chapter by chapter of textbooks, for example.
5. Make the audio library available to students via their computers, iPhones, iPads, iPod Touches, and any other MP3 players to listen to when your class is studying print texts corresponding with the audio files.

Students can also use the CoverLite *http://tinyurl.com/lnsps3c* app for generating live audio or video descriptions of events in their roles as school newspaper reporters, for example, reporting on school meetings or sports games, or in creating reports about issues or civic events in their community. Students can add their own voice-over commentary; publish photos, audio, and video in real time; and e-mail events links or post to Twitter.

## Working With Special Needs and ELL Students

As previously noted, audio is also particularly useful for working with students with learning disabilities that affect language and literacy skills with print. Because these students often have difficulty with reading and/or writing of print texts, listening to a text or using audio apps to produce texts provides them with an alternative way of responding to or producing texts. For example, in lieu of writing an essay, students can create an audio report. Or, as noted in Chapter 6, they can use audio notes or interviews to generate materials for use in writing an essay draft.

Audio is also useful for ELLs or second and world language learners. Students can use a range of apps for listening to and practicing oral language in a different/second language. For example, students can create and share YouTube videos in which they share their facility in using and translating different languages, videos that can be used for second and world language learner instruction.

Or, in literature classes, students can record themselves reading aloud/ performing poetry as a means of enhancing their interpretation of poetry. In his college literature classes, Christopher Phillips (2011) argues for the importance of audio performances of literature that draw on ancient forms of aural learning valued in the past. His students engage in "performed criticism" by creating audio poetry anthologies shared with their class, along with sharing their essays to a Moodle course where they describe their decisions in interpreting and recording their poems.

## Creating Audio Files and Podcasts

One important use of audio to learn involves creating audio files and podcasts. Audio files are simply files that are saved as files on a computer or server. In contrast, podcasts are audio files typically organized as a series of files associated with a topic or radio show with an RSS feed that allows users to subscribe to those podcasts on sites such as iTunes or as links on a blog to download to their iPad, iPhone, or device. The abbreviation RSS stands for Really Simple Syndication, which means that once you subscribe to a podcast, then the information about that podcast is automatically sent to you.

An important literacy practice is the ability to listen to podcasts to garner ideas for creating podcasts. For example, by listening to news podcasts made available using the iOS *http://tinyurl.com/kwtrq6x* and Android *http://tinyurl. com/lc8eunw* CNN Student News apps, students can create their own classroom or school news podcasts as a radio broadcast. Or, by listening to other students from different parts of the world in the iOS *http://tinyurl.com/n4ebmld* or Android *http://tinyurl.com/khxs2jm* Rock Our World app, students gain a sense of cultural beliefs and attitudes that can shape how they communicate their own cultural beliefs and attitudes to these different audiences. Or, in world language classes, students exchange podcasts with other students from all over the world using the eLanguages *http://www.elanguages.org* site as part of learning to communicate using different languages.

Students also indicated that podcasts about the course content helped them review material from a course so that they did not need to be concerned about taking notes about specific details in the course (Tam, 2012). Students also preferred short podcasts—and edited summaries of material of no more than 15 minutes.

## *Accessing Podcasts*

Students can readily access a wide range of podcasts available for subscriptions from the iTunes Store Podcasts and iTunes U. You and/or your students can use keyword searches to find these podcasts, as well as use the podcast access apps listed below.

---

## APPS FOR ACCESSING PODCASTS

**iOS**: Podcasts *http://tinyurl.com/mmtv9cb*, Podomatic Podcast Player *http://tinyurl.com/n4k2w4n*, Podcaster 4 *http://tinyurl.com/7yvszrsor*, Instacast *http://tinyurl.com/cjwqwye*, iCatcher! *http://tinyurl.com/3ctnwp7*, Downcast *http://tinyurl.com/43nuhw2*, RSSRadio Mobile *http://tinyurl.com/6n4bjh2*, Podfisher *http://tinyurl.com/7w7lvrf*, Podcast Box *http://tinyurl.com/64vjxs6*, Podcast Pro *http://tinyurl.com/7ewup24*, and Stitcher Radio *http://tinyurl.com/7m4vr5k*, Education Podcast Network *http://www.epnweb.org*, Podcast Alley *http://www.podcastalley.com*, Podcastdirectory *http://podcastdirectory.com*, Fluctu8 Podcast Directory *http://www.fluctu8.com*

**Android**: PocketCasts *http://tinyurl.com/83mdl4j*, BeyondPod Podcast Manager *http://tinyurl.com/c3woxkv*, Antenna Pod *http://tinyurl.com/crmpwhs*, IPP Podcast Player *http://tinyurl.com/ltm2dh4*, DoggCatcher Podcast Lite *http://tinyurl.com/lxhdgfq*, Cast++ Podcast Player *http://tinyurl.com/n34qqdd*, Podcatcher Deluxe *http://tinyurl.com/177tkrt*

---

Students also access podcasts through the iTunes Store on a desktop and the iTunes app on their iPad or iPhone, which houses audio and video texts for free and for purchase within the categories of Music, Movies, TV Shows, Podcasts, Audiobooks, iTunes U, and Apps. Students can also use iTunes as a storage site to upload songs, audio recordings, or podcasts, as well as video, something we discuss later in this chapter.

The iOS *http://tinyurl.com/cdp9jcj* and Android *http://tinyurl.com/l8hjdr3* iTunes U app provides access to a wide range of college and K-12 courses including video or audio lectures, along with syllabi, texts, notes, and iBooks. Students can also highlight and take notes for inclusion on the iTunes U site. You can also use the iTunes U as a site for sharing your own course materials—assignments, tutorials, readings, videos, images, podcasts, assessments, etc.

When students enter your iTunes U course, they see a bookshelf with your syllabus, Keynote presentations, Pages documents, PDFs, apps, assignments, topics, notes, and announcements on the left site. You can link to specific readings from the iBookstore, including iBooks, as well as videos from iTunes. In the Notes tab, you and/or your students can add and store notes from any texts or course. To create a course, you enroll in the iTunes U portal and then access the support site and the iTunes U Course Manager that provides tutorials on creating course materials. Students can also go to other courses at the Open Culture Links of 400 Free Online Courses from Top Universities.

The iTunes U podcasts are organized both in terms of K–12 schools and universities and by different categories. As you develop your own recordings or videos for students, along with iBook content using the iBooks Author app, you can store them on the iTunes U K–12 site not only for use by your own students within your school iTunes account, but also, if it's open to the public, other teachers. There are also podcasts related to specific subjects listed on the website *http://tinyurl.com/kr73fko*.

## Podcast Production Apps

In addition to listening to podcasts, students can create their own podcasts. In creating podcasts, students should first determine the purpose and audience for their podcasts based on defining a relatively specific focus. Students may also find that rather than engaging in a monologue podcast, they may be more comfortable working with a peer to create a conversational podcast. They may also create a script or set of notes that serves to organize and focus their podcast (for a series of podcasts about creating podcasts as well as use of podcasts in teaching writing, see Bowie, 2012a/2012b).

Audio files or podcasts can be used for a range of different purposes:

- recording presentations and lectures;
- sharing demonstrations;
- posting assignments or reminders;
- listening to historical speeches or news reports of events;
- interviewing people and peers about certain topics or issues;
- creating panel discussions, debates, or radio talk shows;
- listening to and performing literary texts or music;
- providing feedback on students' work;
- employing "autocasting" software such as Talkr to convert their blog posts into audio; or
- creating "soundseeing" audio tours of places.

To record audio you or your students can also use dictation/audio-recording apps described in Chapters 3 and 6 such as Dragon Dictation, Audiotorium, or Audio Memo to record audio. One benefit of using these apps with an iPad or iPhone relates to portability; students can record their observations as they are engaged in an activity, for example going on a field trip or conducting a science experiment. They then have a record of their spontaneous reactions to an activity for use in later writing about those activities.

To create a podcast with an RSS feed so others can subscribe to it on iTunes or a blog, students need to create a 2.0 RSS feed using browser apps such as Feedburner *http://tinyurl.com/lpqbpyv*, FeedForAll *http://www.feedforall.com*, or Podomatic *http://tinyurl.com/8dtoj2a*. In Feedburner, they go to Settings and select Formatting. Then, they find the Show Link Field and click on Yes. To add a feed to a Blogger blog, they first add their MP3 file to their blog by going to Posting-Create, adding a title and show notes, and then adding a link to the file and publish—creating a URL link. They then go to "Setting-Site Feed" to obtain a feed address—which is in Atom format.

## APPS FOR CREATING PODCASTS

**Web-based apps**: GarageBand for Mac *http://tinyurl.com/lemswvx*, Audacity for Windows *http://tinyurl.com/3jcmr* or Mac *http://tinyurl.com/5b8w7*, Spreaker *http://www.spreaker.com* for Mac, Podomatic for Mac *http://tinyurl.com/8dtoj2a*, Podcast Generator *http://tinyurl.com/ks7m5ce*

**iOS**: GarageBand *http://tinyurl.com/mmkcto3*, Soundcloud *http://tinyurl.com/ml4kzjc*, Spreaker *http://tinyurl.com/mh3venz*, Vocaroo *http://vocaroo.com*, Audioboo *http://tinyurl.com/ml6my84*, Audio Recorder *http://tinyurl.com/k62q3ut*, iTalk Recorder *http://tinyurl.com/k243797*, Recorder *http://tinyurl.com/lj3r78v*

**Android**: Audio Evolution Mobile *http://tinyurl.com/bjsnrqd*, Spreader *http://tinyurl.com/6udcasfn*, Track Studio *http://tinyurl.com/kja6x8d*, Virtual Recorder *http://tinyurl.com/lbbwbyl*

One of the primary podcasting apps is GarageBand, which can be used to create an audio recording as well as to produce music or add a music track to an audio recording. In using GarageBand, students choose Track and then the New Track option and then select the option, Real Instrument, because they are recording using their voice. They then select the Male Voice or Female Voice tracks and test out their microphone recording level by noting the amount of green that appears in the right section of the Voice panel. The Podcast Track is for adding images; the Jingles and Radio tracks are for adding music or sounds. The No Effects option is available if they don't want to use the Male or Female Voice options—but it generally works better to select the Male or Female Voice options. They then click Record to record their podcast and click on Record again to stop recording (they can also use the shift bar to start and stop recording).

To edit, students select the track with the waveform at the top that then creates the Track Editor on the bottom for editing that track. To edit a section of the track, they select an area they want to edit and/or to cut—that section then appears in dark blue. They can then select Edit and Cut to remove that section, resulting in a gray gap. To close the gap, they use their finger to slide the right side to close up the gap. They can also use GarageBand to add in "loops"—sound effects, jingles, or music—as well as raise or lower the voice sound, and add in visual images that cue audiences about a podcast's different segments or "chapters."

Because GarageBand doesn't export MP3 files, students first choose Track to go to Show Podcast Track and then Share to Send Podcast to iTunes. They can select Compress to choose MP3 or AAC (if they are adding images, they need to select AAC). They then choose a specific audio quality from the Audio Settings menu. They then select Send Song to iTunes in GarageBand. Then, they find their file in iTunes and, under Advanced, select Convert Selection to iPod. To add ID3 tags, they select File, Get Info, and then fill in information for the name, artist, year, album, track number, composer, comments, and genre (select podcast).

## Studying and Creating Music

Another important use of audio to learn involves studying and creating music. While it is often assumed that studying and creating music is limited to music/band courses, given its high appeal for students, music can be used to foster learning in all subjects. Students in English language arts or art classes study the use of music in film or video productions. Music can also be used to foster writing of stories. In studying the relationship between music and story, Gaetan Pappalardo (2010) had her students view a video of John Williams conducting an orchestra in creating the soundtrack for the movie, *Jaws*, to focus on how the music served to convey the storyline. Or students in history classes can use the History for Music Lovers YouTube channel that includes music videos about specific historical events. (For useful tips on the use of iPad and iPhone apps in teaching music, see Christopher Russell's TeachingMusic blog *http://techinmusiced.wordpress.com* as well as his iBook book, *Practical Technology for Music Educators.*)

### Music Listening Apps

The primary app for accessing music is iTunes, which requires that you and your students have Apple accounts for purchasing songs. You and your students can use iTunes for creating your own playlists of songs based on certain genres, historical periods, or artists. However, students can also access music using the streaming music/radio apps listed below; for example TuneIn Radio that provides access to more than 50,000 radio stations and podcasts.

## STREAMING MUSIC/RADIO APPS

**iOS**: Tuneln Radio *http://tinyurl.com/792de6v*, Pandora *http://tinyurl.com/ybtlxcd*, Spotify *http://tinyurl.com/6uz94yc*, Slacker Radio *http://tinyurl.com/kxcj2k3*, Rhapsody *http://tinyurl.com/6ovhb89*, Sticher Radio *http://tinyurl.com/7m4vr5k*, radio.com *http://tinyurl.com/csy666d*, Tuneln Radio *http://tinyurl.com/792de6v*, ooTunes Radio *http://tinyurl.com/82w3becas*, LastFM *http://tinyurl.com/83n2qz2*, Live365 *http://tinyurl.com/879pw4t*, Internet Radio Box *http://tinyurl.com/7gnwqse*

**Android**: Pandora *http://tinyurl.com/6n7rw9p*, Tuneln Radio *http://tinyurl.com/7bjvjyq*, Slacker Radio *http://tinyurl.com/makw58b*, Spotify *http://tinyurl.com/dym3ogu*, Google Play Music *http://tinyurl.com/77hxf2e*, Android Music Player *http://tinyurl.com/77hxf2e*, MOG Mobile Music *http://tinyurl.com/mjlntwq*, dBstream *http://tinyurl.com/mxx22c6*, Music Stream *http://tinyurl.com/ll58ahq*, Rhapsody *http://tinyurl.com/kevmlhf*

In listening to music, students learn to identify certain songs simply by recalling the song itself. Students can use the Let's Sing! Free *http://tinyurl.com/ck2ue8w* app game that involves one player identifying a song title that another player whistles or hums without using words. The player attempting to guess the title can access Hints for guessing the correct title by providing vowels in the title or the name of the performer.

### Music Production Apps

As is the case with podcasting, the primary app for creating music is GarageBand. Students can use GarageBand to record a range of different instruments simultaneously. The 2012 version of GarageBand includes different Touch Instruments for playing Smart Instruments—pianos, organs, guitars, drums, and basses—as well as recording their own voice. Students can also plug in instruments such as an electric guitar. Using the Multi-Touch keyboard and the Jam Session feature, up to four different students can play different instruments to mix up to eight tracks to create a song.

For example, students in Brock Dubbels's language arts class used GarageBand to create and record songs as members of an imagined band (O'Brien & Dubbels, 2010). To do so, they employed their reading of poems, paragraphs, dialogue, and lyrics to create their lyrics to record themselves reading the text on one of the GarageBand tracks, recording that involved oral interpretation of the lyrics based on their tone, theme, pitch, volume, and emphasis in elongation and breaks. They then added music and beats on another track, drawing on their knowledge of music they liked—and recorded themselves reading as a track on the music software.

For recording using specific instruments, students can employ the apps listed below.

---

## APPS FOR RECORDING SPECIFIC INSTRUMENTS

### Piano

**iOS**: Pocket Piano HD *http://tinyurl.com/833jcps*, Amazing Piano *http://tinyurl.com/6txxtnr*, Virtuoso 3 *http://tinyurl.com/6zxlccy*

**Android**: MyPiano *http://tinyurl.com/m9bv2q7*, Magic Piano *http://tinyurl.com/mmxlg7k*, Real Piano *http://tinyurl.com/n4gsv7v*

### Guitar

**iOS**: Guitar Pro *http://tinyurl.com/6bm6wz3*, Six Strings *http://tinyurl.com/3jggmfu*, Magic Guitar *http://tinyurl.com/74ps657*, Guitar Chords *http://tinyurl.com/6lmotue*, IamGuitar *http://tinyurl.com/7c38odf*

**Android**: MyGuitar *http://tinyurl.com/m9dcye5*, Real Guitar *http://tinyurl.com/k22pw3o*, Guitar! *http://tinyurl.com/meuvb2u*, Guitarist *http://tinyurl.com/kukeoxx*

### Drums

**iOS**: myDrum Pad *http://tinyurl.com/75r7g3h*, Shiny Drum *http://tinyurl.com/77erffd*, Drum Kit *http://tinyurl.com/7rfjko2*, DM1 The Drum Machine *http://tinyurl.com/6tw2rku*, FunkBox Drum Machine *http://tinyurl.com/7ancz75*, and Barrel Tones *http://tinyurl.com/899r3fb*

**Android**: GrooveMixer *http://tinyurl.com/ksl4la4*, Drums *http://tinyurl.com/mczy62f*, Drums Droid HD Free *http://tinyurl.com/m3cl873*, Drum Kit *http://tinyurl.com/boneroa*, Read Drum *http://tinyurl.com/n638osg*

### Synthesizer Music

**iOS**: Animoog *http://tinyurl.com/mrcfevj*, NanoStudio *http://tinyurl.com/kwwtrt3*, Rhythm Studio *http://tinyurl.com/kt6bhvq*, BeatWave *http://tinyurl.com/myzdyba*, SoundPrism *http://tinyurl.com/nyu6sjy*, Music Studio Lite *http://tinyurl.com/msdq586*

**Android**: Musical Studio *http://tinyurl.com/mmgyros*, Music Synthesizer for Android *http://tinyurl.com/m86xbbz*, PocketBand Lite *http://tinyurl.com/mpub8um*, Studio Music *http://tinyurl.com/mpub8um*, EasySynth Synthesizer *http://tinyurl.com/n8znbfa*

---

In addition to recording specific instruments using these apps, students can also use the synthesizer apps to record on different audio tracks to then combine them together into one single track.

Students can also use the iOS *http://tinyurl.com/luwba2w* and Android *http://tinyurl.com/9dotuxs* Songify app that transforms spoken words into songs. Or, they can use the iOS *http://tinyurl.com/mlgw79y* and Android *http://tinyurl.com/mym7ps3* StarMaker: Karaoke + Auto-Tune app to record Karaoke songs.

To create music remixes, students can employ the iOS iRemix *http://tinyurl.com/kb3hyl* and DJ Mixer *http://tinyurl.com/n8pejtm*; iOS *http://tinyurl.com/mcz7qj4* or Android *http://tinyurl.com/c9rnetr* edjing DJ Studio; or Android Music Maker Jam *http://tinyurl.com/lj4ztqn* and DJStudio *http://tinyurl.com/a5hnnq5* that provide access to students' own music library for use in creating remixes, as well as the ability to add their own recording as part of the remix.

## Using Video

There has been a major increase in the uses of videos as an essential learning tool. This is evident in the previously described "flipped classroom" model in which students can access and view instructional videos using apps such as the Khan Academy app that includes short video tutorials as homework so that they can spend time in classes engaged in hands-on work. Ideally, the videos they view are interactive in ways that foster constructivist learning, as opposed to simple lecture videos based on a transmission model of learning.

Videos serve to foster learning through visually portraying ideas or information in ways that engage students. Showing videos of historical events—for example, the bombing of Pearl Harbor—provides a more memorable experience of that event than simply listening to or reading about a description of that event.

Students can also engage in interactive video lessons entitled History Live *http://tinyurl.com/mge8otb* produced by the Minnesota Historical Society in which they use their mobile devices to participate in activities; Minnesota schools pay $75.00 and schools outside of Minnesota pay $120.00 to participate (Hawkins, 2014). Some of the lessons include:

> Media Literacy: 1968: A Year that Changed America (grades 9–12)
> The Dred Scott Family and the National Debate Over Slavery (grades 9–12)
> 1900s Logging Camp: The Life of a Lumberjack (grades 4–6)
> A Voyage Into The Past: The Great Lakes Fur Trade (grades 4–6)
> The Civilian Conservation Corps: A Good Deal from the New Deal (grades 4–6)
> Messages Through Time: American Indian Culture Preserved in Stone (grades 4–6)

For example, in The Dred Scott Family and the National Debate Over Slavery *http://tinyurl.com/mgxb6hk*, students use their mobile devices to revise the Dred Scott family court case decision into their own words, revisions that are then shared for a vote to select the top revisions that are then read aloud by an Uncle Sam avatar.

And, given that videos are now easy to produce, students recognize that from viewing these videos, they can create their own videos to communicate ideas or information.

Videos can also be used to enhance students' digital literacy practices. For example, in reading literature, students may first read a novel, story, or play, and then view a film adaptation of that novel, story, or play to compare their own interpretations with that of the filmmaker, who may produce a very literal versus loose adaptation.

### Accessing Videos Relevant for School Use

The iOS Videos app that comes with the iPad and iPhone serves as a tool for accessing, storing, and playing videos organized according to TV Shows, Movies, and Music Videos, as well as movie rentals from the iTunes Store. There are also a wide range of different apps listed below for accessing videos relevant for school use.

---

## APPS FOR ACCESSING VIDEOS FOR SCHOOL USE

iOS *http://tinyurl.com/coafw5n* and Android *http://tinyurl.com/cqc85sm*
YouTube

iOS *http://tinyurl.com/299auve* and Android *http://tinyurl.com/7eruzhh*
TED Talks

iOS *http://tinyurl.com/849pf7q* and Android *http://tinyurl.com/6ue5l9l*
Khan Academy

iOS *http://www.teachertube.com* and Android *http://tinyurl.com/ljvtomq*
TeacherTube

iOS *http://tinyurl.com/lfbu9mw* and Android *http://tinyurl.com/md2jn4p*
BrainPOP Featured Movie

iOS *http://tinyurl.com/7k99o3a* and Android *http://tinyurl.com/kgyqnvv*
Discovery Channel

iOS *http://tinyurl.com/dyzhshv* and Android *http://tinyurl.com/7wnpk5e*
Vimeo

iOS *http://tinyurl.com/ochblgv* and Android *http://tinyurl.com/khvwj8d*
Frequency

iOS *http://tinyurl.com/mnspv74* and Android *http://tinyurl.com/cbakkk6*
Snagfilms

iOS *http://tinyurl.com/8ecr25h* and Android *http://tinyurl.com/7fcs2nj*
Hulu+

iOS *http://tinyurl.com/3sgon5f* and Android *http://tinyurl.com/kkvswav*
ShowYou

iOS *http://tinyurl.com/mpzjqwu* and Android *http://tinyurl.com/3sgon5f*
PBS Videos

iOS *http://tinyurl.com/m96bvgd* and Android *http://tinyurl.com/mlswtv9*
WatchKnow Educational Videos

iOS *http://tinyurl.com/mg8bd9t* and Android *http://tinyurl.com/2fmdw8j*
Video Science

iOS *http://tinyurl.com/lgqjkw6* and Android *http://tinyurl.com/ndqtkh8*
Video2Brain

iOS *http://tinyurl.com/lo92ymt* and Android *http://tinyurl.com/mp5gzag*
Mobento

---

These apps can be used to access, organize, and/or share videos, including viewing a video at a later time:

- The BrainPOP Featured Movie app provides animated videos related to different subject matter areas, with new videos added each day, providing a vast repository of videos relevant to your instructional needs.
- The Amazon Instant Video app has access to 120,000 videos; if you are an Amazon Prime Member, many of those videos are free. For example, the Video Time Machine provides access to movies from the 1800s to the present for use in film studies or history courses.
- The Vimeo app provides access to an extensive collection of videos for uploading, storing, and organizing according to Groups, Channels, and Albums; user-produced videos can also be uploaded. The Browse feature is particularly useful for finding videos; videos can be put on a Watch Later queue. You or your students can make comments about videos, as well as share them on Facebook, Twitter, Tumblr, WordPress, e-mail, and/or iMessage. Videos can also be edited to add transitions, titles, effects, and music for saving on a camera roll or uploading to Vimeo.
- The Frequency app can be used to determine which topics portrayed in videos are particularly popular within video channels. Students can also create their own Tuner to track topics they are following as well as highlights from challenges in My Feed.
- The SnagFilms app is relevant for accessing 150 biography, history, and music documentaries that are particularly useful for viewing in class using AirPlay and Apple TV. The documentaries on SnagFilms can be used to have students examine issues facing society, as well as serve as stimuli for creating their own documentaries.

Other discipline-based video apps include:

- Video Science app for short videos demonstrating science experiments;
- Discovery Channel HD app that provides extensive videos particularly relevant to science and history;
- Khan Academy app that has thousands of videos on science, math, history, and other subjects;
- PBS video app with more than 300 videos, including Frontline, History Detectives, Masterpiece, Nature, Need to Know, Nova, Secrets of the Dead, and more;
- TED Talks app with video presentations on all disciplines.

## Using YouTube

The major video resource remains YouTube. One English teacher uses YouTube parodies of Shakespeare plays to teach his plays (Desmet, 2009). A math teacher showed videos that include math errors, asking students to identify those errors (Niess & Walker, 2009). Social studies teachers post videos of historical events (Haase, 2009) and science teachers post videos portraying science experiments (Park, 2009).

However, many districts block YouTube given the problematic material or advertising available on it. To address this issue, YouTube created the YouTube EDU *http://www.youtube.com/education* site that includes teachers' playlists of educational videos that are organized by subject and grade, as well as aligned with standards and lessons. They also created the YouTube for Schools *https://www.youtube.com/schools* service that provides schools with controls over which videos are viewable within a school by creating their own YouTube video network within their school. Schools can sign up as Partners so that administrators and/or teachers can log in to preview videos from YouTube EDU, but students cannot log in. Administrators and/or teachers can then create video playlists that are viewable within their school's network. Students can also use YouTube for Schools to create and share videos.

Teachers can also use the following tools for limiting access to content on YouTube: ProTube HD ad-blocker *http://tinyurl.com/7tq46uc*, Subscriptions *http://tinyurl.com/89bqb3u*, A Cleaner Internet *http://clea.nr* (removes extraneous material from YouTube), NowBox *http://tinyurl.com/7ytjeo4*, or Videohunters *http://tinyurl.com/3u7yo2c* (organizes uses and subscriptions to YouTube).

And, you or your students can save a copy of a YouTube video on a computer and then transfer it to an iPad's "Photo Roll" without having to connect the iPad to a computer. In this video (*http://tinyurl.com/6pryz3c*), Wesley Fryer explains how to use the browser app SaveYouTube and the PhotoSync app to save and transfer a YouTube video.

One advantage of YouTube is that its videos are organized into different channels as well as tagged according to keywords, which facilitates finding relevant videos for use in the classroom. For example, the iPedagogy YouTube Channel provides video tutorials on uses of iPads and iPad apps. The Spangler Science channel portrays examples of science experiments. You can also create your own classroom Channel for use by your students to share and/or upload their own videos. The LessonPaths site *http://tinyurl.com/l62pql7* was built by users who create and add videos to playlists relevant to their interests and needs. And, for use in the classrooms, particularly with YouTube videos, LessonPaths eliminates problematic material.

Students can also use YouTube videos for cross-cultural sharing of information about their own cultures as reflected in local media sources (Bloom & Johnston, 2010). Students can share their videos with "video pals" throughout the world and reflect on questions such as:

(1) How does my presentation differ from my video pals? (2) Which, if any, of these differences might be attributed to cultural differences? (3) How did my understanding of this topic change during the process of production? . . . What messages do my video(s) send about my culture? How might someone from another culture interpret my video(s)? How do I interpret my video-pal's production? (pp. 118–119)

Students can also use YouTube to record videos on a webcam directly into YouTube using YouTube Quick Capture. They need to go to "Upload Videos" and provide information about their video. They then select "Use Quick Capture" and then click "Record." Their video will then be stored on YouTube so that they can then copy the "embed" code to their blog.

As previously noted in our description of annotations, students can also use the YouTube Annotations feature to add their annotations to YouTube videos for the purpose of analyzing or sharing reactions to videos (for a video about the use of YouTube Annotations in a "flipped" classroom: *http://tinyurl.com/3mvhwrr*). Students can also use the VideoAnt *http://ant.umn.edu* tool to import YouTube videos to add written annotations to specific images in a video.

Students can also use the Dragontape *http://tinyurl.com/7vuv4z9* app to create remixes of YouTube videos, a primary genre on YouTube. For example, they can create a composite montage of different videos on a certain topic, issue, theme, or object—videos about sports figures highlight performances.

### Creating Videos

In addition to using the screencasting apps described in Chapter 8, students can also use video production apps for creating videos. The newer iPads and Android devices have improved video production features that mean that students can film and edit their videos on these devices without necessarily having to import video from a digital video camera.

Through creating videos, students are learning how to use video as a powerful tool for literacy learning across the curriculum. In their science and math classes, students can use videos to record science experiments or processes involved in solving math problems to not only demonstrate their abilities and knowledge, but also to assist their peers in conducting these experiments or solving math problems. These student-produced videos then contribute to creating a virtual learning commons or databank for teachers to use to discuss different ways of conducting experiments or solving math problems, as well as noting instances of successful versus less successful practices.

For example, in Vito Ferrante's math class, students create their own "think-aloud" videos of themselves addressing math problems (Noonoo, 2012). One student engages in a think-aloud as another student records their think-aloud. Students then switch roles with the other student engaging in the "think-alouds." These videos are then uploaded to their own YouTube Channel for viewing by Ferrante, their peers, and/or parents who can then give the students feedback or share their own experiences. Ferrante notes that creating these videos enhances students' ability to self-correct their mistakes:

> Thinking through the problem forces them to see what they're doing correctly and incorrectly . . . It seems like they're catching their problems a lot more quickly, and they're not just doing the same things over and over again incorrectly. (p. 22)

In social studies, science, or English classes in which students are conducting ethnographic or qualitative research, students can use videos to complement taking written field notes to record their observations of phenomena. For example, in studying students' practices of sitting in cliques in the school lunchroom, students could record videos of these groups (with the students' permission) to document these different groups' actions.

In lieu of writing research papers, over a five-week unit in a twelfth-grade English class on mass media and film production, students collaboratively generated a research paper that served as the basis for a five-minute documentary video that highlighted the material in their research paper (Mallery, 2011). Knowing that they would be creating a documentary video from their writing reshaped their writing to focus on information and visual material relevant to creating their documentary. And, because they were sharing their documentary with their peers, they had a greater sense of audience that itself influenced their writing.

For providing feedback on students' performances in sports, music, or theater, you can use the iOS *http://tinyurl.com/kvqpxhl* and Android *http://tinyurl.com/lqcjbor* Coach's Eye app to record a student's performance. You can then slow down the physical movement for use in providing recorded feedback about the students' use of techniques or form. For example, a coach could record a student's baseball pitch or basketball shot to then share with the student to provide them with feedback.

## Video Production Planning Apps

For planning videos, students need to first create a script and a storyboard to determine the use of certain scenes/settings, types of shots (close-ups, mid-shots, establishing) or angles, use of sound effects or music, and lighting. To do so, they can use scripting apps such as the iOS *http://tinyurl.com/6kf9kvp* or Android *http://tinyurl.com/myuhy32* Celtx Script, the iOS ScriptWrite *http://tinyurl.com/6pnvtxw* or Scriptly *http://tinyurl.com/jvrfl7k* or the Android Scriptwriter *http://tinyurl.com/m2av5rb* or Screenwriter *http://tinyurl.com/m2av5rb* apps. Students can also use Celtx Script app to create their scripts that links to the Celtx desktop version or iCloud so that different students can work together on the same script; they can also e-mail their script as PDFs or text files.

If they are going to be using a lot of different shots in different places, as opposed to just shooting themselves or someone else talking, they should create a storyboard using the storyboard apps listed below to determine the kinds of shots or angles they want to employ: close-ups versus mid-shots (waist up) versus long or establishing shots of a setting, as well as use of cutaway shots showing people's reactions to actions.

---

## STORYBOARDING APPS

**iOS**: Storyboarder *http://tinyurl.com/lhgsyfa*, Storyboards *http://tinyurl.com/m6h6u4n*, Storyboard Composer *http://tinyurl.com/yjxqpoz*, Cinemek Storyboard Composer *http://tinyurl.com/k6xwkq4*, Storyboards 3D *http://tinyurl.com/mrblv3p*, Storyboarder Toolbox *http://tinyurl.com/lhgsyfa*

**Android**: Storyboarder *http://tinyurl.com/nykk5jk*, Storyboard Studio *http://tinyurl.com/k88542t*, Storyboard Maker *http://tinyurl.com/lse8qay*, Storyboard Pro *http://tinyurl.com/ma8qunl*

---

These apps provide students with a wide choice of page templates; students can also import photos, as well as edit or point on those photos. These apps provide options for uses of different types of shots, angles, or framing, and generic objects to add to scenes, as well as the ability to import photos. Students can also use comics apps such as Strip Designer *http://tinyurl.com/3aekl57*, Comics Creator *http://tinyurl.com/6ovrdf8*, PhotoComic *http://tinyurl.com/6qxsjz*, or Comic Touch Lite *http://tinyurl.com/3ov8mfq* to create storyboards. (For a free e-book on use of comics for digital storytelling/storyboarding by Richard Byrne, *Digital Storytelling with Comics*: *http://tinyurl.com/kap43lp*.) Students can also use the Storyboard That *http://www.storyboardthat.com* Web app to collaboratively construct storyboards about literary texts or issues they are studying as a means of demonstrating their understanding of these texts or issues.

## *Video-Editing Apps*

Once they have shot their video, students can then use the video-editing apps listed below to edit their video. Because they are compressing down their video typically to a 320 x 240 screen size for online sharing, they do not necessarily need to do a lot of fancy editing techniques associated with Hollywood movies; employing excessive editing can make a viewer focus more on the use of editing techniques than on the video's content.

---

## VIDEO-EDITING APPS

**iOS**: iMovie *http://tinyurl.com/9y2gab4*, Animoto Video Maker for iPad *http://tinyurl.com/d52y28g*, StoryRobe *http://tinyurl.com/a2pcnbx*, Touchcast *http://tinyurl.com/pocs7b5*, Pinnacle Studio *http://tinyurl.com/kfd2qnh*, Reel-Director *http://tinyurl.com/l8gnuwz*, Videolicious *http://tinyurl.com/85rqdob*, Splice Video Editor *http://tinyurl.com/8y7crbg*, Video Edit *http://tinyurl.com/84vd7wj*, Video Editor Free *http://tinyurl.com/ny9xq2n*, Splice *http://tinyurl.com/mtatdpk*, Magisto *http://tinyurl.com/bpd4mm2*, Movie360 *http://tinyurl.com/mp3xmtj*, Avid Studio *http://tinyurl.com/7zwjh4b*, Silent Film Director *http://tinyurl.com/3qc6xfk*, Movie Looks HD *http://tinyurl.com/7tgd8lk*

**Android**: WeVideo *http://tinyurl.com/mnvgju7*, Video Editor *http://tinyurl.com/ky4dvmp*, Magisto *http://tinyurl.com/cqd8h9e*, Video Maker Pro *http://tinyurl.com/k4ezuw2*, KlipMix *http://tinyurl.com/k9trb8c*, MovieStudio Video Maker *http://tinyurl.com/n7v2zle*, Video Edit *http://tinyurl.com/kt93599*, Video Show *http://tinyurl.com/n6f99nv*

**Chrome OS**: WeVideo *http://tinyurl.com/ldaljcc*

---

The primary video-editing apps are the iOS iMovie app and Android/Chrome OS WeVideo apps. Students import their video or images into iMovie and then employ different "themes" with their own unique transitions, titles, and soundtrack. They can also import photos from their photo library, add sound effects and music, and add their own choice of transitions, including the Ken Burns effect. And, they can create their own recorded soundtrack in GarageBand to import into iMovie. They can also plan and produce their own movie trailers from their video content using nine different pre-set video and music templates. Once they complete their video, they can export it as a QuickTime video or publish it to YouTube, Facebook, Vimeo, and CNN iReport. They can also use AirPlay to show it on a TV. One advantage of the WeVideo app is that because it is cloud-based, it can support students working collaboratively on editing the same video using different tablets or Chromebooks.

The Avid Studio app builds on its storyboard features to organize videos into blocks. It also includes a versatile editing timeline that includes three different audio tracks for combining sound effects, a recorded soundtrack, music, and/or voice-overs.

The ReelDirector app includes a lot of options for transitions and adding text/titles, as well as an easy-to-use timeline. Students can preview their editing choices to test them out, something that helps them in making decisions about editing options

The Silent Film Director app allows students to add and render special effects associated with silent films. Students can also access a gallery of silent films created by other users to gain a sense of the techniques associated with these special effects. The Film Director app is similar to the Silent Film Director app for adding special effects associated with 8mm film—for example, the use of dust & scratches, retro colors, grainy images, flickering, and lighting effects. Students can also use the Movie Looks HD app to add certain Hollywood movie styles to their videos.

## Creating Digital Stories or Music Videos

In their literature classes, students can create personal narrative or digital storytelling videos based on poems, music, and/or pictures that portray certain memories, sounds, smells, and sights, something that we described in Chapter 7 in creating videos of image collections.

In creating these personal narratives or digital stories, students build their stories around a "story core" (Ohler, 2007, p. 72) based on characters' change or growth in coping with challenges or some basic conflict associated with dramatic questions—will the main character be successful in overcoming challenges, who committed the crime, will a relationship between characters develop, etc. Based on these changes or questions, students then create a "story map" (p. 79) that fleshes out the events in a story, leading to a storyboard or script for a digital video production.

Students also need to consider how to engage their audience's emotions through developing characters or situations with which their audiences will identify, for example, the fact that their audiences themselves have faced similar challenges to those facing a main character.

Students then consider how their selection and uses of images and music will serve to foster audience engagement. For example, Jennifer Skalski (2011) had her students create a personal narrative video by first writing a narrative poem based on George Ella Lyon's "Where I'm From" poem in which they describe specific images, artifacts, sounds, descriptions, etc., of the place where they live. Students then used GarageBand to record themselves reading the poem along with a musical song for their poem; they then exported their recording to iLife Preview for temporary saving. Students then collected .jpg images for use in illustrating their poem from sites such as FreeFoto, Gimp Savvy, Pics 4 Learning, Classroom

ClipArt, Free Media Goo, Free Pixels, Free Images, and Nations Illustrated. The students then uploaded and edited their images in iPhoto. Students then imported their soundtrack recording and their images into iMovie. They added transitions, adjusted the timing of images, and added titles and credits. They then shared out their video as a QuickTime video with peers and parents.

To create music videos, students could use iMovie, which includes storyboarding and editing features designed specifically for creating music videos. Students can also create music videos using the iOS *http://tinyurl.com/7vz7ubx* or Android *http://tinyurl.com/qeqvcod* Video Star apps to create music videos; for example, of students singing a Chuck Berry song: *http://tinyurl.com/73rnanl*. Or, they can use the Animoto app to import images and select from a large number of music options to add to a video to create a music-video-like production.

## Creating Animation Videos

Another option for creating videos of live action includes animation videos. One advantage to creating animation videos is that students have relatively more control over the content in that they are creating their own content as opposed to having to shoot live action, which requires dealing with a lot of logistics. For example, in creating stop-motion videos, they can simply move objects, artifacts, or their drawings to create their videos so that they have total control over the content.

There are a wide range of different types or genres of animation videos using the apps listed below.

---

### ANIMATION VIDEO APPS

**iOS**: Animation Desk *http://tinyurl.com/7mufqc2*, Animation Studio *http://tinyurl.com/6pwsmr6*, iAnimator *http://tinyurl.com/798opct*, Toontastic *http://tinyurl.com/8y39ozj*, Animation Creator HD Lite *http://tinyurl.com/7xfwhvc*, iStopMotion for iPad *http://tinyurl.com/6nf9cjk*, Koma-Koma for iPad *http://tinyurl.com/ccr4qak*, Stop-Motion *http://tinyurl.com/ccr4qak*, StopMotion Recorder *http://tinyurl.com/28mvzre*, iMotion HD *http://tinyurl.com/5uym8bd*, Stop Motion Maker *http://tinyurl.com/o6v6oo5*, Puppet Pals HD *http://tinyurl.com/694krvd*, Sock Puppets *http://tinyurl.com/4hs326w*

**Android**: Animation Desk *http://tinyurl.com/kyjau5v*, Animation Studio *http://tinyurl.com/m26f78oor*, Animated Greetings *http://tinyurl.com/kyjau5v*, Android StickDraw *http://tinyurl.com/mcvf8fd*, Stop-Motion *http://tinyurl.com/la9f32o*, Stop Motion Maker *http://tinyurl.com/knfwm4o*, Clayframes *http://tinyurl.com/m3qbtz7*, Comic Puppets *http://tinyurl.com/mxngfqe*, Android Puppet *http://tinyurl.com/lw43m5t*, Puppet Show *http://tinyurl.com/l8o746e*

---

Because many of these apps include content (characters, artifacts, settings, etc.) as well as production tools for recording and editing, they do consume a lot of memory space on an iPad or iPhone. The iOS and Android Animation Desk apps can be used to create three projects of 50 frames using hand-drawn animations on iPad that can be uploaded to YouTube. The iOS Animation Studio app includes various ClipCharacters as well as a ClipSound sound system for recording voice-overs or music. Students can then export their video as a .mov file or stream their video to Apple TV.

For creating cartoon-like animations, students can employ the iOS Toontastic app for younger students that structures creation of a story beginning with selecting a scene based on a "Setup, Conflict, Challenge, Climax, or Resolution"; drawing characters and settings; moving the characters around; recording the characters' voices to create a story; adding music; and then uploading the video to ToonTube.

Students can use the iOS Puppet Pals HD, iOS Sock Puppets, Android Comic Puppets, Android Puppet, or Android Puppet Show apps to select certain puppet characters and settings and then record dialogue for their characters. They can also create characters from imported photos or use photos for their settings.

For creating animations based on their own drawings, students can use the iOS and Android Animation Desk or iOS or Android Animation Studio apps using their fingers as well as different, adjustable brush, crayon, or pencil tools to create drawings for their animations, apps that include layers for foreground and middle-group selections and use of photos for backgrounds, as well as the use of "stamp" features for inserting pictures and shapes. And, students can add background music or sound effects. And, they can save their animations as PDF files, send them as animated e-cards, or upload them to YouTube and Facebook.

For creating stop motion/claymation videos, students can employ PixStop, iStopMotion for iPad, StopMotion Recorder, iMotion HD or Android Stop-Motion, Stop Motion Maker, or Clayframes *http://tinyurl.com/m3qbtz7* apps to create stop-motion/claymation videos. One advantage of claymation videos is that students can move their clay figures to create a relatively realistic portrayal of human-like movement.

## Summary

In this chapter, we described different apps for use in creating audio or video productions for use in the classroom that engage students in multimodal literacies. You can then create activities that exploit the affordances of sound or video for students to communicate their ideas in ways that engage their audiences. Students are then acquiring the literacies of listening and responding to videos in ways that enhance their production of audio and video texts.

# References

Bloom, K., & Johnston, K. M. (2010). Digging into YouTube videos: Using media literacy and participatory culture to promote cross-cultural understanding. *Journal of Media Literacy Education, 2*(2), 113–123.

Bowie, J. (2012a). Podcasting in a writing class? Considering the possibilities. *Kairos, 16*(2). Retrieved from http://kairos.technorhetoric.net/16.2/praxis/bowie/index.html

Bowie, J. (2012b). Rhetorical roots and media future: How podcasting fits into the computers and writing classroom. *Kairos, 16*(2). Retrieved from http://kairos.technorhetoric.net/16.2/topoi/bowie/index.html

Council of Chief State Schools Officers and National Governors' Association. (2010). *Common Core State Standards for English Language Arts & Literacy in History/Social Studies, Science, and Technical Subjects.* Washington, DC: Author. Retrieved from http://www.corestandards.org

Desmet, C. (2009). Teaching Shakespeare with YouTube. *English Journal, 99*(1), 65–70.

Haase, D. (2009). The YouTube makeup class. *The Physics Teacher, 47*(5), 272–273.

Hawkins, B. (2014, March 10). New interactive technology turns classrooms into time machines. *MinnPost.* Retrieved from http://tinyurl.com/m4qwxhn

Mallery, S. (2011). Using a USB microphone with an iPad [Web log post]. Retrieved from http://tinyurl.com/kzj6f4a

Niess, M. L., & Walker, J. M. (2009). This rock 'n' roll video teaches math. *Learning and Leading with Technology, 36*(8), 36–37.

Noonoo, S. (2012, February 6). BYOD class takes their learning to YouTube. *THE Journal.* Retrieved from http://tinyurl.com/764k4fk

O'Brien, D., & Dubbels, B. (2010, May 13). Technology and literacy: Current and emerging practices with Student 2.0 and beyond. *Video Games as Learning Tools.* Retrieved from http://tinyurl.com/7fxtoed

Ohler, J. B. (2007). *Digital storytelling in the classroom: New media pathways to literacy, learning, and creativity.* Los Angeles: Corwin Press.

Pappalardo, G. (2010, November 15). Using music in the classroom to inspire creative expression [Web log post]. Retrieved from http://www.edutopia.org/blog/music-classroom-gaetan-pappalardo

Park, J. C. (2009). Video allows young scientists new ways to be seen. *Learning and Leading with Technology, 36*(8), 34–35.

Phillips, C. (2011). Performing criticism: How digital audio can help students learn (and teach) poetry. *Transformations: The eJournal of inclusive scholarship and pedagogy, 22*(1), 52–67. Retrieved from http://web.njcu.edu/sites/transformations

Searfoss, L. (1975). Radio reading. *The Reading Teacher, 29*(3), 295–296.

Skalski, J. (2011, December 9). Using GarageBand and iMovie to build personal narratives. 2011 TIES Conference, Minneapolis, MN. Retrieved from http://tinyurl.com/lj7krd7

Tam, C. O. (2012). The effectiveness of educational podcasts for teaching music and visual arts in higher education. *Research in Learning Technology, 20.* 14919—DOI: 10.3402/rlt.v20i0/14919

# 10

# USING APPS FOR GAMING/SIMULATIONS

One of the important developments in education in the past decade has been the increased use of games and simulations to foster learning. There are a large number of games apps designed for educational purposes that certainly have their use in the classroom.

Adolescents devote a considerable amount of time to playing video/digital games; one survey found that 8–18-year-olds spend an average of 73 minutes per day in this activity (Rideout, Foehr, & Roberts, 2010). The estimated time devoted to playing video games in the United States in 2012 was a total of 142 hours per person, double the amount of time from 2002 (Kopf, 2012a).

At the same time, there has been a shift from purchase of video games to mobile digital games, including mobile apps and social network gaming; 38% of US households' games are played on smartphones and 26% of games on wireless devices; in 2012 over 100 million mobile phone users played games on their phones (Kopf, 2012b).

## Use of Games in the Classroom

The current popularity of video games among adolescents has led teachers to employ games in the classroom. A survey of 505 K-8 teachers on their attitudes regarding the use of digital games in the classroom indicated that teachers who identify as very or moderately comfortable in using digital games in the classroom use games more frequently with their students than teachers who are less comfortable (Levine & Millstone, 2012). And 32% of these teachers use games 2–4 days per week while 18% use them every day; these teachers also spend $50 or more per year on games or game subscriptions. Of the sample, 70% of teachers agree that using digital games increases motivation and engagement with content/curriculum; and 60% say that using digital games helps personalize instruction and provide data on student learning.

Unfortunately, games are also often dismissed in education because they are perceived as simply a form of diversionary *play* that, in turn, is perceived as antithetical to *work* or study. However, the assumption that games are simply play, as opposed to work, ignores the ways in which games and simulations involve different forms of social, cognitive, and creative work that contributes to learning. In playing games, students are actually learning how to "work the system" through defining goals and rules constituting, receiving feedback from, and engaging in, a system. Jane McGonigal (2011) posits that games have "four defining traits: a goal, rules, a feedback system, and voluntary participation" (p. 21). (See also Jane McGonigal's videos on Gaming for Education and the Social Good: *http://tinyurl.com/ay9o8j6*).

## Acquiring "Gaming Literacy" Practices

Through playing games, students acquire "gaming literacy" practices of problem-solving, perspective-taking, identity-construction, collaboration, and knowledge-construction practices that can transfer to lived-world contexts (Gee, 2007; McGonigal, 2011). Playing the game Evoke *http://www.urgentevoke.com*, in which players are given a new issue for each week—issues such as food shortages, massive power outages in cities, water security, disaster relief, poverty, pandemics, education, and human rights—requires crowdsourcing collaboration, collaboration that can transfer to addressing specific problems in players' own lives (McGonigal, 2011).

## English Language Arts Common Core State Standards Related to Using Games and Simulations for Learning

The following are Common Core Standards related to the use of games and simulations (Council of Chief State Schools Officers and National Governors' Association, 2010).

### *Writing Standards*

- Use technology, including the Internet, to produce, publish, and interact with others about writing. (p. 37)
- Gather relevant information from multiple print and digital sources, assess the credibility and accuracy of each source, and integrate and cite the information while avoiding plagiarism. (p. 37)

## Speaking and Listening Standards

- Participate effectively in a range of interactions (one-on-one and in groups), exchanging information to advance a discussion and to build on the input of others. (p. 44)
- Integrate and evaluate information from multiple oral, visual, or multimodal sources in order to answer questions, solve problems, or build knowledge. (p. 44)
- Make strategic use of digital media and visual displays of data to express information and enhance understanding. (p. 44)
- Adapt speech to a variety of contexts and communicative tasks, demonstrating a command of formal English when indicated or appropriate. (p. 44)

## Game-Based Learning and Design

The use of games and simulations in the classroom has larger implications for the design of learning. What is known as game-based learning (GBL) or "gamification" goes beyond just promoting uses of games or simulations in the classroom to apply the literacy practices associated with games or simulations to all forms of learning (Gee, 2011; Miller, 2011a, 2011b). This does not necessarily imply just the use of games; it may also involve creating face-to-face activities that involve students in game-like learning activities. For example, students may address challenges or problems by engaging in quests to achieve the goal of finding certain resources to address these challenges or problems; for example, creating a crime lab to achieve evidence to determine who committed a murder (Miller, 2011a). In the Quest to Learn schools located in New York City and Chicago, students engage in various quests as defined by the Institute of Play. The involved schools work on these goals:

- Collect Quest Goal is to collect/harvest x resources.
- Puzzle Quest Goal is to solve a problem (might also be called a Code Cracker Quest).
- Share Quest Goal is to share x resources.
- Drama Quest Goal is to enact a system or behavior.
- Conquest Goal is to capture a territory or resource.
- Spy or Scout Quest Goal is to observe and gather information and report back.
- Research Quest is to research a question and return with the answer. This research might take any number of forms, from questioning friends and teachers to ascertain their viewpoints to reading and more. (Miller, 2011b)

Students may also engage in different levels of challenging missions that involve synthesizing what they have learned from engaging in their quests. To be successful, you provide students with the relevant background knowledge they will need to succeed in their quests or "boss levels," as well as helping student learn from their failures.

However, GBL can be misapplied to instruction. Game players are assumed to be driven by acquiring external rewards like points or badges or by winning against competitors. However, it is important that GBL should not emphasize extrinsic motivation like winning points or badges or beating competitors, but be more intrinsically motivated by participating in the game itself (McGonigal, 2011).

## Acquiring Literacy Practices Through Playing Games or Simulations

In creating activities using games apps to foster literacy learning, you can consider the degree to which use of these game apps fosters the following literacy practices.

### Engaging in Problem-Solving

Games often begin with relatively simple problems or challenges and become progressively more complex or challenging as players advance through different levels. These different sets of levels of problems are also structured in a manner so that students must learn to solve the initial problems before they advance to more difficult problems (Gee, 2011).

Problem-solving in games entails more than just cognitive processing; problem-solving also involves emotions, attitudes, and values that reflect students' epistemic frames or value systems (Shaffer, 2006). For example, in making decisions about how to raise a child in The Sims FreePlay *http://tinyurl.com/mkfh37o* simulation, students draw on their emotions, attitudes, and values.

To address problems, games provide students with relevant "just in time" information for solving problems associated with disciplinary knowledge when they need or want that information. Many game apps related to math or physics pose problems that require students to make calculations or to draw on knowledge of physics to address these problems. The popular iOS *http://tinyurl.com/pjnwxm7* and Android *http://tinyurl.com/764f4zg* Cut the Rope game poses the challenge of having to feed a monster with candy that is lowered down to the monster on ropes. Because there are traps that will steal or smash the candy, students must cut the ropes so that it reaches the monster's mouth, requiring application of physics.

When students are playing the iOS *http://tinyurl.com/lendf6w* or Android *http://tinyurl.com/8ufvszn* iBlast Moki 2 game, they have to engage in various calculations to determine how much force to apply to assist the Mokis against their enemies. Students at Baruch College Campus High School in New York used their experience with the iOS *http://tinyurl.com/bpgfbo7* or Android *http://tinyurl.com/7o32jfc* Angry Birds game to study physics equations to predict the arc of flying birds and tumbling rocks in the game (Chu, 2012).

Students also draw on disciplinary knowledge to define rules or norms related to adopting appropriate strategies and roles/identities. For example, in playing the iOS *http://tinyurl.com/mrzj8ff* or Android *http://tinyurl.com/ctshy8b* Angry Birds Space HD game, in which the birds must fly through space according to the laws of gravity, students apply their knowledge of physics to determine how to manipulate their birds. In playing the iOS *http://tinyurl.com/adgkktfin* and Android *http://tinyurl.com/82vmk7w* Plants Vs. Zombies, where students need to grow a wide variety of different types of plants to create weapons for fighting zombies, students are applying knowledge of rules of biology to determine how to grow and use plants.

Students also learn how to address problems through working collaboratively with other players. For example, the *http://tinyurl.com/nelkq46* and Android *http://tinyurl.com/prpkutm* FarmVille 2: Country Escape game apps based on Zynga's FarmVille 2 desktop game involve the challenges of running a small farm that includes animated weather effects, moving animals, and flying planes (Takahashi, 2014). To address the challenges of purchasing or generating water, acquiring sugar, creating flour from wheat, etc., players can recruit their peers to assist them with farming tasks, for example, by having peers catch fish in the farm's pond or purchasing ingredients from a local farm co-op; players can also chat online about these tasks. Through interacting with peers to solve problems or address challenges, students are learning how to work collaboratively with others.

Students can also use simulation apps to engage in problem-solving when placed within a certain virtual context that requires them to address particular problems using:

- iOS Virtual Manipulatives *http://tinyurl.com/mjgrcuu* app: share math calculations using percentages, fractions, or decimals within a vitual space;
- iOS *http://tinyurl.com/pjjpzqo* and Android *http://tinyurl.com/q55hyeo* Chemist app: simulated chemistry lab for conducting experiments;
- iOS *http://tinyurl.com/q5k3fvo* and Android *http://tinyurl.com/lckyqby* Virtual Human Body app for studying human anatomy;
- iOS *http://tinyurl.com/d69353g* and Android *http://tinyurl.com/o377t2k* Frog Dissection app for dissecting frogs in biology;
- iOS Leafsnap *http://tinyurl.com/nuh46t7* app for identifying leaves and other types of plant life growing in the same area as the leaf's tree. (Dennen & Hao, 2014, pp. 33–35)

## Achieving Goals

When they play games, students are attempting to achieve certain goals related to addressing or solving problems, often defined in terms of "quests." These "quests" include coping with challenges at increasing levels of difficulty that serve to motivate students to employ those actions designed to achieve a goal. When they recognize that their actions are not achieving a goal, students will then adopt an alternative action. If that action succeeds, then students gain a sense of satisfaction because their actions are productive.

Having clearly defined goals that direct their achievement helps students learn to cope with the inevitable failures they experience in playing a game. Knowing that they will eventually achieve their goals means that students will keep trying to succeed in a game. McGonigal (2011) notes that in games, the ways in which players fail can often be engaging in positive ways. She cites a study from the M.I.N.D. research center (Ravaja, Saari, Laarni, Kallinin, & Salminen, 2005) in which researchers found that players of the iOS *http://tinyurl.com/l7b8zj8* and Android *http://tinyurl.com/7uhv4dc* Super Monkey Ball 2 game actually enjoyed failing because when they failed, the monkeys "went whirling and wailing over the edge and off into space" (p. 66). The failure served as an entertaining reward and provided players with a sense of agency in that they "had failed spectacularly, and entertainingly" (p. 66). As a result, players had a sense of optimism that they can keep trying until they succeed, a sense of optimism that can transfer to a sense of agency in one's ability to cope with lived-world failures.

### Acquiring and Employing Feedback Related to Achieving Goals

Within the game space, students are continually receiving feedback as to whether and how they are achieving their goals. This feedback system provides them with criteria for achieving certain levels or giving them scores, points, or a progress bar—feedback that encourages them to continue playing. Moreover, players are performing with others in a multiplayer game by sharing both success and failure with others playing the same game, a way of helping players learn to share both their successes and failures with others, another set of important social skills.

McGonigal cites the example of the online video game iOS app, Rock Band *http://tinyurl.com/y9st6rn* that involves up to four avatar players mimicking popular rock songs based on cues for how to play these songs. The more successful each player is in playing their instrument or singing the song, the closer the song sounds to the original song. The less successful, the less the song sounds like the original, resulting in an animation audience booing the band off of the stage.

The game provides feedback in terms of the percentage of successfully mimicking the original song, so that players can gauge their level of success each time they attempt to play a song; players can also get a visual confirmation of whether they have or have not played a correct note. And, if one player does poorly, other players can compensate for that failure by playing or singing successfully.

Learning to operate within a feedback system involves students in learning how to receive feedback when they experience setbacks or failures so that they can change or revise their practices, which is itself a form of play. John Seely

Brown (2012) posits that learning to play involves having the permission or support to fail numerous times until one achieves a goal. When students receive feedback, they then reframe or redefine their perceptions of the game space through tinkering or playing around with different options, a practice that transfers to a willingness to tinker with a problem, for example, a computer glitch, until that glitch is addressed.

Brown also perceives learning as tinkering or reframing reality as leading to knowing how to critique and change systems:

> You get a sense for what can be pushed around. You get the sense of what the pushbacks are all about. You start to develop an almost intimate familiarity with the system itself and with the material at hand. It is a form of being embodied, you're embodied, a kind of a form of embodied immersion and you start to develop an instinct, and of course, [it] is deeply situated. So this is kind of a deep structure type of tinkering that I think we're looking at that leads to this reframing that is completely aligned with this sense of the epiphany stuff, and how do you kind of play with really radically changing the context, which starts to build new lenses that you can use.

## Constructing Identities

In adopting an avatar or role in a game, students are experimenting with adopting different identities in ways that are shaped by the game. James Gee (2007) describes students' "projective identities" that consist of three different identities: (1) the student's lived-world identity; (2) the virtual identity of the role or avatar adopted by the lived-world identity but that is also controlled by the game; and (3) their projective identity in which the lived-world identity employs certain actions consistent with succeeding in the game (p. 55).

Adopting these "projective identities" entails students learning to take on different perspectives consistent with the goals and rules of the game world that differs from their lived-world goals and rules, a process of socialization in learning how to operate in different worlds. Moreover, the game itself provides positive feedback depending on how well the student adopts their "projective identity" so that the student is rewarded for their ability to assume this different identity or role.

## Collaborative Learning

Many games involve more than one player as members of teams playing against other teams. Learning how to be an effective member of a team requires the ability to collaborate effectively with other members of that team. To help students learn these collaboration literary practices, you can employ the iOS Group Games *http://tinyurl.com/8a8nngm* app that includes guides and reference materials to over fifty different games that deliberately focus on developing leadership, collaboration, and trust.

This shared space includes players playing collaboratively as teams or "guilds" in popular video games such as World of Warcraft (WoW), as well as online forums surrounding the games in which they are using videos, blogs, "walkabouts," "paratexts," or cheat sheets to assist each other on how to play the game. The fact that players codify these strategies in a "paratext" or "walkabout" guide leads them to reflect metacognitively on their use of these strategies, particularly because they are having to explain them to novice players.

Games also provide rewards for learning to work collaboratively. McGonigal (2011) cites the example of the Facebook FarmVille *http://tinyurl.com/3x5npo4* game in which players plant and harvest crops and take care of animals. She notes that a key aspect of this popular game is that players can take care of other players' farms as well as sharing gifts as a means of building social connectivity and collaboration, which, in turn, enhances players' "sense that we're creating a global community with a purpose" (p. 94).

## Operating In and Redesigning Systems

Playing games also involves an awareness of operating within systems—what Gee (2011) defines as "systems thinking" about how their avatars' actions impact others' actions within a system. This involves perceiving the game itself as a system based on shared norms, roles, beliefs, and goals that simulates lived-world systems such as the military, legal, government, workplace/retail, the environment, housing, banking/finance, entertainment, family, community, or school. Understanding how to address contemporary problems requires complex thinking about how these systems operate.

For example, in playing the iOS *http://tinyurl.com/akjurer* or Android *http://tinyurl.com/d8assc7* Tiny Tower game, players are building an urban tower floor-by-floor that includes stores, restaurants, housing, and laundromats. Players earn money from tenants paying rent, which then is used to build more floors to create more stores, restaurants, housing, and laundromats. Players can also acquire "Tower Bux" to employ for building or restocking stores. In doing so, they need to find ways to please the "bitizens" who shop or live in the tower and then comment on their experiences, as well as visit other players' towers using the Apple Game Center.

Learning how the retail or housing systems works as a system requires an understanding of how people in these systems acquire certain roles and responsibilities as builders, retailers, tenants/owners, customers, or sales persons; how actions are shaped by rules and norms associated with legal requirements or norms for conducting business; and how systems themselves are driven by certain larger objects or motives related to making money or pleasing tenants/owners and customers.

In similar games, iOS CityVille Hometown *http://tinyurl.com/7pq2sd5* and My Town 2 *http://tinyurl.com/7y4qdk3* or the Android Tiny Village *http:// tinyurl.com/cn4hjeo* apps, players are creating towns by building homes and businesses designed to attract new people to these towns. Or, in using the iOS *http:// tinyurl.com/krov8ew* and Android *http://tinyurl.com/mbgehko* Trade Nations app, players create a small village and attempt to build it into a city through making trades with others to build the village. And, as in the previously mentioned Farm-Ville, in the Farm Story online-only game app, students design, decorate, and manage a farm on which they can grow hundreds of different kinds of crops and then interact with other farmers.

Engaging in problem-solving in these systems entails recognizing that problems they are addressing are constituted by systems themselves and how those systems operate. Players coping with the spreading virus in Whyville *http://tinyurl. com/33tmj6*, discussed later in this chapter, face the problem that current vaccines are ineffective in stopping the virus—that the medical system itself isn't able to cope with the virus.

And, recognizing the problematic nature of a system leads students to critique how systems operate in ways that can lead to redesigning systems to address the limitations of a system. In playing Tiny Tower, students are grappling with the challenges of the finance and legal systems in terms of trying to make money and follow the law. They must therefore create alternative systems designed to address the problems with the status quo systems.

## Apps for Playing Games Organized by Disciplinary Literacies

We've organized our recommended game apps according to disciplinary literacies constituting various subjects, recognizing that many of these games can be played across different subjects.

### *Disciplinary Literacies Shaping Game Playing*

In playing games, students are applying disciplinary literacy knowledge to cope with the challenges facing them (Nelson & Erlandson, 2012). In coping with the virus in Whyville, players draw on their knowledge of science to keep records of the virus, investigate possible causes, and develop potential vaccinations, an essential disciplinary literacy in science.

Game design therefore frames disciplinary literacies in terms of the kinds of problem-solving specific to different disciplines defined more in terms of engaging in activities than in terms of acquiring content (Squire, 2011). Applying disciplinary knowledge is therefore equated with learning to play the game(s) constituting uses of disciplinary literacies unique to a certain game—that engaging in a discipline is itself a "game." As Gee (2011) notes:

A science like biology is not a set of facts. In reality, it is a "game" certain types of people "play". These people engage in characteristic sorts of activities, use characteristic sorts of tools and language, and hold certain values; that is, they play by a certain set of "rules". They *do* biology. Of course, they learn, use, and retain lots and lots of facts—even produce them—but the facts come from and with the doing. Left out of the context of biology as activity, biological facts are trivia. So, ironically, just as what you learn when you learn to play a good video game is how to play the game, so too, what you learn when you learn biology should be how to play that game. (p. 3)

Consistent with a constructivist approach, effective game or simulation apps therefore engage players in actively applying and constructing disciplinary knowledge. This differs from many games/simulation apps that simply reify a transmission model as reflected in the development of quiz app games designed to test students on what they have learned in a certain subject, as opposed to the use of imaginative, problem-solving methods associated with a constructivist approach. As Kurt Squire notes in an interview with Henry Jenkins (2012):

Unfortunately, very few "educational" games go beyond simple "drill-and-practice" pedagogy. The educational "content" is added onto familiar game formulas such as shooting, matching, or jumping games. In these games, the computer is essentially a flashcard machine that presents the players with prescribed problems, monitors the player, adjusts the type of problem to match player performance, and then records player progress. This type of game, while useful in some contexts, does not take advantage of the computer's ability to represent complex visual phenomena, create rich interactive microworlds, model dynamic systems, or allow creative expression . . . A challenge for designers of educational games is to find ways to fuse educational content with the gameplay, so that students are solving authentic problems, engaging in meaningful scientific, mathematical, or engineering practices, thinking creatively within games.

## Using Multiplayer Games on Game Center

In recommending these apps, we note that some of these apps employ the Apple Game Center feature that allows students to play with other players. While multiplayer games are more likely to be online video games, students can play multiplayer app games in which they collaboratively work with or compete against other students. They can do so in several different ways (Rich, 2012). They can use one iPad or iPhone device and pass their device around between students or they can create a link between devices on which the same game is installed.

Or, and this is the better option, they can employ the free, online Apple Game Center iOS service, which allows players from anywhere to play collaboratively on the same game. Students will need an Apple account to use the Game Center. Students can create an online profile on the Game Center and then search for other Contacts to request if they want to play a game. Students can also find games in the Game Center that are compatible with the Game Center multiplayer features.

When students access a game app that is compatible with Game Center, they can then turn on the Game Center option to have it work with Game Center. By doing so, they can invite friends to play that game or share game results. And, they can find other multiplayer games that are compatible with Game Center.

## English Language Arts

There are a large number of games that involve learning or using words similar to games such as Scrabble. One of the more popular ones is the iOS *http://tinyurl.com/ye5l3k7* and Android *http://tinyurl.com/75yoz3c* Words With Friends app in which students can play with other students to string together words; if one player doesn't add another word within seven days, they are eliminated from the game. Another popular word-game app is the iOS *http://tinyurl.com/6wewqco* and Android *http://tinyurl.com/7q27ouz* Draw Something app in which one player selects a word, creates a drawing that represents the meaning of that word, and then sends the drawing to another player who must guess the word. This game can lead students to reflect on how the quality of their images or drawings themselves serves to communicate certain intended meanings.

One of the more challenging word-game apps is the iOS *http://tinyurl.com/7xqzjrp* and Android *http://tinyurl.com/kdpsrrw* SpellTower app in which players build towers by creating words from rows of letters. And, the iOS *http://tinyurl.com/yzaoees* and Android *http://tinyurl.com/n65nv5f* Wordle game involves 3,500 puzzles requiring knowledge of word definitions. However, one limitation of these word-based games is that they can reify the notion of English language arts as simply acquiring or using words in isolation, rather than using language for social purposes.

Students can also use games to develop ideas for their own creative writing activities. For example, based on playing the iOS *http://tinyurl.com/26f3vzb* and Android *http://tinyurl.com/m6ztd9b* Epic Citadel game in which students move around a medieval fantasy town with a cathedral and circus, students created their own short digital stories, slideshow, video, comic, poem, or collages (Department of Education, Victoria, Australia, 2013).

They can also employ interactive-fiction-game apps in which they enter into a fictional world based on epic novel series. For example, in the iOS *http://tinyurl.com/yj4ojqa* and Android *http://tinyurl.com/82578cs* role-play

Zenonia series, students assume the role of the hero engaging in quests and battles between the forces of good versus evil. The iOS *http://tinyurl.com/ccbg2mv* and Android *http://tinyurl.com/mant6f3* Terra-Eternal Chaos app involves 17 different "dungeon quests" requiring highly adaptive skills.

There are also a large number of interactive fiction role-plays that are typically based on series of epic books in which students assume the role of the main character who makes decisions about taking certain actions. These include the *Rimelands* series, for example, the iOS *Rimelands: Hammer of Thor http://tinyurl.com/lq2d5bu*, the iOS *Forest of Doom http://tinyurl.com/ke4d2cb* as part of the Fighting Fantasy series, the iOS *Gamebook Adventures: Infinite Universe http://tinyurl.com/l6ue23x*, the Android *Forging of a Legend http://tinyurl.com/c3wb6j7*, or the *Blackout Gamebook http://tinyurl.com/mao67ep* interactive fiction apps. Students can also create their own interactive fiction using games written for the Z-Machine such as *Legends of Zork* using the Frotz *http://tinyurl.com/yll87bz* app in which they write commands according to the characters' actions in these games. And in the iOS *http://tinyurl.com/mm75qaw* and Android *http://tinyurl.com/jvmel2f Hamlet* app, players attempt to assist Hamlet in coping with his challenges.

There are also game apps based on popular fiction or movies series that students could play in conjunction with reading fiction and/or studying film. For example, in playing the iOS *http://tinyurl.com/2e7t9ck* and Android (walkthroughs) *http://tinyurl.com/k6t56vb* LEGO Harry Potter: Years 1–4 game based on the *Harry Potter* series, students adopt different characters based on their familiarity with the first four books and movies about Harry's initial four years at Hogwarts. Students could also play the iOS *http://tinyurl.com/7phzq49 Hunger Games: Girl on Fire* game in which they assume the role of Katniss coping with her adversaries. Or, they can play the iOS *http://tinyurl.com/7ld8dyr* and Android *http://tinyurl.com/mjbfz7c Avatar* game based on the movie, in which they enter into the world of Pandora to determine whether to side with the Na'vi native people or the humans seeking to exploit their world. And, based on their familiarity with the mystery genre, they can play mystery app games such as the iOS *http://tinyurl.com/d9yglwu* Puzzle Agent 2 HD game in which students adopt the role of an FBI agent attempting to solve the case of a missing factory foreman.

There are also a number of role-play games (RPGs) apps that involve students assuming roles related to addressing issues. For example, the iOS *http://tinyurl.com/6u7er42* and Android *http://tinyurl.com/mtnjnbd* Saturday Morning RPG app is a role-playing game in which a high school student must make decisions to cope with the threat of an evil villain to attempt to save the world, a game that draws on Saturday morning cartoons. The iOS *http://tinyurl.com/ygyqh69* and Android *http://tinyurl.com/lprgve6* Surviving High School game involves adopting the role of a new female high school student coping with getting to know students in her school or a male assuming the role of a member of the high school football team. The game includes new weekly episodes with both familiar and new characters. However, given the somewhat sexist portrayals of these main characters with the focus of the female character on building relationships and the male character on sports, students could also critique the gender stereotyping in this game.

## Social Studies

Younger students can play the iOS *http://tinyurl.com/4xzlssz* and Android *http://tinyurl.com/mxw2r4l* American Presidents app in which they can read biographical essays of about 1,500 words about each president, as well as photos, maps, speeches, portraits, and a timeline of related historical events. Younger students can also play the iOS *http://tinyurl.com/7qkbf2p* and Android *http://tinyurl.com/kmfesva* Stack the States app to learn about different states or the iOS *http://tinyurl.com/7ns5f3p* or Android *http://tinyurl.com/m2guznt* Stack the Countries app to learn about countries throughout the world. When students respond correctly to questions about information for different states or countries, the states or countries are stacked up on the bottom of the screen; when they reach a line a third up from the bottom, they are then awarded a state or a country.

Students draw on their knowledge of geography in playing the iOS *http://tinyurl.com/2c7ac8x* and Android *http://tinyurl.com/myja9xf* GeoMaster app, which involves identifying various sites or places on a map of the United States. The iOS *http://tinyurl.com/m5dwyhz* World Countries or Android Countries of the World *http://tinyurl.com/cnyaozd* or World Countries *http://tinyurl.com/k5w4249* apps involve students in learning information and gaining access to maps of different countries.

Based on the original The Oregon Trail game, the iOS *http://tinyurl.com/7qg6h5t* and Android *http://tinyurl.com/m3ondz5* The Oregon Trail app involves learning to settle in a frontier village through farming, hunting, adding buildings, and coping with challenges such as storms or buffalo stampedes, as well as interacting with historical figures. In playing the iOS *http://tinyurl.com/73mz6nb* and Android *http://tinyurl.com/m55jhog* Expedition Africa app, students journey on the same route through Africa that Henry Stanley took to find Dr. David Livingstone.

Younger students can participate as avatars in the 1000 different worlds on the 3D Active Worlds *http://tinyurl.com/mkrvs7l* site to engage in chat with each other that appears not only above their heads, but also on a chat log at the bottom of the screen. For example, in the "Barnsborough" world, they explore a deserted town to identify clues such as notes, links, posters, or sites to determine why the town is deserted (Merchant, 2010).

Students studying psychology and neuroscience can use the iOS *http://tinyurl.com/pcrn6md* and Android *http://tinyurl.com/kkh8gcf* Einstein BrainTrainer app to test out their cognitive processes, memory, attention, and problem-solving through a series of games, and then track their progress over time to reflect on how learning is influenced by the brain.

Students in civics classes can play the iOS *http://tinyurl.com/lyfc2ts* Pocket Law Firm game that is a part of the iCivics project (most of the iCivics games are flash-based desktop games that won't work on the iPad or iPhone; Pocket Law Firm is an exception). In this game, students draw on their knowledge of the Constitution to determine whether potential clients have a right to a trial. They then match clients with the appropriate lawyer and seek to win their cases. As they win more cases, their law firm grows larger.

There are also a number of previously-mentioned game apps that involve creating or constructing towns or cities that require making decisions about building communities related to social studies issues having to do with civic engagement and governmental structures. Based on The Sims computer games, the iOS *http://tinyurl.com/mkfh37o* and Android *http://tinyurl.com/bqev6pl* Sims FreePlay and iOS SimCity Deluxe Free *http://tinyurl.com/79saacu* game apps involve building homes or growing gardens in neighborhoods designed to support families, as well as coping with daily issues faced by family or community members. The iOS *http://tinyurl.com/7fxx8mm* and Android *http://tinyurl.com/kmz9zmv* Tiny Village app includes creating a prehistoric village by building homes and buildings, starting up shops, and harvesting crops for the town market.

The iOS *http://tinyurl.com/6v3hddn* and Android *http://tinyurl.com/m2j3ca8* Virtual Villagers 2 Lite app is part of the Virtual Villagers series that involves teaching survival strategies to members of a tribe living in a remote village. In the iOS *http://tinyurl.com/78jelky* The Settlers game, students create a new settlement by collecting resources and building a town, as well as coping with conflicts between Romans, Vikings, and Mayans. Similarly, in playing the Android *http://tinyurl.com/k45vkuu* The Townsmen students construct a medieval town by coping with a series of challenges. In playing the iOS *http://tinyurl.com/7y6qyfz* and Android *http://tinyurl.com/l4w88ap* Venture Towns game, students are addressing economic and social issues involved in creating a town that will best serve its residents. In the iOS *http://tinyurl.com/7styffbm* and Android *http://tinyurl.com/kr4jmgx* Virtual Families game, students adopt a new family member and then raise that child or they build a home, start and raise a family, begin a career, and/or have children at college, while facing continuous challenges in doing so.

## Science

Students can play the iOS *http://tinyurl.com/84mppca* and Android *http://tinyurl.com/pe43mr9* SporeOrigins game that involves understanding of evolution associated with development of animal life and cells to help a "Spore" grow through eating smaller creatures to avoid the threat of being eaten by bigger creatures based on 30 different levels of challenge. The iOS *http://tinyurl.com/66zqdwa* and Android *http://tinyurl.com/lrncoej* Plants Vs. Zombies app involves use of biological knowledge of 49 different plant species to ward off attacks from the zombies.

There are a large number of games that build on knowledge of physics to move or create objects/structures. Students can employ the iOS *http://tinyurl.com/7jqdctx* and Android *http://tinyurl.com/m8c3ac9* SimplePhysics app to design and build different structures in competition with other players based on certain principles of physics related to the strength and cost of a structure, so that if there is too much strain on a structure, then that area of the structure shows up as red. Similarly, the iOS *http://tinyurl.com/7l5cyp3* Touch Physics app poses the challenge of guiding a wheel up to a star by drawing objects using crayons to move the wheel up to the top of the screen through different levels. The iOS *http://tinyurl.com/ksa9ssy* and Android *http://tinyurl.com/as57ea9* Contre Jour app makes use of physics to assist an animal to cope with various challenges. And the Android Newton *http://tinyurl.com/l9meld8* game involves negotiating objects in ways that are consistent with Newton's Laws. Another physics game is the iOS *http://tinyurl.com/7wjrq65* or Android *http://tinyurl.com/le9vngq* Drop the Box app in which players build structures to deliver boxes.

The iOS *http://tinyurl.com/3davok9* and Android *http://tinyurl.com/klu6cwj* Feed Me Oil game requires knowledge of physics to move oil through broken pipes. And, the popular iOS *http://tinyurl.com/3nbqwnh* and Android *http://tinyurl.com/885ubg4* Where's My Water? game involves knowing how to provide water for an alligator who lives in a sewer, water that is continually being cut off by his enemies.

Based on the desktop Minecraft software, the iOS *http://tinyurl.com/6uaz5ra* or Android *http://tinyurl.com/7zjc5yk* Minecraft Pocket Edition involves creation of buildings or worlds. For students playing Minecraft on their desktop, students can also use the iOS *http://tinyurl.com/7zdtlw2* or Android *http://tinyurl.com/ldy8pnh* Minecraft World Explorer app to move between their desktop and their iPad/iPhone, which includes a strategy guide of recipes for creating worlds. Students can use Minecraft to study actual buildings such as the Roman Coliseum or the Globe Theatre that can be imported into the game, create scale models of buildings requiring knowledge of ratio and proportion, and visualize buildings or story events drawn from their reading (Miller, 2012).

The iOS *http://tinyurl.com/7r5f8vt* and Android *http://tinyurl.com/n2cbxxs* SpaceChem Mobile game app involves assuming the role of an engineer working for a chemical synthesizer company for frontier colonies by transforming raw materials into chemical products.

Students can also participate in the science inquiry browser app, Whyville *http://tinyurl.com/33tmj6*, with a particular focus on science learning designed for younger students, in which they adopt avatars and engage in dealing with various challenges. For example, students grapple with how to cope with the Whypox plague or the WhyFlu in terms of vaccines or cures.

There are also games that combine knowledge of physics and astronomy. The iOS *http://tinyurl.com/7cqryyx* and Android *http://tinyurl.com/lewjg6w* Angry Birds Space HD game, created in conjunction with NASA, expands the popular Angry Birds game by pitting the Angry Birds against the space pigs throughout different parts of space. The iOS *http://tinyurl.com/23ztlsn* and Android *http://tinyurl.com/cue3r36* Osmos game involves growing an asteroid-like object by absorbing matter in space while at the same time attempting to move in space by eliminating matter which causes the object to shrink. The iOS *http://tinyurl.com/7z77ncw* and Android *http://tinyurl.com/l2kjjde* Gravity 2.0 game involves either creating a solar system, requiring knowledge of gravity to put the planets in orbit around a sun, or building a solar system to fight opponents based on who creates a better system.

## Math

The iOS *http://tinyurl.com/7y9w5ok* Rocket Math game for younger students involves 56 different missions requiring different specific math strategies to support a rocket in space. For learning prime numbers that cannot be divided into smaller whole numbers, younger students can play the iOS *http://tinyurl.com/3jzv3aj* and Android *http://tinyurl.com/lnl8y5t* Factor Samurai in which the Samurai attempts to slice the numbers. The iOS *http://tinyurl.com/7q2bpzp* Answer 2 Equations game involves learning arithmetic functions (+ − x /) at different levels of difficulty by using the correct function to solve problems. The iOS *http://tinyurl.com/7vozt49* and Android *http://tinyurl.com/kqqexnv* Freddy Fraction game draws on students' knowledge of fractions, while the iOS *http://tinyurl.com/7e7w7vo* Algebra Champ requires students to draw on knowledge of algebra to solve increasingly more difficult problems.

## Second/World Languages

Students can play the iOS MindSnacks *http://tinyurl.com/7smtyrq* language learning games, for example the MindSnacks Spanish game, in which an avatar acquires points based on learning different Spanish, French, Italian, German, and Chinese words. In the iOS Smash The Word *http://tinyurl.com/7yo4knb* game, students adopt the role of "Wordliths" to learn and destroy Spanish, French, Italian, German, and English words. For learning Mandarin Chinese, students can play the Mandarin Madness game in which they play an arcade game involving uses of Chinese. Similarly, the Android Learn Spanish Vocabulary *http://tinyurl.com/ljo36zh* also employs an arcade game format for learning Spanish.

For ELL students, the iOS Mega Multilingual Word Find *http://tinyurl.com/7vtpkcu* game includes word search puzzles based on uses of English, as well as other languages, which assists students with translations. They can also play the iOS *http://tinyurl.com/8yxcyy3* and Android *http://tinyurl.com/km4mmxz* English Ear Game in which they listen to an English word and choose the right one from similar words.

The iOS *http://tinyurl.com/7mky2br* and Android *http://tinyurl.com/mkvw8fc* English Monstruo game, designed to help Spanish-speaking students acquire English, is based on a database of common errors made by Spanish speakers learning English. Students are challenged by a monster who assumes that a student will make mistakes until a student begins to correct those mistakes to resist the monster.

## Music

The iOS *http://tinyurl.com/7f4ku8m* Guitar Rock Tour 2 game involves players as members of a band on a virtual tour playing popular songs by hitting notes on the screen. There are three different levels of difficulty requiring physical dexterity in holding the iPad or iPhone in a certain way to play the guitar or drums. When the band successfully plays a song at a certain tour venue, they then advance on the tour to play new songs.

One popular music game app is the iOS *http://tinyurl.com/33hsb54* Tap Tap Revenge 4 in which players connect with others who make up 15 million members of the Tap Tap community to compete in the ability to accurately tap the screen according to the beat of popular songs. Players can also access songs from the Android Tap Tap Revenge 4 Cheats Songs *http://tinyurl.com/qgz2wyt*.

The iOS Tap Studio *http://tinyurl.com/odrftmq* and Tapic Free *http://tinyurl.com/qj62cbg* or Android Beat Tapper *http://tinyurl.com/kuc9saf* apps involve creating taps for music. Another popular game is the iOS *http://tinyurl.com/myywvot* and Android *http://tinyurl.com/lq8n3p2* Rhythm Racer 2, which involves moving a flying plane according to the rhythm of the music.

There are also music app games for learning to play instruments. The iOS Piano Dust Buster Song Game *http://tinyurl.com/n92j37d* challenges students to correctly match the notes on a virtual piano keyboard or their own actual piano with popular songs. The iOS *http://tinyurl.com/mnmqjxs* and Android *http://tinyurl.com/lhlp9xf* Flashnote Derby game for younger students has students identify appropriate musical notes so that their horse and jockey can gain ground in a horse race. The Android Tap the Music *http://tinyurl.com/ptudvm6* game involves playing instruments within a set time period.

Students can also play games involving their knowledge of music. The iOS *http://tinyurl.com/7u55qej* Music Library Quiz and Android Music Quiz *http://tinyurl.com/ksqyjew* games build on knowledge of song snippets in a music library that is based on which player can first identify song titles, artists, album covers, or album titles.

## Art

In playing the iOS *http://tinyurl.com/mtbsjvg* and Android *http://tinyurl.com/ku4c5g5* Greatest Artists, iOS *http://tinyurl.com/7smuast* or Android *http://tinyurl.com/kfc45jh* Art Puzzle, iOS *http://tinyurl.com/ksfg9pb* or Android Art Puzzles *http://tinyurl.com/pgffpq2*, or Android Art Museum *http://tinyurl.com/mgna7xe* apps, students complete puzzles related to their understanding of famous painters' paintings, as well as completing quizzes about their knowledge of these painters. With the iOS Faking It *http://tinyurl.com/qja5png* or Android Art Curator *http://tinyurl.com/ljspaf6* app, students detect forgeries from authentic paintings.

In the iOS *http://tinyurl.com/ldygnqo* and Android *http://tinyurl.com/cc69415* Sketch W Friends, iOS Sketch n' Guess! Lite *http://tinyurl.com/6salu6l*, iOS Draw N Guess *http://tinyurl.com/l5uaaqm*, Android Sketch Guess *http://tinyurl.com/k2v2b2o*, Android Sketch It Online *http://tinyurl.com/cvs77gw*, and Android Draw and Guess *http://tinyurl.com/l3twvrd* apps, students as members of competing teams attempt to guess what the other team is drawing in their sketches.

## Creating Games

Students can also create games using various programming tools such as Gamestar Mechanic *http://gamestarmechanic.com*, Inform 7 *http://inform7.com* (for interactive fiction), Scratch *http://scratch.mit.edu*, Alice *http://www.alice.org*, Stencyl *http://www.stencyl.com*, GameSalad *http://gamesalad.com/creator*, Game Maker *http://game-maker.en.softonic.com*, Codea *http://twolivesleft.com/Codea*, XCode *https://developer.apple.com/xcode*, and Objective-C *http://www.tucows.com/preview/7937/GNOME-Objective-C* (Crooks, 2012; Daley, 2010; Ford, 2011; Moore, 2011; Salter, 2011).

They can also create geography games that involve guessing the location of a certain place based on a Google Street View image of the place, as is the case with the GeoGuessr *http://geoguessr.com* game (Byrne, 2014). To create such a game, you or your students can use the GeoSettr *http://geosettr.com* site that includes a map with a Pegman and a Street View image for the Pegman's location, so that students can then move the Pegman to determine a location that players are required to identify (Byrne, 2014). Or, you or your students can use the Mission Map Quest *http://tinyurl.com/chyjlvz* site to create clues for players to use to identify places around the world (Byrne, 2014).

For working with his students in a Geology unit, Kevin Hodgson's (2014) sixth-grade students created their own games using the online Gamestar Mechanic game-design training site. Students created games based on narrative quests. Students created games such as Layers of the Earth *http://tinyurl.com/mnrfbtd*, Adventures in Geology *http://tinyurl.com/kwde7vn*, A Journey Through Layers *http://tinyurl.com/lutbjka*, and Science Videogame Project (plate boundaries) *http://tinyurl.com/nxkdmn7* (Hodgson, 2014).

In one study, high school students used the Game Maker program to create a game, Immune Attack, based on their study of immunology as part of their participation in a STEM program that involved study of 3-D computer modeling and animation, computer programming concepts, and video game design (Khalili, Sheridan, Williams, Clark, & Stegman, 2011). In the game, players controlled a "nanobot" that moves through the body to repair breakdowns in the immune system. Analysis of the students' work found that they learned to question their own knowledge and understanding of the science concepts; assumed a sense of ownership and responsibility to make the game attractive, engaging, and scientifically accurate; and defined the purpose for their games as related to acquiring certain knowledge required for playing the game.

To create games for younger children in a manner similar to using e-book apps to create children's books for younger children, students can use the iOS Tiny-Tap *http://tinyurl.com/lxcs3sg* app for designing games. In using this app, students add their own or online photos, type or record questions for children to answer about these photos, and then add answers for children to select. And, for thinking about the kinds of games to develop or what games may be popular with certain audiences, students can use the iOS *http://tinyurl.com/35tgmn7* and Android *http://tinyurl.com/c8bcgcj* Game Dev Story app in which players are creating games within a company, requiring analysis of game design and marketing.

## Summary

We argue that students are highly engaged in playing games, engagement that can be tapped for use of gaming to acquire certain disciplinary literacies as well as certain socio-emotional practices and dispositions such as goal-setting, coping with and learning from failure, engaging in productive problem-solving, collaborating with others, adopting different roles and perspectives, and learning to draw on feedback to improve one's learning. In addition to those game apps we cite in this chapter, there are also thousands of other games that you can employ to foster learning across the curriculum.

## References

Brown, J. S. (2012). *Cultivating the entrepreneurial learner in the 21st Century.* Digital Media and Learning Conference 2012, San Francisco.

Byrne, R. (2014, March 6). Create your own geography games with these free tools [Web log post]. Retrieved from http://tinyurl.com/kfw43wz

Chu, E. (2012, April 19). At Baruch High School, Math takes the prize [Web log post]. Retrieved from http://www.wnyc.org/story/302708-at-baruch-high-school-math-takes-the-prize

Council of Chief State Schools Officers and National Governors' Association. (2010). *Common Core State Standards for English Language Arts & Literacy in History/Social Studies, Science, and Technical Subjects.* Washington, DC: Author. Retrieved from http://www.corestandards.org

Crooks, C. E. (2012). *iPhone game development for teens.* Independence, KY: Course Technology PTR.

Daley, M. (2010). *Learning iOS game programming: A hands-on guide to building your first iPhone game.* New York: Addison Wesley.

Dennen, V. P., & Hao, S. (2014). Paradigms of use, learning theory, and app design. In C. Miller & A. Doering (Eds.), *The new landscape for mobile learning* (pp. 20–40). New York: Routledge.

Department of Education, Victoria, Australia. (2013). iPads in education: Epic Citadel. Author. Retrieved from http://tinyurl.com/lrt6ffy

Ford, J. L. (2011). *Scratch programming for teens*. Independence, KY: Course Technology PTR.

Gee, J. P. (2007). *What video games have to teach us about learning and literacy*. New York: Palgrave Macmillan.

Gee, J. P. (2011, June 13). Good video games and good learning [Web log post]. Retrieved from http://dmlcentral.net/resources/4578

Hodgson, K. (2014, January 27). Game on! Our student videogames in action [Web log post]. Retrieved from http://tinyurl.com/llpfngj

Jenkins, H. (2012, March 7). What we've learned about games and learning: An interview with Kurt Squire (Part One) [Web log post]. Retrieved from http://tinyurl.com/7edts8v

Khalili, N., Sheridan, K., Williams, A., Clark, K., & Stegman, M. (2011). Students designing video games about immunology: Insights for science learning. *Computers in the Schools, 28*(3), 228–240.

Kopf, S. (2012a, April 16). Ten facts about the videogame industry [Web log post]. Retrieved from http://www.trenditionist.com/2012/04/16/ten-facts-about-the-videogame-industry

Kopf, S. (2012b, July 30). The videogames industry is changing: Mobile gaming expected to rise [Web log post]. Retrieved from http://tinyurl.com/cguuwb6

Levine, M., & Millstone, J. (2012, May 5). Teacher attitudes about digital games in the classroom. New York: Joan Ganz Cooney Center at Sesame Workshop. Retrieved from http://tinyurl.com/kmks2n9

McGonigal, J. (2011). *Reality is broken: How games can make us better and how they can change the world*. New York: Penguin.

Merchant, G. (2010). 3D virtual worlds as environments for literacy teaching. *Education Research, 52*(2), 135–150.

Miller, A. (2011a, September 26). Game-based learning units for the everyday teacher [Web log post]. Retrieved from http://www.edutopia.org/blog/video-game-model-unit-andrew-miller

Miller, A. (2011b, October 17). Get your game on: How to build curriculum units using the video game model [Web log post]. Retrieved from http://www.edutopia.org/blog/gamification-game-based-learning-unit-andrew-miller

Miller, A. (2012, April 13). Ideas for using Minecraft in the classroom [Web log post]. Retrieved from http://tinyurl.com/7z4skrz

Moore, T. (2011). *Tap, move, shake: Turning your game ideas into iPhone & iPad apps*. Sebastapol, CA: O'Reilly Media.

Nelson, B. C., & Erlandson, B. E. (2012). *Design for learning in virtual worlds*. New York: Routledge.

Ravaja, N., Saari, T., Laarni, J., Kallinin, K., & Salminen, M. (2005, June). The psychophysiology of video gaming: Phasic emotional responses to game events. Changing views: World in play. Digital Games Research Association, Vancouver, British Columbia. Retrieved from http://www.digra.org/dl/db/06278.36196.pdf

Rich, J. R. (2012). *iPad and iPhone tips and tricks*. Indianapolis, IN: Que.

Rideout, V. J., Foehr, U. G., & Roberts, D. F. (2010, January 1). Generation M2: Media in the lives of 8- to 18-year-olds. The Kaiser Family Foundation. Retrieved from http://www.kff.org/entmedia/8010.cfm

Salter, A. (2011, August 30). Games in the classroom (part 1). *ProfHacker: Chronicle of Higher Education.* Retrieved from http://chronicle.com/blogs/profhacker/games-in-the-classroom-part-1/35596

Shaffer, D. W. (2006). *How computer games help children learn.* New York: Palgrave.

Squire, K. (2011). *Video games and learning: Teaching and participatory culture in the digital age.* New York: Teachers College Press.

Takahashi, D. (2014, March 3). Zynga tries to retake mobile gaming with FarmVille 2: Country Escape [Web log post]. Retrieved from http://tinyurl.com/pv9mp48

# 11

# USING APPS FOR REFLECTION/ ASSESSMENT

In this chapter, we discuss the use of assessment to foster student reflection for learning. Learning to reflect on one's work is essential for growth or change— for learning. By reflecting on their use of literacy practices, students are identifying those practices and then determining their effectiveness in using those practices.

As you are aware, students do not necessarily reflect on their own. They need feedback from you or their peers that encourages them to reflect. And, they need some criteria—for example, the degree to which they provide supporting evidence for their claims, to help them articulate their self-reflections.

In this chapter, we describe ways of using different apps for providing such feedback to foster reflection that supports learning, as well as suggest some criteria for fostering self-reflection.

## Assessment *of* Learning Versus *for* Learning

A primary purpose for assessing students is to foster their learning of literacy practices. You may certainly use assessment *of* their learning by giving them a grade or rating their abilities to employ certain literacy practices. For example, having created a digital map of the different characters in a novel, you might give students a grade or score based on the degree of specificity or elaboration of their map.

However, assessment *of* student learning may not provide useful feedback and encouragement *for* learning (Black, Harrison, Lee, Marshall, & Wiliam, 2003). For the purposes of assessment *of* learning, students take standardized reading, writing, and math tests that are assumed to be valid and reliable measures of their learning of reading, writing, and math. In his critique of decontextualized, standardized tests as measures of "reading ability" or "writing ability," James

Gee (2003) argues that these tests fail to recognize that students learn uses of literacy tools within specific contexts or what he defines as "semiotic domains":

> Just as we don't read "in general", but read specific sorts of texts in specific ways, we don't learn "in general", but learn specific "semiotic domains". Indeed, any text is itself associated with one or more specific semiotic domains. By a *semiotic domain* I mean a set of practices that recruit one or more modalities (e.g. oral or written language, images, equations, symbols, sounds, gestures, graphs, artifacts, and so forth) to communicate distinctive types of meanings. Here are some examples of semiotic domains: cellular biology, postmodern literary criticism, first-person-shooter video games, high fashion advertisements, Roman Catholic theology, modernist painting, midwifery, rap music, wine connoisseurship. (p. 31)

## Use of Formative Assessment to Provide Descriptive Feedback to Foster Reflection

Assessment *for* learning involves providing ongoing, descriptive feedback as students are working on their tasks that foster students' use of reflection on their uses of literacy practices. The NCTE Formative Assessment that *Truly* Informs Instruction (National Council of Teachers of English, 2013) statement posits that formative assessment involves the following processes:

Formative assessment:

1. Requires students to take responsibility for their own learning.
2. Communicates clear, specific learning goals.
3. Focuses on goals that represent valuable educational outcomes with applicability beyond the learning context.
4. Identifies the student's current knowledge/skills and the necessary steps for reaching the desired goals.
5. Requires development of plans for attaining the desired goals.
6. Encourages students to self-monitor progress toward the learning goals.
7. Provides examples of learning goals including, when relevant, the specific grading criteria or rubrics that will be used to evaluate the student's work.
8. Provides frequent assessment, including peer and student self-assessment and assessment embedded within learning activities.
9. Includes feedback that is non-evaluative, specific, timely, and related to the learning goals, and that provides opportunities for the student to revise and improve work products and deepen understandings.
10. Promotes metacognition and reflection by students on their work. (p. 2)

By providing formative assessment through descriptive feedback to students, you are providing students with your perceptions of their use of literacy practices. For example, in responding to their creation of a digital story, you may note that you enjoyed how they employed fade transitions and music to heighten the suspense in developing the story, but I wasn't clear about the setting of the story and got lost at the end in terms of knowing what happened to the main character.

In doing so, you are explicating your descriptive reactions to their digital story without making judgments about the story—for example, the fact that the student was using effective transitions and music but needed to clarify the ending of their story.

Providing this descriptive feedback then helps students themselves judge whether they have achieved their intended effects. By doing so, they are learning to engage in metacognitive reflection about their uses of specific literacy practices, reflection essential to developing future uses of these literacy practices. In working on their digital story, having received your descriptive feedback, the student could assess what they did well and what they needed to improve, for example, clarifying their setting and story ending. Students ultimately need to learn how to engage in their own self-assessing so that, when they are not receiving feedback, they can assess their own work in the future.

You can also provide feedback to foster students' reflection on how certain affordances helped them employ specific disciplinary literacies practices. For example, in responding to students' use of annotation apps to synthesize their responses to reading science reports, you can note how students are using their annotations to identify claims and cite evidence to support those claims, as well as challenge their peers' claims.

At the same time, given large class sizes, it is often difficult for you to provide every student with descriptive feedback as they are working on their projects. You can therefore train peers to provide additional feedback by modeling your use of specific, descriptive feedback. Without such training, peers often provide only vague, general comments such as "nice work" out of concern for offending their peers.

## Apps for Giving Descriptive Feedback

There are a number of different kinds of apps that you can employ to provide descriptive, audience-based feedback to students' work, apps we've previously described in this book.

### Apps for Providing Audio Feedback

You can employ audio recording apps to provide audio descriptive feedback, apps described in Chapters 3, 6, and 9 such as Dragon Dictation, Audiotorium, or Audio Memos to create audio files—using Dropbox or Google Drive to store and share audio files. To use these apps, you or peers simply record feedback to a student's work and then share an audio file with that student.

One advantage of using these audio recording apps relates back to portability—that students can listen to them on their phones or iPods while engaged in other activities. Using audio recording apps, as with screencast apps, also encourages you to adopt a dialogic, conversational stance in providing feedback. At the same time, in contrast to screencasts, you will need to reference the specific sections or aspects of a student's work so that students know what sections or aspects you're describing.

It's also the case that using audio feedback may encourage you to adopt a more dialogic, conversational mode for providing descriptive, audience-based feedback in which you're talking with a student as if you were in a face-to-face conference with that student. And, in contrast to reading written comments, students can then hear how the inflections in your voice imply certain meanings.

For providing audio feedback to students' writing on Google Docs or Forms, you can use Kaizena *https://kaizena.com*, one of the Google Drive tools, to provide audio comments to students' writing. To use Kaizena, you first activate it in Google Drive and then add voice comments just as you would written comments to students' Google Docs or Forms files. Once you have completed your comments, you can then share the link to the document to the student for them to access your comments.

## Apps for Providing Annotation Feedback

You can also use annotation apps such as iAnnotate, GoodReader, Diigo, or Evernote Web Clipper that include both written and audio annotation features so that you can provide students with written or audio comments at specific places in students' drafts. Using the iAnnotate PDF app, you can select either a written or audio annotation mode to provide feedback with either the written annotation or an icon for the audio feedback "pinned" to the section of the PDF file you are commenting on. In providing such multimodal feedback, you are describing students' abilities to employ affordances to acquire disciplinary literacies. For example, in responding to drafts of students' writing, you can record your responses to specific places in the drafts using GarageBand, and then save your comments as a file to send to your students, or use iAnnotate to embed audio comments in sections of the written product.

Because many of these apps work on PDFs, you can ask your students to save their written drafts as a PDF file to submit to you to use the apps to add annotations. You can then email back the files or save them on Dropbox for students to review. Then, when students go through their draft, they have a record of your comments for use in self-assessing and revising their draft linked to specific parts of a draft (Yeh & Lo, 2009). As they are going through their draft, they can then respond to these annotations by making needed revisions.

For giving annotation feedback to students' videos, you can upload those videos to VideoAnt *http://ant.umn.edu* or VoiceThread to provide written annotations targeted to specific places in the video.

### Video Chat and Conferencing Apps

Another set of apps for providing feedback are synchronous video chat conferencing apps described in Chapter 7: FaceTime, Skype for iPhone and iPad as well as Android Skype for iPad, Google+ Hangouts, Share Board, ClickMe Online Meetings, GoToMeeting, Adobe Connect for iOS, Fring: Video Calls + Chat, BT Chat HD, ooVoo Video Chat, Vtok: Google Talk Video, and Chat for GoogleTalk.

You can use these apps to engage in virtual teacher/student as well as peer conferences. Using these video chat/conference apps is particularly useful for peer-group feedback in which peers respond to each other's writing or work, something that could be done outside of class time (Herrington, Hodgson, & Moran, 2009). One advantage of using video chat/conference is the fact that participants can view each other's faces, which adds the value of nonverbal communication. Videoconferencing can also be used to train students to provide peer feedback by using examples of their feedback to model feedback strategies. One study of 184 tenth-graders' use of online peer-assessment indicated that students significantly improved their writing due to the peer feedback and that peers' scores were highly correlated with expert scores, suggesting a high validity for the peers' scores (Tseng & Tsai, 2007).

Engaging in online peer-group feedback can foster a sense of community between students and students' ability to critically read their peers' writing (Beach, Anson, Kastman-Breuch, & Reynolds, 2014). And, in contrast to just receiving feedback from screencast or audio feedback, based on the feedback they receive, student writers have the opportunity to engage in sharing their self-assessing and exploration of potential revisions.

### Asynchronous Forum Apps

One alternative to synchronous chat is the use of asynchronous forums found on course management systems (CMSs) such as Moodle, Desire2Learn, WebCT/ Vista, Angel, Brainhoney, Blackboard Mobile Learn, Blackboard Illuminate, Pearson's PowerTeacher 2.0, LanSchool, Collaborize Classroom, Schoology, Canvas, or iTALC, or classroom social networking sites such as Ning, Grou. ps, Mixxt, Soceeo, Lefora, Webjam, Youth Voices, or Qlubb, as well as a class blog or wiki. Students can also submit their fiction writing to sites such as fanfiction.net for feedback from others on this site. Students can use these sites or apps to post their writing or work and you and/or peers can provide feedback on that work.

One advantage of using an asynchronous as opposed to a synchronous platform is that you or your students have time to reflect on the feedback you or they are providing, which is sometimes not the case in providing synchronous feedback (Black, 2005; Breuch, 2004). A comparison of the benefits of asynchronous and synchronous online peer feedback found that the feedback in an asynchronous forum was more effective than feedback in a synchronous forum (Liu & Sadler, 2003). At the same time, if peers in the synchronous forum wrote feedback on the student's paper and returned the paper to the student, then the synchronous feedback was more effective than the asynchronous feedback. This study points to the critical factor of whether a student has a record of the feedback referencing specific features of a student's writing or work. Because students can refer back to feedback in an asynchronous forum, they actually do have a record of that feedback for use in revising their writing or work.

## Observation Notes

Another form of feedback involves keeping observation notes about students' work, for example, observations related to their participation in discussions. To do so, you can use note-taking apps such as the iOS Confer *http://tinyurl.com/k87ug6l* app to record notes you take about your students. One advantage of Confer is that it allows you to organize your notes on a spreadsheet to view students based on your tags such as "strength," "teaching point," or "next step," as well as by name, date, level, group, or flag. Having taken notes about a students' discussion contributions, you can then search back through those notes by name to evaluate that particular student's progress in their discussion participation. And you can search by date to determine changes in their participation over time. You can also use the Formative Feedback for Learning *http://tinyurl.com/loz26cp* app to give feedback to students' videos of, for example, their public speeches or drama performance.

## Apps for Fostering Student Self-Assessing

Another important aspect of assessment for learning is the degree and quality of students' reflection through self-assessing—their ability to summarize their learning and reflect on their own effectiveness in employing certain literacy practices mediated by uses of apps. For example, students are creating podcasts using the GarageBand app based on interviews with residents of a local senior citizens' home in which the seniors were asked to describe a memorable experience in their lives. Creating these podcasts required students to develop open-ended interview questions, interact with the senior citizens, effectively record their interviews, and then edit those interviews to add their own commentaries about the interviews. As they are working on these projects, students can describe their ability and effectiveness in using these literacy practices. For example, they may note that they had difficulty posing open-ended questions in ways that facilitated the seniors expressing themselves.

Students can use Twitter or blogging apps to share written summaries, or screencasting or presentation apps to create short presentations of their learning. For example, junior high students used the iOS Haiku Deck *http://tinyurl.com/k8bh2mk* presentation app to use visual analogies for what they had learned about certain concepts (Fritz & Hahn, 2013). In doing so, they also had to select certain images that best represented what they learned and explain why they chose certain images to represent the concepts they acquired.

Students can also record self-assessments using Google Drive Forms *http://tinyurl.com/pahen25* employing a form for students to respond to general questions about their learning (Frey & Fisher, 2011):

- Where am I/are we going?
- What am I/we trying to accomplish?
- How am I doing?
- Where am I now?
- Where am I going next? (pp. 45–47)

To have students reflect on their uses of apps, you can have them respond to these questions:

- What happened when I used an app in this activity or event?
- How engaged was I in using this app?
- What is my purpose for using an app within a specific event or context?
- What are the challenges and difficulties that I faced in achieving these purposes?
- How well did I work together with others to achieve these purposes?
- How can I use this app in another context or discipline?
- How have I changed in my use of this app over time?

One advantage of using Google Drive Forms is that the students' answers are published in a spreadsheet on Google Drive. In creating questions you can require students to answer a question or give them the option to skip a question. You can also create scale questions in which students rate their perceptions of certain phenomenon, for example, their perception of their level of engagement in an activity ("6" high vs. "1" low).

Once you complete a form, you can share it by providing students with a link to the form, using a code to embed it on a class site or blog, or emailing it to students. You can then collect students' answers for an entire class to perceive variations in students' responses. And, by having students complete forms over time, you can track individual students' changes in their self-assessment. If you wish to share the composite results with students, you can create graphs or charts to show students' results, ideally without having to identify individual students.

Students could also provide narrative descriptions or "learning stories" (Swaffield, 2008) describing their experiences of using certain literacy practices.

For example, for their project interviewing seniors, students could describe the different steps they took in preparing for, recording, and then editing their interviews with senior citizens. Students are more likely to go into some detail about their experience by using narratives than by using expository analysis.

## Self-Assessment of Dispositions

Another factor shaping students' learning is their dispositions towards learning—how their level of interest, engagement, motivation, sense of responsibility, persistence, etc., is shaping their effectiveness in using literacy practices. A joint statement by the Council of Writing Program Administrators, National Council of Teachers of English, and National Writing Project (2011) on assessing writing identified the following dispositions that are important for learning to write effectively:

- *Openness*—the willingness to consider new ways of being and thinking in the world.
- *Engagement*—a sense of investment and involvement in learning.
- *Creativity*—the ability to use novel approaches for generating, investigating, and representing ideas.
- *Persistence*—the ability to sustain interest in and attention to short- and long-term projects.
- *Responsibility*—the ability to take ownership of one's actions and understand the consequences of those actions for oneself and others.
- *Flexibility*—the ability to adapt to situations, expectations, or demands.
- *Metacognition*—the ability to reflect on one's own thinking as well as on the individual and cultural processes used to structure knowledge.

You can have students reflect on their dispositions by responding to questions such as:

- How open was I in entertaining alternative perspectives or approaches in this activity?
- How engaged was I in this activity and what were the reasons for my high or low engagement?
- How did I employ my creativity in this activity?
- How persistent was I in completing this activity and what were the reasons for my high or low persistence?
- To what degree did I assume responsibility for contributing to a group project?
- How flexible was I in adopting alternative perspectives or in working with others?
- How easy or difficult was it to reflect on my participation in this activity?

For example, a student working on producing a podcast with a group of peers may recognize that she has difficulty working with her peers because she's not open to their suggestions, leading her to not assume responsibility for her own contribution to the group's work. You can also use other apps such as iResponse *http://tinyurl. com/mw7ncvd* or eClicker *http://tinyurl.com/lno3d9f* to obtain students' responses to questions related to their perceptions of dispositions associated with their sense of engagement, self-confidence, or persistence to complete a task.

## Record-Keeping/Grading Apps

One major challenge for teachers involves keeping track of information about students' work. You can also use record-keeping apps listed below for storing and organizing information about students as well as to provide them with grades or assessments about their growth over time.

---

### STUDENT RECORD-KEEPING/GRADING APPS

**iOS**: Class Pro *http://tinyurl.com/leffwet* (for use with Engrade *https://www. engrade.com*), PowerTeacher Mobile *http://tinyurl.com/kbjx5xt* (for use with PowerSchool *http://tinyurl.com/o6mvgy*), PowerSchool for Students *http:// tinyurl.com/k2cueka*, TeacherKit *http://tinyurl.com/n3c2cu2*, Essay Grader *http://tinyurl.com/n558kfx*, Collaborize Classroom Pro *http://tinyurl.com/ mwbsxno*, Easy Assessment *http://tinyurl.com/7zbmotb*, Teacher Assistant Pro: Track Student Behavior *http://tinyurl.com/lw275hc*, Duper Data Tracker *http://tinyurl.com/7ls9kpc*, Classroom Manager *http://tinyurl.com/my4a8u9*, iDoceo *http://tinyurl.com/kr2qpkk*, Teacher's Assistant for iPad *http://tinyurl. com/kaa6fql*, Gradekeeper *http://tinyurl.com/726m5b5*, iHomework *http:// tinyurl.com/y9m3p92*, MyRubrics *http://tinyurl.com/kllhzfs*

**Android**: Engrade *http://tinyurl.com/mkcet92*, PowerSchool Access *http:// tinyurl.com/khsxgut* (for use with PowerSchool *http://tinyurl.com/o6mvgy*), PowerSchool for Students *http://tinyurl.com/n8hcsaa*, Easy Assessment *http://tinyurl.com/lrhrv3e*, Teacher Aide Pro *http://tinyurl.com/n7a7wzb*, Random Student *http://tinyurl.com/momwdde*, Student Logs *http://tinyurl. com/mk8hpfy*, Teacher Book Lite *http://tinyurl.com/mwk4uxx*, Grade Rubric Pro *http://tinyurl.com/mgp4mc7*, Teacher App & Grade Book *http://tinyurl. com/lm8hkkw*, Homework *http://tinyurl.com/jwmsa9k*

---

These apps assist you in creating extensive databases about your students' work so that you can keep track of each student's progress over time, as well as adding notes about particular aspects of individual student records, information that can be linked to students' portfolios or shared with parents at parent conferences. These apps can store student data across devices and computers, which means that you can share information with students, parents, and administrators, who in turn can readily access information about students' performance over time. You can also use many of these apps such as Engrade to connect student data to specific standards operating in your school, so that, for example, you can show how students are effectively addressing those standards.

One app that does support open-ended feedback is the iOS Essay Grader designed particularly for use in giving feedback to students' writing that allows you to create a feedback comment form for providing feedback to students to e-mail to students or store on your iPad. It also includes a holistic rubric for rating students' writing. At the same time, it includes "pre-written comments" related to praise, organization, content, mechanics, style, and documentation, whose use may involve providing "canned" responses to students' writing.

You can also use the iOS Collaborize Classroom Pro *http://tinyurl.com/mctdhkr* classroom management system app described in Chapter 7 for use in assessing students' work, particularly their online discussion participation. This app can be used to track each student's discussion participation and for building online portfolios for storing and sharing student work. Similarly, the Easy Assessment app can be used to provide students with open-ended feedback, including adding images or video clips of a student's performance.

You can also use these apps to keep records of your student assessments, as well as comments about individual students and information about students, including their attendance records. For example, the PowerTeacher Mobile apps can be used to include student demographics, keep records of student work/ performance, add observations, and provide results to both students and parents simultaneously.

The iOS and Android Easy Assessment, iOS MyRubrics, and Android Grade Rubric Pro include development of rubrics, use of images or video notes for recording students' performances or work, written comments, creation of spreadsheet results, and sharing of results with students and parents. At the same time, because many of these apps employ or support rubrics in ways that can limit self-reflection, it's important to consider their limitations in using these apps. You may want to employ those apps that value open-ended feedback as opposed to those apps that are simply based on rubric scoring.

To keep track of students' reading performance, you can use the iOS *http:// tinyurl.com/mzh7ahh* or Android *http://tinyurl.com/n4lw42m* Reading Log or the Record of Reading *http://tinyurl.com/pesl6dl* apps for recording changes in students' reading scores over time.

## Using Summative Assessments to Foster Reflection

In contrast to ongoing formative assessment, summative assessments provide students with more final or summary assessments of their learning, often based on their performance on final exams/essays or mandated standardized tests. All of this raises the question as to whether summative assessment *of* learning can, as is the case with formative assessment, be used as assessment *for* learning. One limitation of current summative assessments is that they are largely print-based, for example, multiple-choice reading tests or expository essay-writing tests, which may be inconsistent with the use of apps to construct and share knowledge. However, the Common Core Partnership for Assessment of Readiness for College and Careers (PARCC) and Smarter Balanced summative assessments involving use of computers for open-ended tasks will result in an increased focus on summative assessments involving uses of digital tools.

One app that you can employ to provide summative feedback regarding changes in the uses of both positive and problematic practices is the iOS *http://tinyurl.com/aog3bxt* and Android *http://tinyurl.com/keujquv* ClassDojo app. ClassDojo provides students with certain feedback points for employing positive practices such as participation, helping others, creativity, having useful insights, hard work, and effective presentations, as well as problematic practices such as disruption, being late, not turning in homework, showing disrespect, and interrupting peers. When you perceive a student engaging in these different practices, you use your iPhone, iPad, or laptop/tablet to note their use of those practices. Students then receive this feedback instantly on their own device, for example, the fact that they provided an insightful comment in a discussion.

One advantage of using ClassDojo for summative assessment is that it keeps track of students' practices over time as data to share online with students, administrators, or parents—for example, data showing that while a student was initially not turning in their homework, later in the year, they began to turn in their homework, a reflection of positive growth. Teachers can also customize their feedback for use of their own criteria or rubric. And, they can use the iOS *http://tinyurl.com/aog3bxt* and Android *http://tinyurl.com/qg6gtte* ClassDojo Messaging app to send messages to parents regarding assignments or information on students' practices.

One limitation of an app such as ClassDojo is that it can be overused as a behavior reinforcement tool so that students become dependent on receiving feedback for their use of positive practices. They then perceive the use of positive practices as simply a means to receive positive reinforcement as opposed to engaging in these practices to improve their learning or relationships with others.

## Use of E-portfolio Apps to Foster Summative Assessment for Reflection

All of this raises the question as to how apps themselves can be used for summative assessment to foster reflection on development in the use of literacy practices over time, for example, how students have developed a strong sense of voice in their discussions or writing over time.

Students can use e-portfolios for collecting their work and then reflecting on changes in that work, as well as planning needed future goals for improving their work. Rather than use commercial, Web-based e-portfolio platforms that are relatively expensive and often overly structured, we recommend that you consider employing some of the writing apps described in Chapter 6 for use in creating e-portfolios. For example, students can use the blog containing their entries as an e-portfolio by adding some reflections associated with e-portfolio reflection to their blog.

Students can also self-assess their own learning using iPads or smartphones to collect or curate samples of their work as an e-portfolio collection designed to foster reflection about their learning (Barrett, 2007). Students can reflect on how patterns in their work over time lead to reflection about their interest in certain topics or issues, as well as changes in how they are improving or developing over time. They can use annotation apps to note specific instances of these patterns or changes, as well as share their reflections with their teachers, parents, and peers.

## E-portfolio-specific Apps

One limitation of using note-taking, blogging, wiki, or writing apps to create e-portfolios is that you still need to provide students with the structure and directions for converting their writing into an e-portfolio. You can therefore turn to e-portfolio-specific apps that provide more structure for creating and organizing e-portfolios.

---

### E-PORTFOLIO APPS

**iOS**: Portfolio for Ipad *http://tinyurl.com/mhdl9tt*, Philio *http://tinyurl.com/kf7s42x*, PadFolio *http://tinyurl.com/my8v4es*, Three Ring *http://tinyurl.com/k789t5u*, Easy Portfolio *http://tinyurl.com/n6ec3oq*, Minimal Folio *http://tinyurl.com/m3dxgmx*, Teacher's Wire *http://tinyurl.com/kc5ywhl*, Open-School ePortfolio *http://tinyurl.com/kdx2ta2*

**Android**: Easy Portfolio *http://tinyurl.com/maql5l3*, Three Ring *http://tinyurl.com/knsm4ml*, Desire2Learn ePortfolio *http://tinyurl.com/mjj7xoh*, Portfolio for Android *http://tinyurl.com/k32cdga*, Fotolio *http://tinyurl.com/k5a6pvb*

---

The iOS and Android Three Ring provides you with a means to collect and organize your students' writing or presentations. You can use Three Ring to take pictures of student work to store and tag for inclusion in their e-portfolio, as well as email the students' work to parents. With Teacher's Wire, you can also upload your learning objectives or outcomes to then link students' work as evidence for achieving these objectives or outcomes (for examples, go to *http://www.teacherswire.com*). If you want to collect students' photos, images, artwork, or videos, you can use the iOS Portfolio for iPad or Android Portfolio for Android apps that include ways of organizing collections of photos, images, artwork, or videos into galleries for tagging and reflection on patterns or development as evident in these gallery collections.

## Steps in Creating and Using E-portfolios

There are a number of steps involved in creating and using e-portfolios.

### Collecting and Storing Student Work

Students need to be continually collecting and storing their work *during* an entire course or school career, as opposed to waiting until the end of a course or school year, so that the collection process is ongoing throughout the year. For collecting work not in text form, students can use their iPads or iPhones to take screenshots of their work or use screencasting apps to record their activity on the iPad that then provides teachers with information about successes and issues in using their iPads (Ash, 2012).

### Storage Versus Showcase/Display E-portfolio

By collecting and storing their work, students are creating what could be called a storage e-portfolio. From this storage e-portfolio, students could then create a showcase or display portfolio that includes representative samples of their work. These different samples can be used to illustrate different types or genres of their work, for example, what they consider to be their best essay, digital story/poem, video/slideshow, etc., created in an English class; or work from the beginning, middle, and end of a course. In doing so, they can organize their showcase or display their portfolio using a table of contents referencing the categories containing different types or genres of their work (Beach et al., 2014).

### Student Reflection on Their Work

To foster student reflection on their work, you can have students review back through their work to note consistent thematic patterns in the work. For example, a student may note that across their writing, they continually focused their attention on the issue of gender roles and identity in writing about literature and films, as well as in their own lives. In writing their reflections on these thematic patterns, students can use hyperlinks to specific illustrative examples as a means of connecting their work.

One of the primary challenges in fostering student reflection in use of portfolios is that students may have difficulty engaging in authentic, thoughtful, self-critical reflection, often treating it as just a pro-forma school assignment, resulting in superficial, inauthentic reflection. To foster authentic reflection, you can model what constitutes an authentic versus less authentic reflection. It is also useful to have students work collaboratively on their e-portfolios so that they can give feedback to each other's work, feedback that may foster more authentic reflection.

You can also provide prompts or questions designed to encourage authentic reflection related to students' learning and change, as well as goals and areas for improvement in the future. Jonathan Mueller (2014) proposes using the following questions to foster reflection.

### Selection Questions/Prompts

Why did you select this piece? Why should this sample be included in your portfolio? How does this sample meet the criteria for selection for your portfolio? I chose this piece because . . .

### Growth Questions/Prompts

What are the strengths of this work? Weaknesses? What would you work on more if you had additional time? How has your _____ (e.g., writing) changed since last year? What do you know about _____ (e.g., the scientific method) that you did not know at the beginning of the year (or semester, etc.)? Looking at (or thinking about) an earlier piece of similar work, how does this new piece of work compare? How is it better or worse? Where can you see progress or improvement?

### Overall Portfolio Questions/Prompts

What would you like your _____ (e.g., parents) to know about or see in your portfolio? What does the portfolio as a whole reveal about you as a learner (writer, thinker, etc.)? A feature of this portfolio I particularly like is . . . . In this portfolio I see evidence of . . .

You can also provide students with criteria related to your learning objectives and/or Common Core Standards to have students use material from their portfolios to reflect on how they have achieved these learning objectives and/or Common Core Standards. For example, for the criterion "employ mind-mapping apps to brainstorm and connect relevant ideas in specific, logical ways for use in extended writing," students could compare their mind maps from the beginning, middle, and end of a course to note how their maps became more elaborated during your course. In his science classes at La Junta High School, East Otero,

Colorado, Chris Ludwig (2012) has his students use their e-portfolios on Google Sites websites to reflect on achievements in nine different science standards, one of which is a standard involving self-reflection:

> A blog is organized chronologically by date of publication, but an ePortfolio is organized by skill and content area standards and represents an attempt to prove that those standards have been met . . . . Students not only have to include links to relevant blogposts or other artifacts that they have created, but they also need to justify to the portfolio reviewers why they feel that a particular artifact meets the goal of that particular section of the portfolio. So on each portfolio page, if done well, there exist links to student products and the students' rationale for why they believe that those artifacts demonstrate that they have mastered a particular standard.

Students then have to reflect on how their blog posts served to achieve each of the nine science standards:

> Students have to look through all the blog posts that they have written so far and select which ones will go into their portfolio and on which pages to include them. This leads naturally to a discovery of which standards have a lot of evidence of mastery and which have less. Furthermore, there is a page within the portfolio that is for evidence of self-reflection, either in blog posts or as demonstrated while completing the portfolio. Many students used this page to assess the current status of their learning as shown by the portfolio.

## Assessing and Sharing E-portfolios

Once students have completed their e-portfolios, you can provide your own assessments based on criteria such as students' ability to:

- select a wide range of different work from a course representing different types and genres of work;
- clearly organize this work in a recognizable manner based on a table of contents or categories related to objectives or standards;
- select relevant, illustrative work to demonstrate learning and change based on certain objectives or standards;
- formulate specific, authentic reflections in terms of how one has changed in a course, along with goals for further growth.

You can also share e-portfolios with parents through e-mails or in conferences to provide them with information about their students' work in your course. For example, Rob Van Nood's (2012) students use Evernote to create their e-portfolios. Students take pictures of their work or scan their writing to store in their Evernote e-portfolio, using the tagging features of the Evernote app to label their work. He then adds his own notes about how this work represents student progress and then emails these notes to parents, as well as drawing on one example of work from math, writing, art, and kinesthetics to share with their parents:

> With Evernote, I'm able to show parents their kids' progress in school in real time. They don't have to wait for report cards. Evernote has really changed the way I've been thinking about report cards all-together. With Evernote, we're constantly documenting what students are doing and sharing this feedback with parents.

Students can also continue to use their e-portfolio across different grades, providing current and future teachers, college admissions officers, and employers with a record of their work. In doing so, they can then reflect on their long-term changes over a period of years, reflections that themselves provide teachers, college admissions officers, and employers with insights into their ability to be self-reflective about their work.

## Summary

In this chapter, we discussed the use of formative assessment techniques to provide students with descriptive feedback to foster self-reflection. And, we described the use of audio, annotation, video/chat, asynchronous forum, and observation recording apps for providing this feedback, as well as the use of apps for student self-assessment and record-keeping. We also discussed the use of apps for summative assessment, particularly e-portfolio apps students can use to collect and reflect on their work over time.

## References

Ash, K. (2012). Rethinking testing in the age of the iPad. *Education Week, 5*(2), 36–38. Retrieved from http://www.edweek.org/dd/articles/2012/02/08/02mobile.h05.html

Barrett, H. C. (2007). Researching electronic portfolios and learner engagement: The REFLECT Initiative. *Journal of Adolescent and Adult Literacy, 50*(6), 436–449.

Beach, R., Anson, C., Kastman-Breuch, L., & Reynolds, T. (2014). *Understanding and creating digital texts: An activity-based approach.* Lanham, MD: Rowman & Littlefield.

Black, A. (2005). The use of asynchronous discussion: Creating a text of talk. *Contemporary Issues in Technology and Teacher Education, 5*(1), 5–24.

Black, P., Harrison, C., Lee, C., Marshall B., & Wiliam, D. (2003). *Assessment for learning: Putting it into practice.* Maidenhead, UK: Open University Press.

Breuch, L. (2004). *Virtual peer review: Teaching and learning about writing in online environments.* New York: State University of New York Press.

Council of Writing Program Administrators, National Council of Teachers of English, and National Writing Project. (2011). *Framework for success in postsecondary writing.* Authors. Retrieved from http://tinyurl.com/k5wfutf

Frey, N., & Fisher, D. (2011). *Formative assessment action plan: Practical steps to more successful teaching and learning.* Alexandria, VA: American Society for Curriculum and Development.

Fritz, B., & Hahn, D. (2013, December 10). Creative real-time formative assessments. Presentation at the TIES conference, Minneapolis. Retrieved from http://goo.gl/TnUeBv

Gee, J. P. (2003). Opportunity to learn: A language-based perspective on assessment. *Assessment in Education, 10*(1), 28–46.

Hawkes, M. (2006). Linguistic discourse variables as indicators of reflective online interaction. *The American Journal of Distance Education, 20*(4), 231–244.

Herrington, A., Hodgson, K., & Moran, C. (Eds.). (2009). *Teaching the new writing: Technology, change, and assessment in the 21st-century classroom.* New York: Teachers College Press.

Liu, J., & Sadler, R. W. (2003). The effect and affect of peer review in electronic versus traditional modes on L2 writing. *Journal of English for Academic Purposes, 2,* 193–227.

Ludwig, C. (2012, March 26). 3rd Q recap: Why I'll keep using ePortfolios [Web log post] Retrieved from http://tinyurl.com/mfwleqq

Mueller, J. (2014). Authentic assessment toolbox. Retrieved from http://jonathan.mueller.faculty.noctrl.edu/toolbox/portfolios.htm

National Council of Teachers of English. (2013). Formative assessment that *truly* informs instruction. Urbana, IL: Author. Retrieved from http://tinyurl.com/lu5aa2e

Swaffield, S. (Ed.). (2008). *Unlocking assessment: Understanding for reflection and application.* New York: Routledge.

Tseng, S., & Tsai, C. (2007). On-line peer assessment and the role of the peer feedback: A study of high school computer course. *Computers & Education, 49,* 1161–1174.

Van Nood, R. (2012, February 28). How to create a portfolio with Evernote. Evernote Education Series. Retrieved from http://tinyurl.com/7yug3qf

Yeh, S. W., & Lo, J. J. (2009). Using online annotations to support error correct and corrective feedback. *Computers and Education, 52,* 882–892.

# PART III

# Professional Development

# 12

# PROFESSIONAL DEVELOPMENT ON USING APPS

In this book, we've described the use of a wide range of different apps to foster learning with literacy in all subjects. For many of you, becoming familiar with and trying out these apps in the classroom can be a challenge, given all of the demands on your time. This raises the question as to how you, as a busy teacher, can learn to effectively employ these apps in the classroom through professional development opportunities.

You can certainly learn to acquire and use these apps on your own. There are a lot of online resources for app recommendations and descriptions of teachers using apps in the classroom. Many of these online resources are created by teachers who want to share their own experiences in using apps in their classrooms (for more on online professional development sites see *http://tinyurl.com/799hguu*).

In this chapter, we provide you with information about these various online resources for helping you effectively employ apps in the classroom. At the same time, later in the chapter, we also want to suggest that you consider engaging in collaborative professional development with your colleagues through participation in a school-wide professional learning community (PLC).

## Online Resources on Uses of Apps in the Classroom

There are a considerable number of different kinds of resource sites related to uses of apps in the classroom.

### Information and Review Sites for Apps

The following are some selected sites that include descriptions of different apps as well as reviews of those apps. In most cases, they include information and reviews for both iOS and Android apps.

---

## INFORMATION AND REVIEW SITES FOR APPS

**iOS and Android apps**: Chalkable *http://chalkable.com*, Appolicious *http://tinyurl.com/l3bwbew*, AppAdvice *http://appadvice.com/appnn*, Appitism *http://www.apptism.com*, AppsZoom *http://tinyurl.com/mc93743*, 148Apps *http://www.148apps.com*, Apps in Education *http://appsineducation.blogspot.com*, CrazyMike'sApps *http://crazymikesapps.com*, Educational App Store *http://www.educationalappstore.com*, Common Sense Media *http://tinyurl.com/l47fe7o*, Texas Computing Education Association (TCEA): Apps *http://tinyurl.com/7skn7ym*, Fun Educational Apps *http://www.funeducationalapps.com*, App+Acessories *http://www.appcessories.info*

**iOS apps**: iPad Apps for School *http://ipadapps4school.com*, iPads in Education *http://tinyurl.com/38amkkb*, Cybraryman: iPad Apps *http://cybraryman.com/ipad.html*, High School iPad apps *http://tinyurl.com/7zrgeh7*, AppStart for iPad *http://appadvice.com/appnn*

**Android apps**: AppBrain *http://www.appbrain.com*, AndroidTapp *http://www.androidtapp.com*

---

Many of these sites have educators engaged in reviewing and recommending apps. For example, the Apps in Education site provides extensive information about apps organized according to different subject matter areas. The Appolicious and Chalkable sites include recommendations by teacher members of the site in terms of the relevancy of apps for use in the classroom.

On the other hand, as we argued in Chapter 3, while these recommendations are useful, they may not describe the particular affordances associated with how you plan to use an app given your learning objectives.

## Curriculum Resources Sites

There are also a number of curriculum resource sites listed below that provide resources related to larger issues of technology support/curriculum development, including lesson plans, teaching ideas, and links to different resources.

---

## CURRICULUM RESOURCES SITES

PBS for Teachers *http://www.pbs.org/teachers*, ReadWriteThink *http://www.readwritethink.org*, Sophia *http://www.sophia.org*, Share My Lesson *http://www.sharemylesson.com*, iTunes U *http://tinyurl.com/mt52smg*, Explore Learning *http://www.explorelearning.com*, Discovery Education *http://*

*www.discoveryeducation.com,* Curriki *http://www.curriki.org,* EdSitement *http://edsitement.neh.gov,* Education World *http://www.educationworld. com/a_tech,* Thinkfinity *http://www.thinkfinity.org,* 4Teachers *http://www. 4teachers.org,* Annenberg Learner *http://annenberg.org,* LearningFront *http://learningfront.com,* Connexions *http://cnx.org,* EduTeacher *http://www. eduteacher.net,* English Companion Ning *http:// englishcompanion.ning.com,* California Learning Resource Network *http://www.clrn.org/home*

The PBS for Teachers site provides extensive video resources on topics in all subject areas, along with well-designed lesson plans associated with these videos. The Sophia lesson plans are submitted by teachers and are rated for quality by experts; they also include professional development resources. The ReadWriteThink and Share My Lesson sites also include an extensive number of lesson plans submitted by teachers for use in all subject matter areas. The Explore Learning and Discovery Education sites have resources for teaching math and science. The iTunes U site/iOS app includes thousands of courses with vetted curriculum content that includes activities, videos, podcasts, texts, etc. (for more on curriculum resource sites see *http://tinyurl.com/7hfqf6x*).

## Technology Support Sites

There are also many technology support sites listed below devoted to the uses of technology tools and devices in general in the classroom.

## TECHNOLOGY SUPPORT SITES

Classroom 2.0 *http://www.classroom20.com,* School 2.0 *http://school20.ning,* iOS *http://tinyurl.com/n8rt3nr* and Android *http://tinyurl.com/kxuw6mu* EduTeacher Backpack, Tech&Learning *http://www.techlearning.com/ index,* Technology Integration in Education (TIES) *http://www.technology integrationineducation.com,* Atomic Learning (videos on technology) *http:// www.atomiclearning.com/k12,* Learning.com: Digital Literacy *http://www. learning.com/digital-literacy,* Apple Distinguished Educators *http://tinyurl. com/735q7pj,* Educational Technology and Mobile Learning *http://www. educatorstechnology.com,* iEARN *http://www.iearn.org,* International Society for Technology in Education (ISTE) *http://www.iste.org,* National Writing Project (NWP) Digital IS *http://digitalis.nwp.org,* Digital Media and Learning Central *http://dmlcentral.net,* Kathy Schrock's Guide to Everything *http:// www.schrockguide.net,* Teach With Tablets *http://www.teachwithtablets. co.uk,* Langwitches *http://langwitches.org/blog*

**iOS devices**: Teach With Your Ipad *http://teachwithyouripad.wikispaces.com*, iPads in Education *http://ipadeducators.ning.com*, iPads in Schools *http://tinyurl.com/7fjpvh2*, iPad Academy *http://ipadacademy.com*, iPads for Learning *http://www.ipadsforeducation.vic.edu.au*, Tony Vincent's Learning in Hand: iPad resources *http://learninginhand.com/ipad*, Apple: IT in the Classroom *http://www.apple.com/education/it*, iPads in Education *http://tinyurl.com/38amkkb*, Learning and Teaching with iPads *http://learningwithipads.blogspot.com*

**Android devices**: Android in Education *http://tinyurl.com/lxdkasx*, Android 4 Schools *http://android4schools.com*, Educational Technology Guy: Android in Education *http://tinyurl.com/n727j9l*, LinkedIn Group: Android Tablets for Education and Training *http://tinyurl.com/kxu6s44*

---

The Classroom 2.0 and School 2.0 sites include members sharing their uses of technology in the classroom. The National Writing Project (NWP) Digital IS site provides extensive resources on digital writing. The Digital Media and Learning Central (DML) site includes current methods and ideas related to uses of different digital tools and media, particularly in terms of literacy practices and critical inquiry methods. The iOS and Android EduTeacher Backpack app provides teachers with access and reviews of relevant websites for use in their instruction (for more on online technology training modules see *http://tinyurl.com/bpuze3h*).

## Podcasts

There are also a number of different professional development podcasts listed below on uses of mobile devices and apps, as well as uses of technology. Even if you can't listen to these podcasts, you can access their "show notes" for links to different resources.

---

### PODCASTS

#### Technology Use in the Classroom

EdReach channel (MobileReach, Google Educast, Te@cher Tech T@alk) *http://edreach.us*, TeacherCast *http://teachercast.net/teachercastpodcast*, Teachers Teaching Teachers *http://tinyurl.com/lb6wh4p*, The Future of Education *http://tinyurl.com/7dmsjn*, EdTechCrew *http://www.edtechcrew.net*, Tech Chick Tips *http://techchicktips.net*, Education Talk Radio *http://tinyurl.com/829x9nv*

**iOS apps**: Appy Hours 4 U *http://www.blogtalkradio.com/techchef4u*, iPad Today *http://twit.tv*, Today in IOS *http://tinyurl.com/7uhfruk*, iMore *http://tinyurl.com/7a96kdh*, The iPad Show *http://tinyurl.com/7wfl2t8*, iPad 365 *http://www.ipad-365.com*, Two Guys and Some iPads *http://tinyurl.com/nxqumb4*, The B&B Podcast *http://5by5.tv/bb*

**Android apps**: AndroidGuys *http://www.androidguys.com*, TWIT: All About Android *http://twit.tv/aaa*, This Week in Google *http://tinyurl.com/n6f9ka*, Android and Me *http://androidandme.com*, That Android Show *http://tinyurl.com/m888dwy*, Droid Life Show *http://tinyurl.com/n5eozmz*

---

One advantage of some of the podcasts such as MobileReach, Google Educast, Te@acher Tech T@alk, Appy Hours 4 U, TeacherCast, EdTechCrew, and Tech Chick Tips is that they are produced and recorded by teachers describing specific ways in which they or their students are using apps in the classroom as well as issues that occur with the use of these apps.

The iPad Show, iPad 365, and Two Guys and Some iPads provide current information about the uses of iPads in the class, while the AndroidGuys, All About Android, This Week in Google, Android and Me, That Android Show, and Droid Life Show describe uses of Android devices in the classroom (for more on classroom/school podcasts *http://tinyurl.com/83hcdcl*).

## Twitter Sites

You can also use the Twitter app as well as other Twitter-like apps to acquire information about uses of iOS, Android OS, and Chrome OS apps. One advantage of using Twitter is that you can receive continuous updates with links related to your specific needs, as well as readily share information with your peers and other Twitter followers. One study analyzing Twitter feeds employed by classroom teachers found that teachers engaged in conversations with peers using Twitter 61% of the time, with the majority of their posts related to education, particularly in terms of practice, questions, and resource sharing (Alderton, Brunsell, & Bariexca, 2011). For 82% of the time, they followed experts in the field to obtain information related to building their personal learning networks.

Central to effective use of Twitter is finding experts to follow who can provide you with relevant information. You can also use Twitter hashtags listed below to follow people organized according to topics relevant to uses of apps, for example, #ipaded and #elapse (for suggestions: *http://tinyurl.com/bdcx7lb*).

## TWITTER HASHTAGS ORGANIZED BY TOPIC OR SUBJECT MATTER FOCUS

**General education topics**: #edchat, #lrnchat, #spnchat, #teachchat, #teaching2030, #edblogs, #schools, #pgce

**Technology**: #4productivity, #smedu (social media), #BYODchat, #musedchat, #web20chat, #tichat, #BYOT, #smchat (social media), #vitalcpd, #slide2learn, #edapp, #elearning #mlearning, #edtech, #gbl (games based learning)

**English**: #engchat, #FYC (First-year composition), #yalitchat (young adult literature)

**Social Studies**: #sschat, #historychat, #HistoryTeacher, #GeographyTeacher

**Math**: #mathchat

**Science**: #scichat, #asedchat, #PhysicsEd

**World/English language teaching**: #ELTchat, #langchat

**Music**: #musedchat

**Art**: #artsed

**Special education**: #spedchat

You can also use these hashtags to organize weekly live chats on Twitter about topics specific to their topic focus (for a schedule of live chats *http://tinyurl.com/bctdmem*; for more on professional development Twitter tools *http://tinyurl.com/7ca6mys*).

## Conferences/EdCamps

You can also attend face-to-face or access online conferences or local Google in Education Summits or EdCamps related to technology integration. The fact that many of these conferences provide access to presenters' materials and handouts means that, even if teachers are not able to attend a conference, they can still access online resources from the conference site for professional development.

## CONFERENCES/EDCAMPS

International Society for Technology in Education (ISTE) *http://www.iste.org*, Digital Media and Learning (DML) Conference *http://dml2012.dmlcentral. net*, K12 OnLine Conference *http://k12onlineconference.org*, Google in Education Summits *http://www.appsevents.com*, EdTechTeacher iPad Summits *http://tinyurl.com/k5nwyet*, Classroom 2.0 Live *http://live.classroom20.com*, EdTechTeacher *http://edtechteacher.org*, Florida Educational Technology

Conference *http://tinyurl.com/nypj82e*, Texas Computer Education Association (TCEA) *http://tinyurl.com/kmcymon*, Mobile Learning Conference *http://mobile2012.org*, EduCon *http://educon24.org*, Technology Information Education Services (TIES) *http://www.ties.k12.mn.us/Conferences.html*, Cybraryman: Webinars *http://cybraryman.com/webinars.html*, EdCamp Wiki: information about EdCamps *http://edcamp.wikispaces.com*

---

The International Society for Technology in Education (ISTE) conference is a large annual conference that focuses on both technical and pedagogical aspects of technology integration, while the Digital Media and Learning (DML) Conference focuses more on uses of digital media in the classroom, and the Mobile 2012 Conference includes a lot of sessions on the use of apps (see the Mobile 2012 wiki for resources). There are also totally online conferences such as the K12 OnLine Conference and the Classroom 2.0 conferences that provide specific examples of classroom uses of technology.

The Google in Education Summits and EdTechTeacher iPad Summits are regional face-to-face conferences related to use of Google apps or iOS apps in the classroom. And the EdCamp meetings provide opportunities for teachers to interact with each other on an informal level about technology integration.

## Online Journals/Magazines

There are also a number of online journals/magazines focused on uses of mobile devices and apps in the classroom.

---

### ONLINE JOURNALS/MAGAZINES

Edudemic *http://edudemic.com/magazine*, Apps Magazine *http://tinyurl.com/lmvan98*, T.H.E. Journal *http://www.thejournal.com*, Edutopia *http://www.edutopia.org*, MacWorld AppGuide *http://tinyurl.com/nyzeyj*, Learning and Leading with Technology *http://tinyurl.com/7c8h2tr*, MERLOT *http://www.merlot.org/merlot/index.htm*, Tech & Learning Magazine *http://www.techlearning.com*, Educause Review Online *http://www.educause.edu/eq*, Computers in the Schools *http://www.tandfonline.com/toc/wcis20/current*, Computers & Education *http://tinyurl.com/8y5a6q2*, Computers & Composition *http://tinyurl.com/8a9tjn4*, eSchool News *http://www.eschoolnews.com*, EdTech Magazine *http://www.edtechmagazine.com/k12/magazine/archives*, Electronic School *http://www.electronic-school.com*, Internet@Schools *http://tinyurl.com/6wxjyrh*

---

The *Edudemic, T.H.E. Journal, Edutopia, Learning and Leading with Technology,* and *MERLOT* magazines provide reports on use of apps and devices in the classroom, while the *Apps Magazine* and *MacWorld AppGuide* provide specific descriptions and recommendations for use of apps.

## Apps for Training in Instructional Design

There are also a number of apps that can be used to assist you in designing lessons or curriculum. For example, the iOS *http://tinyurl.com/cpyk5wo* and Android *http://tinyurl.com/kgu6luv* Common Core State Standards app includes all of the standards and related resources for addressing the standards. For other resources on implementation of the CCSS and resources associated with a book on implementation of the CCSS for English language arts see Beach, Haertling-Thein, and Webb (2012), along with its resource website *http://englishccss.pbworks.com.*

The iOS Arizona State University NETS Video Library *http://tinyurl.com/mh4z6oh* app includes videos of classrooms, lesson plans, teacher handouts, and student work linked to these videos. This project is related to the Arizona Technology Integration Matrix designed to foster reflection about five different degrees of levels of technology use consistent with the idea of curriculum redefinition and transformation discussed in Chapter 1:

> *Entry*: The teacher uses technology to deliver curriculum content to students.
> *Adoption*: The teacher directs students in the conventional use of tool-based software. If such software is available, this level is recommended.
> *Adaptation*: The teacher encourages adaptation of tool-based software by allowing students to select a tool and modify its use to accomplish the task at hand.
> *Infusion*: The teacher consistently provides for the infusion of technology tools with understanding, applying, analyzing, and evaluating learning tasks.
> *Transformation*: The teacher cultivates a rich learning environment, where blending choice of technology tools with student-initiated investigations, discussions, compositions, or projects, across any content area, is promoted.

You can also use the iOS Snapguide *http://tinyurl.com/d3njb8q* app to create how-to descriptions for your colleagues or students on how you employ certain apps in the classroom. This app includes the ability to combine text with images, audio, and video to create appealing how-to tutorials or guides. If you anticipate that students may have difficulties completing an activity employing a certain app, you can address these difficulties in your tutorial or guide.

The iOS Classroom Management Essentials *http://tinyurl.com/lkbjby9* and Android HP Classroom Manager *http://tinyurl.com/kk7sele* apps provide resources and tools for addressing classroom management issues, including video clips, and interactive features on how to define rules/routines, create positive social relationships, and distinguish minor versus serious misbehavior incidents.

## Creating a School-Wide Professional Learning Community (PLC)

In addition to using these online resources, you may also want to engage in professional development with your own colleagues through your school or district. Unfortunately budget cuts to schools have led to reductions in professional development opportunities. In a national survey of literacy and language arts teachers (Hutchison & Reinking, 2011), 81.6% of teachers report that a lack of professional development on how to integrate technology is a barrier to its integration. Further, 73% of teachers report that they do not have time to teach students the skills needed for complex tasks, with 45.7% of teachers reporting their own inability to use technology.

And, the professional development teachers do receive is often ineffective. A report on research on professional development (Gulamhussein, 2014) indicated that:

- most teachers only experience traditional, workshop-based professional development, even though research shows it is ineffective;
- the largest struggle for teachers is not learning new approaches to teaching but implementing them;
- in order to truly change practices, professional development should occur over time and preferably be ongoing;
- coaches/mentors are found to be highly effective in helping teachers implement a new skill;
- professional development is best delivered in the context of the teacher's subject area;
- research on effective critical thinking strategies is lacking, but teachers don't have to wait and can lead the way by establishing professional learning communities.

Technology training sessions often do not include opportunities for you and your colleagues to go beyond learning about apps to implementing use of apps in the classroom and to jointly engage in redefining the curriculum as well as share ideas about your own uses of apps. One study found that in a program in which there was no direct technology training of teachers, but with a focus on teachers working together to plan curriculum around technology, the teachers made major gains in their use of technology in their teaching (Blocher, Armfield, Sujo-Montes, Tucker, & Willis, 2011).

This suggests the importance of collaborating with some other colleagues to work together on planning curriculum related to redefining the curriculum around new ways of learning disciplinary literacies. Given the ways in which your school's curriculum is framed according to addressing your state's Common Core Standards in terms of how certain standards will be addressed at certain grade levels, redefining the curriculum often requires teachers' school-wide participation in which you collaboratively determine what content and learning objectives will be addressed at what grade levels.

## Organizing a PLC Using Online Interaction

To engage in collaborative professional development with your colleagues in your school, you can create a professional learning community (PLC) organized around a school website or wiki as a central online repository or "learning commons" for sharing resources, curriculum documents, lessons plans, and students' work/e-portfolios (Beach, 2012; Baker-Doyle, 2011; Koechlin, Luhtala, & Loertscher, 2011; Richardson & Mancabelli, 2011). Teachers within your school could then use Moodle, Ning, Google+ Hangout, Desire-2learn, EDU 2.0, Edmodo, Schoology, LearnBoost, Tappedin.org, or Blackboard Collaborate to engage in synchronous or asynchronous chat (for resources on creating PLC, see the All Things PLC website *http://www.allthingsplc.info*; for more on professional development wikis *http://tinyurl.com/8x67tme*; and on social networking sites used by educators *http://tinyurl.com/84y2t82*).

The fact that you have a central online repository for lesson plans, curriculum documents, resources, and students' work/e-portfolios means that you and your colleagues can readily access the same materials for shared discussions of these materials. And, the fact that teachers from different disciplines are sharing their perceptions about the same work enhances the likelihood of interdisciplinary curriculum planning.

You and your colleagues can then share ideas about using apps throughout your school in all subjects based on your school's own unique curriculum and student demographics. You can also work with administrators and technology coordinators to develop Internet use policies, device and app purchasing strategies, and wireless support ways of integrating uses of apps in the curriculum.

You can also include links to teacher and/or student e-portfolios described in the previous chapter. In your own or your colleagues' teacher e-portfolios, you can include examples of your teaching philosophy/beliefs, curriculum materials, student work, professional development activities, and examples of your students' work. By including and sharing student e-portfolios in a PLC repository, you and your colleagues can all access the same student e-portfolio work to discuss your perceptions of student learning in your school, for example, how well students are acquiring certain disciplinary literacies, and, if they are having difficulties, methods for addressing those difficulties.

## Apps for Teacher Observations by Administrators and Peers

Another important component of a PLC involves administrators or teachers providing feedback to teachers based on classroom observations or "walkabouts." As we noted in the previous chapters on student evaluation, both students and you, as the teacher, may be more likely to engage in self-reflection if you receive specific, descriptive feedback focused on particular teaching activities as well as how students are responding to those activities. If you receive only cursory, pro-forma feedback on a check-list, they are then not receiving this specific, descriptive feedback.

There are a number of different apps for use in conducting teacher observations. The iOS Teachscape Reflect Live *http://tinyurl.com/mr8e9cg* and Android Teachscape Mobile DCT *http://tinyurl.com/lutpchm* apps can be used to enter in observational data into an iPad, or the iOS Teachscape Instruction Mobile *http://tinyurl.com/mqnnglp* app or Android Reflect Walkthrough *http://tinyurl.com/m9vwgfv* for entering data into devices that is then sent wirelessly to the Teachscape website for alignment with the Charlotte Danielson Framework for Teaching to rate teachers on rubrics, as well as for summarizing feedback and noting changes over time. These apps also include a dictation feature and forms for teachers to complete before and after the observed lesson, as well as the ability to attach a lesson plan.

The iOS *http://tinyurl.com/m8hkbhd* and Android *http://tinyurl.com/mlvjk8j* Teacher Compass app includes teacher observation tools and self-diagnosis features that are linked to videos, tutorials, and online modules. For mathematics teachers, the iOS Ci2 Protocol Mathematics *http://tinyurl.com/lloumfn* app also includes teacher observation tools linked to the math Common Core Standards, along with videos modeling instruction.

Other apps include the iOS *http://tinyurl.com/ladl6f6* and Android *http://tinyurl.com/lsawuel* Administrator Edition: eCOVE Observation Software for use with the eCove General Edition for iPad *http://tinyurl.com/lwr8oby* and the Android eCove General Edition *http://tinyurl.com/kuey2h8*; the iOS *http://tinyurl.com/lgc5yfm* and Android *http://tinyurl.com/m6d3mj7* Assessa apps, iOS *http://tinyurl.com/lm7mdpe* and Android *http://tinyurl.com/n556p3p* Observation 360 for generating assessments that are then linked to relevant PD 360 professional development video resources; iOS GoObserve Classroom Observation and Walkthrough Tool *http://tinyurl.com/lmc3a5j*, and the Android EZ Walkthrough *http://tinyurl.com/krn5rsq* app. Another option to using these apps is to create your own forms using Google Forms or note-taking apps for uploading observations to

Dropbox or iCloud for sharing with teachers used in addition to open-ended notes (Stephenson, 2012).

## Using the PLC to Address Issues in Uses of Apps and Devices

You can use PLCs for you and your colleagues to collaboratively address a number of issues that often arise in using apps in schools, discussions that can lead to establishing policies or procedures that enhance students' uses of apps.

One major challenge facing schools is the issue of access to websites consistent with federal policies related to children's access to problematic online material using browser apps. It's important to have school Internet policies related to guidelines as to what types of online content should or should not be blocked, as well as clear identification as to who is responsible for blocking these sites. Unfortunately, schools often outsource this work to companies outside of the school, who may employ arbitrary criteria as to which sites should be blocked.

A related policy issue has to do with BYOD (bring your own devices), described in Chapter 1. It's important for a school to establish clear policies related to when and where devices can and cannot be used, as well as how these devices can be connected to the school's Wi-Fi network. For examples of BYOD policies established for use in the Forsyth County Schools see *http://tinyurl.com/3qwkycp*; or for the Hanover Public Schools *http://byod.hanoverpublic.org*.

Another challenge has to do with students who have a limited number of devices available for their use in school given the costs of these devices. For example, a classroom may have only a few devices for use by an entire class. You and your colleagues can share strategies for having only a few devices: the use of a projector to show students a screen for them to collaboratively work off of a single device or creating activities in which students pass around a device to engage in collaborative reading or writing activities.

You may also find that students often have difficulty initially employing certain apps simply because they do not exploit all of the affordances of an app. To address this problem, you could discuss the importance of modeling your own uses of apps for students to show them how to exploit the affordances. You could also discuss creating a database of how-to videos or tutorials using screencasting apps such as ShowMe, Explain Everything, VoiceThread, or Snapguide to demonstrate uses of apps for students to view on their own, particularly outside of school.

As noted in Chapter 11, you and your colleagues may often struggle with how to employ effective formative and summative assessments of students' growth in disciplinary literacies, particularly assessments that are consistent across an entire school. To do so, you and your colleagues could develop some shared criteria or rubrics that can be employed throughout your school so that students are being evaluated in their uses of literacy practices based on the same criteria across different subjects, while also recognizing how these criteria may vary according to different disciplinary literacies. And, by employing a shared e-portfolio system across different subjects, in which students are including their work from different subjects, you and your colleagues can then gain a better understanding of how a student is performing in all of their classes. And, as previously noted, you can then discuss the effectiveness of certain teaching methods in fostering student learning.

## Concluding Remarks

We hope that you will benefit from the ideas and materials in this book, particularly in thinking about how effective implementation of apps entails more than simply using apps for their own sake—that what's important is to think about how app affordances are being used to foster disciplinary literacies across the curriculum. We also hope that you find that students will be engaged in using these apps for fostering learning in your classrooms and that you can share your experiences with your colleagues about such engagement so that those colleagues will also perceive the value of using apps.

If you do want to share your own links or resources related to uses of apps in the classroom you can do so by adding them to the book's wiki (*http://usingipads. pbworks.com*). You can request editing privileges from Richard: rbeach@umn. edu, or send links or resources directly to Richard who will add them to the wiki. You can also comment on our Apps for Learning Literacies website (*http://www. appsforlearningliteracies.com*).

## References

Alderton, E., Brunsell, E., & Bariexca, D. (2011). The end of isolation. *MERLOT Journal of Online Learning and Teaching, 7*(3), 354–365. Retrieved from http://jolt.merlot.org/vol7no3/alderton_0911.pdf

Baker-Doyle, K. J. (2011). *The networked teacher: How new teachers build social networks for professional support.* New York: Teachers College Press.

Beach, R. (2012). Can online learning communities foster professional development? *Language Arts, 89*(4), 256–262.

Beach, R., Haertling-Thein, A., & Webb, A. (2012). *Teaching to exceed the English language arts Common Core State Standards: A literacy practices approach for grades 5–12.* New York: Routledge.

Blocher, J. M., Armfield, S. W., Sujo-Montes, L., Tucker, G., & Willis, E. (2011). Contextually based professional development. *Computers in the Schools, 28*(2), 158–169.

Gulamhussein, A. (2014). *Teaching the teachers: Effective professional development in an era of high stakes accountability.* Alexandria, VA: Center for Public Education/ National School Boards Association.

Hutchison, A., & Reinking, D. (2011). Teachers' perceptions of integrating information and communication technologies into literacy instruction: A national survey in the U.S. *Reading Research Quarterly, 46*(4), 308–329.

Koechlin, C. K., Luhtala, M., & Loertscher, D. V. (2011). Knowledge building in the learning commons. *Teacher Librarian, 38*(3), 20–26.

Richardson, W., & Mancabelli, R. (2011). *Personal learning networks: Using the power of connections to transform education.* Bloomington, IN: Solution Tree.

Stephenson, C. (2012, October 2). Using iPads for classroom observations [Web log post]. Retrieved from http://tinyurl.com/cphr43p

# INDEX